Ultimate
THE ^STUDENT
TEACHING GUIDE

Second Edition

Ultimate
THE ^STUDENT
TEACHING GUIDE

Second Edition

Kisha N. Daniels
North Carolina Central University

Gerrelyn C. Patterson
North Carolina Central University

Yolanda L. Dunston
North Carolina Central University

⑤SAGE

Los Angeles | London | New Delhi
Singapore | Washington DC

SAGE

Los Angeles | London | New Delhi
Singapore | Washington DC

FOR INFORMATION:

SAGE Publications, Inc.
2455 Teller Road
Thousand Oaks, California 91320
E-mail: order@sagepub.com

SAGE Publications Ltd.
1 Oliver's Yard
55 City Road
London EC1Y 1SP
United Kingdom

SAGE Publications India Pvt. Ltd.
B 1/I 1 Mohan Cooperative Industrial Area
Mathura Road, New Delhi 110 044
India

SAGE Publications Asia-Pacific Pte. Ltd.
3 Church Street
#10-04 Samsung Hub
Singapore 049483

Acquisitions Editor: Theresa Accomazzo
Editorial Assistant: Sarita Sarak
Production Editor: Melanie Birdsall
Copy Editor: Janet Ford
Typesetter: C&M Digitals (P) Ltd.
Proofreader: Caryne Brown
Indexer: Jean Casalegno
Cover Designer: Karine Hovsepian
Marketing Manager: Terra Schultz

Printed in the United States of America

Library of Congress Cataloging-in-Publication Data

Daniels, Kisha N.

The ultimate student teaching guide / Kisha N. Daniels, North Carolina Central University, Gerrelyn C. Patterson, North Carolina Central University, Yolanda L. Dunston, North Carolina Central University. —Second edition.

pages cm.
Includes bibliographical references and index.

ISBN 978-1-4522-9982-2 (pbk. : alk. paper)

1. Student teaching—United States—Handbooks, manuals, etc. 2. Student teachers—Training of—United States—Handbooks, manuals, etc. I. Patterson, Gerrelyn C. II. Dunston, Yolanda Lyght. III. Title.

LB2157.U5D36 2015

370.71′1—dc23   2013035369

This book is printed on acid-free paper.

14 15 16 17 18 10 9 8 7 6 5 4 3 2 1

Brief Contents

Detailed Contents

PART II. POLITICS

Preface

OVERVIEW

The need for effective teachers to prepare students for global citizenship is more urgent now than ever before. Consequently, initial training for novice teachers is even more critical to the success of teacher effectiveness. Thus, the mission of this text is to offer a guide replete with practical, yet research-based, field-tested strategies to assist novice teachers during the most pivotal experience in their teacher education or licensure program—the student teaching internship.

As veteran educators with more than 30 years of combined experience teaching and supervising preservice teachers in schools and universities, we continually search for resources that can assist our students currently in the field. Although several excellent texts are available, we were unable to locate one with the appropriate blend of theory, practical strategies, and supplemental activities specifically designed for the student teaching internship. Also, our students expressed dissatisfaction with the assignment and reading selections from certain texts during the internship. Instead, they chose to focus on completing tasks directly related to their responsibilities in the field (e.g., lesson planning, creating portfolios, studying for Praxis examinations, and applying for teaching positions). We needed a text with supplemental activities that didn't feel like "busy work"; it needed to speak directly to the students' current field experiences.

In addition, the types of preservice teachers we were seeing enter the program began to change dramatically. A text for the traditional undergraduate student was insufficient. Instead, we needed a text appropriate for the diverse population of students we served: traditional undergraduate students, second-degree students, second-career students, lateral entry teachers seeking certification, and instructional assistants transitioning into lead teaching roles. No text seemed to address directly the unique circumstances and experiences these varying types of students brought to the internship. Plus, because these students were entering the internship with varying levels of experience in schools, we needed a text that was not only inclusive of current best practices in teaching (e.g., differentiation, technology integration, and brain-friendly teaching strategies) but also readable and accessible to diverse types of preservice teachers.

Finally, as university supervisors of student teachers in the field, we realized we were spending an inordinate amount of time explaining issues omitted from the textbooks (legal and ethical issues, cooperating teacher conflicts, school politics, classroom management without "real" power, and more). As a result, we ceased using a text altogether and allowed the themes of our student teaching classes to emerge. Several themes consistently emerged across disciplines and grade levels: professionalism, the cooperating or mentor-teacher relationship, managing the workload, stress and organization, classroom management, teacher confidence, and life after the internship. Furthermore, there was a clear correspondence between the themes discussed and the trajectory of the student teaching internship. *The Ultimate Student Teaching Guide* is a compilation of those themes.

Teacher education and licensure programs do an excellent job of preparing preservice teachers, and this text in no way disputes the quality of these programs. Additionally, there are many excellent texts that help to prepare novice teachers. *The Ultimate Student Teaching Guide*, however, serves as a fresh approach to supporting a broad range of students dealing with issues and events likely to occur during the internship. Using a lighthearted tone, it candidly addresses the totality of the student teaching internship: its complexities, joys, frustrations, and challenges.

USES OF THE TEXT

This is an excellent textbook for preservice teachers about to enter a student teaching internship or those who are currently in an internship. It is also useful to novice teachers in developing fundamental skills, such as lesson planning, instructional strategies, classroom management, and understanding school culture. Students enrolled in alternative licensure programs will find this text useful as well. Additionally, those in nontraditional programs for preparing teachers (e.g., complete distance education instruction or distance education combined with face-to-face classes) will find *The Ultimate Student Teaching Guide* an invaluable resource that clearly explicates the universal experiences of the internship.

ORGANIZATION OF THE TEXT

The Ultimate Student Teaching Guide is divided into four parts: Part I: People, Part II: Politics, Part III: Planning, and Part IV: Performance. Part I provides readers with an overview of the *people* they will encounter during the internship, such as school personnel and the cooperating teacher (CT). School culture, legal and ethical issues, and general professionalism are addressed in Chapter 1 (Welcome to Student Teaching: The Open House). The relationship with the cooperating teacher is addressed in Chapter 2 (Meeting Your Cooperating Teacher: The Teacher Conference), which examines different types of leadership models and how they change over the course of the internship.

Part II focuses on *politics*—or the activities involved in managing the internship—including matters involving relationships, workload, and student behavior. An overview of the relationship between personality theory, strategic problem solving, and the development of a positive relationship with the cooperating teacher is presented in Chapter 3 (Understanding Your Cooperating Teacher: The Rules). Stress management and strategies for handling the various responsibilities that run concurrently with the internship are addressed in Chapter 4 (Managing the Workload: The Late Bell). A review of well-known classroom management plans and strategies for responding to management issues that arise during the internship are provided in Chapter 5 (Classroom Management During Student Teaching: The Principal's Office).

In Part III, which focuses on *planning*, special attention is given to effective instruction. A review of assessment-based instruction, brain-friendly teaching, and technology infusion is provided in Chapter 6 (Strategies for Effective Teaching: The Planning Period), and fundamentals for developing sound instructional plans that meet the needs of all learners are discussed in Chapter 7 (Preparation and Performance: The Lesson Plan).

Part IV concludes the book with an emphasis on *performance*. Readers are challenged to view student teaching as a process, to think about how that process affects self-confidence and impacts teaching assignments, and to use reflection as a tool for professional growth in Chapter 8 (Developing Confidence in Your Teaching Ability: The Evaluation). Finally, guidelines for developing portfolios and résumés, studying for specialty area exams, applying for licensure, and applying for jobs are provided in Chapter 9 (The Last STEP: Student Teacher Exit Plan).

FEATURES OF THE TEXT

We have taken great care to write this book with the reader in mind. Over the years, we've received comments from many students about textbooks, and the feedback is always the same: "They are so boring." As a result of their feedback, we've chosen to incorporate two special features to make the text reader-friendly: a conversational tone and a visual presentation.

The reader will find that the tone of this book is less technical and more conversational than that of other textbooks. However, ample theory is interwoven into the content. There are references to the many significant educational, psychological, and social learning theories that support and extend the objectives listed in the chapters. Furthermore, many chapter titles and headings refer to a specific school experience and/or phase.

The text is also supported by a variety of visuals (figures, checklists, pictures, diagrams, etc.) that encourage differentiated learning styles. It incorporates a glossary of professional terms that students need to know and use, as well as an appendix of templates to help take the guesswork out of creating documents, such as lesson plans and résumés.

Additionally, *The Ultimate Student Teaching Guide* maintains the spirit of the tone by incorporating the following features that are similar to those in other texts, but are presented in a new format.

Letter to the Student Teacher. The reader will find these friendly letters at the beginning of every chapter. They are informal yet provide useful information about the context and contents of the chapter.

Special Feature Section. This section speaks directly to the special populations that are often overlooked (lateral entry, licensure only, instructional assistants, paraprofessionals, men, etc.). It provides specific information for candidates whose experiences may be different from those of traditional audiences.

Bulletin Board. Bulletin boards are used to convey and present important information. Similarly, in this text, the Bulletin Board references all of the information that you need to know about a chapter. Essentially, it is the chapter summary presented to look like a bulletin board.

Extra Credit. The text is extended by suggested activities that allow the reader to further examine, reflect on, and activate content themes. Each chapter has an "Extra Credit" section; however, the activities vary. Within each section you will find these features:

Read About It. This section includes a list of web-based and traditional resources that provide additional information about methods, strategies, or research.

Think About It. By utilizing a variety of strategies that offer opportunities to reflect on the content themes and how they affect experiences, this section provides systematic methods for communicating successes, problems, and challenges.

Try It. Students will find activities, from the basic to the specific, that encourage the direct application of methodology and/or theories. The section may include worksheets or reference resources from the "Read About It" section.

For the second edition, we've kept all of the features that make the text unique and added updated information to provide you with even more support. New to this edition is an expanded section on workplace professionalism in Chapter 1, which offers a historical look at professionalism and gives the reader insight into what potential employers look for in top-notch employees. Chapter 2 introduces you to the wonderful world of accreditation (CAEP, or the Council for the Accreditation of Educator Preparation) and the national Common Core standards. The new standards have impacted instruction; therefore, in Chapter 6 we've included new information on instructional strategies that support teaching and learning, including technology—and at the rate that technology changes, we'll probably be updating this chapter again really soon. Last, the section in Chapter 9, titled "Getting to and Through the Interview," has been expanded to include additional advice and steps to get new graduates closer to signing their first teaching contracts.

Acknowledgments

This textbook would not have been possible without our student teachers. We experienced such joy watching you develop into effective, passionate educators. Without you, there would be no stories to share. We sincerely thank you because you provided us with constant reminders of why we love teaching and learning.

Our thanks to the cooperating teachers and university supervisors who worked so diligently to provide nurturing and support for our student teachers. Without you, the internship would not have been possible.

We also extend deep and sincere gratitude to the never-ending support of our families and friends. No one could ask for better parents, siblings, in-laws, neighbors, co-workers (the list could go on and on). We are eternally grateful for the many ways you all pitched in so that we could have uninterrupted time to work on this project. Your support and encouragement were invaluable. But above all else, special thanks go to our children and husbands. While writing this book, we received over 100,000 kisses and hugs, 5,000 caffeinated drinks, 1,000 pieces of chocolate, and 500 "I Love Mommy" pictures from our children. Priceless! And finally, to our husbands, Shan, Brandon, and Phil, thank you for being our number one fans, for believing in us, and for making it possible for us to follow our dreams.

Thank you also to the following prospectus and draft chapter reviewers:

Patrice Boyles, Chicago State University

Hazel A. Brauer, University of San Francisco

Donna J. Cole, Wright State University

Melissa R. Gibson, University of the Cumberlands

Lyman Goding, Bridgewater (MA) State College

Robert D. Kefferstan, Waynesburg University

Edward J. Lazaroff, University of Hartford

Terri B. Pantuso, Governors State University

Richard T. Scarpaci, St. John's University

Thomas J. Troisi, Hofstra University

Barbara Torre Veltri, Northern Arizona University

Diantha B. Watts, SUNY Geneseo

Cindy Wilson, University of Illinois at Springfield

Jeffrey Winter, National-Louis University

Part I

People

Welcome to Student Teaching

The Open House

Dear Student Teacher:

Congratulations! You have worked really hard, and all of the late nights, presentations, papers, exams, and endless studying—not to mention the fights with your computer and hours of field experience—have finally paid off. You are ready for student teaching. It's an exciting experience filled with many unknowns. Most of you will spend at least 600 hours meeting your new "family," learning new rules, and navigating new experiences. If you aren't familiar with your placement site or your cooperating teacher, you probably have a million questions in preparation for your first day: What should I wear? What will my school be like? Will I get along with my cooperating teacher? Does the cafeteria serve good food?

While these questions are all relevant, you may not have thought to ask yourself additional questions: What is the school culture? Who is the principal? What is the role of parent involvement at the school?

Every school has its own unique spoken and unspoken way of doing things. These rules can present themselves as specific policies in the teacher handbook or as vague guidelines for workplace etiquette. We've observed student teachers in many diverse schools, and some of the best student teachers struggle with this transition. So trust us when we say that you'll want to read this chapter thoroughly (we won't waste your time with useless information). In our experience, understanding these politics (or at least knowing the questions to ask) can help you realize how you fit into the system and provide you with the first of many steps toward a successful experience.

Sincerely,

Your School Culture Coaches

CHAPTER OBJECTIVES

After reading this chapter, you will be able to

- define the importance of school culture;
- appreciate how school culture affects the organizational structure of schools;
- recognize the legal and ethical issues surrounding the teaching profession;
- identify the various functions of school employees; and
- describe the dos and don'ts of workplace professionalism.

SCHOOL CULTURE

What Is School Culture?

The concept of *culture* refers to a group's shared beliefs, customs, and behaviors. A **school's culture** includes the obvious elements of curriculum and policies, as well as the social interactions that occur within those structures that give a school its look and feel. This look and feel often lead to school labels, such as "friendly," "elite," "competitive," "inclusive," and so on. Frequently, it is the unwritten rules about interactions, problem solving, and decision making that give schools a "unique character," and almost everything in a school can have a set of unwritten rules about how to behave. These unwritten rules often reflect what the school and staff members care about (school mission and/or philosophy), what they are willing to spend time doing (actions in the classroom and parent involvement), how and what they celebrate (career accomplishments, birthdays, weddings, births, etc.), and what they talk about (the all-important school newsletter and teachers' lounge conversations).

School culture is *not* about

- **Race:** The categorization of humans into populations or ancestral groups on the basis of various sets of heritable characteristics
- **Socioeconomic status (SES):** A measure of a person's work experience and of an individual's or family's economic and social position relative to others, based on income, education, and occupation
- **Size of the school:** The population and whether it is considered large or small
- **Religion:** A set of beliefs concerning the cause, nature, and purpose of the universe

Let's make this conversation a little more tangible. Think about your family and all of the habits, relationships, celebrations, and kitchen table conversations that make it unique. Would you ever say that your family is like every other family? Absolutely not. It may seem difficult to understand why one family celebrates the Christmas season throughout the year (really—365 days, Christmas tree and all), or why a family enjoys going ice fishing as a tradition on birthdays, or the unusual practice of another particular family who hurl dinner rolls across the table instead of calmly passing around the breadbasket. It might be easy to judge these families if their experiences are vastly different from yours. Are these customs considered bad manners or just common courtesy? Would a visitor from another family instantly understand the unwritten rules of your family? Probably not at first, but over time the family choices would become quite clear to visitors because either: (a) they stay for an extended time indicating they agree with and appreciate your family's ideas and practices, or (b) they thank you for the evening and sneak out the back door, never to be seen again.

In either case, you probably agree that knowing some basic elements of culture helps others understand how your family "does the things that they do."

We trust that no one will be throwing dinner rolls at you as you walk into the school cafeteria, but what they will be doing remains an open question. How will you know what is valued and expected of you in the school where you will be spending the majority of your waking hours for the next 10,000 weeks? (Just kidding; the length will vary by program.) And if you find out, why does it matter?

Why Is School Culture Important?

Have you ever heard the saying, "What you don't know might hurt you?" Well, you may want to replay this phrase as you think about the "unwritten and unspoken rules" of the school where you will complete your student teaching internship. This will be helpful as you understand and find your place in this new family. By focusing on the importance of school culture, it is our intention to give you some points to think about as you prepare for and establish yourself in the student teaching experience. Throughout this guide, we refer to the uniqueness of the student teaching experience. There is no place where the uniqueness of this experience is more apparent than in understanding how it is connected to the culture of your placement school. This sentiment is echoed by Cherubini (2009), who found that the student teaching experience is often marked by tensions relating to the difference between teacher candidates' expectations of school culture and their observed realities. He further noted that this is due mostly to the unique and distinctive circumstances of the student teaching practicum.

For a moment, let's discuss these unique circumstances:

- Student teachers are not paid employees of the school system,
- Student teachers are expected to fulfill the vast majority of the same responsibilities as teachers (within legal parameters),
- Student teachers are acknowledged as part of the staff, but may not be afforded the same privileges,
- Student teachers are students, and
- Student teachers are also viewed as professionals (and expected to act as such).

School Culture and School Roles Work Together

The student teaching experience typically puts you in a problematic spot where you often straddle the fence (or live in the two worlds) as both student and teacher. In order to hurdle the fence, you must teach for a predetermined amount of time under the supervision of a certified teacher; thus, we now have your new title of **student teacher (ST)**. You don't have the same privileges as your **cooperating teacher (CT)**, who is an experienced teacher selected to be a mentor, model, and guide, or the other teachers in the building, but you are expected to live by the same rules—whether they are spoken or unspoken. You could say that you are being held to a higher standard because you need to prove yourself, whereas the other teachers and staff already have their seal of approval—a signed employment contract. (However, if you are a lateral entry teacher, you may have other unique circumstances that we address throughout the book, so keep reading.) Since you probably didn't have the luxury of selecting the school (or the culture) of your student teaching experience, you need to take the steps to ascertain information about the school culture and get some immediate on-the-job training as to how to fit in. Specifically, you want to think about the ways in which the school culture impacts the following:

- The school's **mission statement**, which is a formal, short, written statement of the purpose of a company or organization (What are the academic goals? How does the school involve families?)
- The school's roles (What are the various school roles? Who does what job?)
- The school's relationships (What type of decision making is valued? How are conflicts handled?)
- The school's workplace **professionalism**, which refers to adhering to a set of values composed of standards, obligations, formally agreed on codes of conduct, and informal expectations (What can I wear? What is not appropriate to say in the hall?)

Consequently, how you respond to the culture most often sets the tone for how you are received and viewed as a student professional (and possibly a new hire). Of course, you won't be a student teacher forever. Therefore, it is also important to have a holistic perspective of school culture and take note of the impressive research that strongly correlates positive school cultures with:

- increased **student achievement** (an evaluation of performance based on a measurable standard);
- increased student **motivation** (the intrinsic or extrinsic activation of goal-oriented behavior);
- teacher productivity; and
- teacher satisfaction.

This is important to think about as you search for schools where you want to work in the future (we discuss this further in Chapter 9).

ORGANIZATIONAL STRUCTURE

Who Are the People in Your Neighborhood?

School cultures may differ, but one thing that all schools have in common is an **organizational structure**. This structure (or neighborhood) is defined as the form of an organization or entities that collaborate and contribute to serve one common goal and is devised to clearly delineate various roles and day-to-day job responsibilities of everyone inside and outside of the school building. However, if we refer back to our earlier discussion, remember that you may need to look deeper and examine the culture of your school in order to discover the unspoken roles and day-to-day tasks of each of its members. Table 1.1 provides you with a basic chart that defines the most common school roles and their corresponding tasks. Additionally, we've given you some top secret information to help give you a complete picture of what it takes to make any school run smoothly. You'll be surprised at how much goes on behind the scenes.

Table 1.1 The School Directory

Title	Role	Additional Responsibilities (These are generalizations based on our years of experience. Specific roles and responsibilities differ at every school.)
Principal	The leader who provides guidance to teachers, students, staff, and community members (when appropriate)	• Fortune teller: Predicts the future • Juggler: Juggles many things at one time • Conflict mediator: Has to be able to resolve conflicts and counsel • Magician: Makes things appear out of nowhere • Politician: Makes sure everyone's needs are being voiced
Assistant Principal	Assists the principal in the general governance and leadership of a school	• Educational researcher: Conducts classroom observations • Detective: Solves "Whodunits" • Creative director: Supports and manages curriculum and instruction • Transportation supervisor: Facilitates and organizes the smooth transportation of precious cargo (the students)
Secretary (VIP = Very Important Person. Secretaries tend to be "in the know" about everything in the school building)	Answers telephone to provide information, take messages, and transfer calls May order and dispense school supplies	• Nurse: Takes care of basic medical needs • Mind reader: Remembers everyone's names and needs • Activities director: Schedules and organizes the school calendar
Bookkeeper	Inputs, classifies, and records numerical data to keep financial records complete	• Auditor: Makes sure the financial records are in line and well organized
Counselor	Counsels individuals to help them understand and overcome personal, social, and/or behavioral problems affecting their educational or vocational situation Maintains accurate and complete student records as required by laws, district policies, and administrative regulations Confers with parents or guardians, teachers, other counselors, and administrators to resolve students' behavioral, academic, and other problems Meets with parents and guardians to discuss their children's progress and to determine their priorities for their children and their resource needs	• Social worker: Helps children or families who are experiencing a crisis (especially if the school does not have a full-time social worker) • Testing consultant: Organizes, coordinates, and supports the myriad assessments that kids have to take • Trainer: Ensures that teachers are trained in new test administrations • Tour guide: Gives tours to prospective families

Title	Role	Additional Responsibilities (These are generalizations based on our years of experience. Specific roles and responsibilities differ at every school.)
Teacher (includes teaching assistants)	Establishes and enforces rules for behavior and procedures for maintaining order among the students for whom they are responsible Observes and evaluates students' performance, behavior, social development, and physical health Prepares materials and classrooms for class activities Adapts teaching methods and instructional materials to meet students' varying needs and interests Plans and conducts activities to create a balanced program of instruction, demonstration, and work time that provides students with opportunities to observe, question, and investigate Instructs students individually and in groups using various teaching methods, such as lectures, discussions, and demonstrations Establishes clear objectives for all lessons, units, and projects, and communicates those objectives to students Assigns and grades classwork and homework Reads books to entire classes or small groups Prepares, administers, and grades tests and assignments in order to evaluate students' progress Confers with parents or guardians, teachers, counselors, and administrators in order to resolve students' behavioral and academic problems	• Nurse: Takes care of basic medical needs • Social worker: May be called on to help children or families who are experiencing a crisis • Event planner: Plans special projects, birthdays, coordinates assemblies, etc. • Editor: Checks lots of homework; helps students revise and edit their work • Lobbyist: Lobbies for the needs of the students, the school, and themselves • Sociologist: Carefully studies the behaviors of kids and how they form relationships (this helps teachers understand cooperative learning and playground behavior) • Judge: Has to decide and enforce consequences
Cafeteria manager (VIP—if you are really nice to the cafeteria manager, you might be	Determines production schedules and staff requirements necessary to ensure timely delivery of services	• Event planner: Coordinates lunches for special occasions, and may need to rearrange the entire lunch schedule to accommodate special school functions

(Continued)

Table 1.1 (Continued)

Title	Role	Additional Responsibilities (These are generalizations based on our years of experience. Specific roles and responsibilities differ at every school.)
able to get the cookies that come right out of the oven)	Estimates amounts and costs of required supplies, such as food Inspects supplies, equipment, and work areas to ensure compliance with established standards	• Health inspector: Serves healthy meals and ensures that the workspace is in top shape
Custodial staff (VIP—never overlook the knowledge of a well-informed custodian; plus, a custodian probably has the keys to the supply closet where the extra paper is kept)	Keeps the school building clean and in orderly working condition Inspects supplies, equipment, and work areas to ensure compliance with established standards	• Inspector: Makes recommendations to the administration for new products and designs to make the building more efficient, and ensures that the facilities are in working order • Security specialist: Secures and protects the building
Community (While not on the payroll, no one can dispute the fact that neighboring communities are a part of a school's organizational structure)	Community members and activists work in the community to create positive social change in the school and surrounding the school, helping communities come together to solve problems	• Fundraiser: Helps to raise money for school needs • Writer: Writes countless letters, articles, and speeches for causes that he or she supports • Visionary: Works for the vision of equal justice and social change

So, perhaps it really does take a village (or maybe a small army) of dedicated professionals to run a school. Now, what is your role in this army? The decision is totally up to you. It has often been said that student teaching is like a long job interview. Even if you do not want to be employed in that school, you will eventually want a job teaching in somebody's school, and you'll need a reference. You can jump in and work for the greater good, or you can choose to stand on the sidelines and watch from afar (we do not recommend the latter). Set your sights on being a part of the team, not just in your cooperating teacher's classroom but in other aspects of the school as well. As you work toward being a team player, it is equally important to understand the legal and ethical issues that impact your profession.

LEGAL AND ETHICAL ISSUES

In many aspects of education, the impact of laws has intensified since the landmark *Brown v. Board of Education* decision of 1954. It is clear that laws have substantial implications on teacher preparation and practice. For example, based on state teaching qualifications and regulations, you spent several years in school working toward your teaching certification. Directly and indirectly, laws influence the learning environment for children and for the adults who teach them. Moreover, whether you agree or disagree with the current educational laws (and policies), realize that as a teacher they shape what you can and cannot do within the educational environment.

Definitions of Important Terms

Interestingly, we found that although there are a few (relatively minor) laws dealing with student teachers, overall, the majority of the legal problems that apply to student teachers are the same ones that affect the entire profession. So, our conversations in this section largely pertain to general **legal** (concerning the protections that laws or regulations provide) and **ethical** (concerning what is moral or right) issues in teaching. Any good lawyer advises that you can't begin until everyone has all of the facts, so let's get on the same page with the terms and definitions that we use throughout this guide.

- *Legal* (lee-guhl), adjective: Permitted by law; of or pertaining to law; connected with the law or its administration; appointed, established, or authorized by law; deriving authority from law.
- *Law* (law), noun: A system of rules enforced through a set of institutions. It shapes politics, economics, and society in numerous ways and serves as a primary social mediator of relations between people. Additionally, the word applies to any written rule or collection of rules prescribed under the authority of the state or nation, as by the people in its constitution.
- *Ethics* (eth-iks), noun: The rules or standards governing the conduct of a person or the members of a profession.
- *Ethical* (eth-i-kuhl), adjective: Concerning a set of principles of conduct or a theory or system of moral values.
- *Issue* (ish-oo), noun: Any matter of dispute in a legal controversy or lawsuit.

Legal Versus Ethical

Now that we've presented the definitions of the above terms, we'd like to spend a moment discussing the distinct differences. It is often the case that people tend to use words like *legal* (or *the law*) and *ethical* (or *ethics*) interchangeably, but they are in fact quite different. They are separate concepts and are not dependent on each other. Laws are enacted by an authority, whereas ethics attempts to determine morals. Ethical issues have no force of law to uphold them, but they can affect the society around you. However, depending on the law, what is legal may also be construed as unethical (e.g., slavery).

Most licensing, professional institutions prescribe ethical principles with the expectation that their members adhere to those standards. This is most often a direct result of the culture of the professional community. In this example, violations of the ethical culture are not criminally actionable, but you can be penalized and/or even expelled from the organization according to the contract you signed. Simply put, don't break the law and don't act in an unethical manner. A violation of either the law or school ethics will more than likely result in losing your job. We address some of the most common ethical violations in the "Workplace Professionalism" section below, but first let's review some legal history specific to the field of education.

A History Lesson

Here are some landmark decisions that affected teaching. It is important to take this brief journey, as the decisions of these cases shaped the teaching profession. In an effort not to bore you with legal jargon, we present this information in a handy reference chart. Table 1.2 summarizes some of these historic cases and explains how they may affect your day-to-day teaching experiences. Of course, this list is not inclusive of every key decision but highlights major ones in the educational field.

Table 1.2 Landmark Education Cases

Landmark Case	Why It Matters to You	What You Should Do
Brown v. Board of Education (1954) Issue: Should Blacks and Whites receive an education integrated with or separate from each other? The U.S. Supreme Court declared that state laws establishing separate public schools for Black and White students and denying Black children equal educational opportunities are unconstitutional. Chief Justice Warren said the Court concluded that in the United States "the doctrine of 'separate but equal' has no place. Separate educational facilities are inherently unequal."	While some critics argued that the Brown decision did more to help other institutions and left the schools largely where they were in 1954, others believe that the spirit of the law moved people to serve as catalysts for social justice and change. It helped to shed light on the things that you can change within your own classroom, school system, and state.	The issues surrounding equity in the schools are very large (achievement gaps, disproportionate funding that relies on property taxation, teacher quality, etc.), and many of these issues are out of the hands of teachers, but you can make a difference. Make a pledge to be an advocate for the students in your class. Work through your local teacher associations to say the things that some of your students and their families cannot. Do the hard work of making high-quality education nonnegotiable for all students, regardless of race, gender, or creed.
Florence County School District Four v. Carter (1993) IDEA (Individuals with Disabilities Education Act) (1990) Issue: Should public schools be held accountable for teaching children with exceptionalities and disabilities? Shannon Carter had dyslexia, which compromised her school performance. In desperation, her parents placed her in a private school for disabled children, where she jumped several grade levels within a few years and graduated reading on grade level. The Carters then sued the school system for the private school tuition they'd paid. At the time, the law limited the school choice of parents with disabled children to state-approved schools. In this case, however, the court ruled that the school system failed to provide an "appropriate public education."	Children who have disabilities and/or exceptionalities in your classroom are your responsibility, regardless of any additional staff working to support and facilitate their education. If they are in your class, you must work to design instructional strategies to meet their needs. Every local education agency (LEA) has a method for identifying and supporting children with exceptionalities.	What you should do if you suspect that a child has an exceptionality: Talk to your CT. Ask about the process for identification. Observe the child. Take detailed and objective notes. Revisit your textbooks (or consult new books) that focus on strategies for working with children with special needs.

Landmark Case	Why It Matters to You	What You Should Do
IDEA governs how states and public agencies provide early intervention, special education, and related services to more than 6.5 million eligible infants, toddlers, children, and youth with disabilities. The act has been reauthorized and amended a number of times, most recently in December of 2004. Other documents often associated with this law include Americans with Disabilities Act (ADA, especially Section 504); Education for All Handicapped Children Act (EAHCA) (PL 94-142); Free Appropriate Public Education (FAPE); Individualized Education Program (IEP) (PL 99-142); Least Restrictive Environment (LRE).		
Norwalk Teachers' Association v. Board of Education (1951) Issue: Do teachers have the right to organize and/or strike? Should the Board of Education recognize the Teachers' Association as the bargaining agent? Are arbitration or mediation acceptable methods? Dispute over salaries involving stalwart negotiations between the Teachers' Association and the Board of Education led to a legal decision that prohibited public employees' method of conflict resolution. (It's important not to confuse striking with protesting. Striking is leaving work or stopping work as a coercive measure, whereas protesting is making a formal declaration of disapproval or objection; both can involve a concerned person, group, or organization.) The court held that since government is established by and run for all people (not for the benefit of any one person or group), to strike is a contradiction. A strike by public employees is in effect a strike against the government and hence goes against public policy.	It is a given that during your long, happy career as a teacher, you might have a dispute with someone else in the organization. If and when this happens, be glad that you can go to your local or national teacher association. This law helped to support the creation of local, state, and national teacher organizations as well as solidify their place in aiding teachers through myriad issues.	Teacher associations work hard on your behalf. Their roles include (but are not limited to) grassroots efforts involving collective bargaining for better pay, workloads, and working conditions; and they use negotiations, arbitrations, and mediation to achieve their purposes. But in order to take advantage of all that these organizations have to offer, there are some things that you have to do: Find out more about teacher organizations, associations, and unions. Locate your local, state, and national representatives. Decide which organization is best for you.
New Jersey v. T.L.O. (1985) Issue: Can schools search students' possessions?	The assistant principal probably looks back on that search and seizure and is thankful that there was	If you have a suspicion that a student has done something or is in possession of something

Table 1.2 (Continued)

Landmark Case	Why It Matters to You	What You Should Do
T.L.O. was 14 years old at the time that she was caught smoking cigarettes in a public school bathroom. When she denied the accusation, the assistant principal demanded to see the contents of her purse. Inside he found not only a pack of cigarettes, but rolling papers, marijuana, and a list of names of students who owed her money. T.L.O. was later charged with drug dealing. Her family argued that the school was unlawful in their search of T.L.O.'s property. However, the U.S. Supreme Court stated that searches and seizures may be conducted by school officials based on "reasonable suspicion."	enough evidence to make a case, because without it, he would have lost his job. The moral to this story is, make sure that you have a good reason to search a student's locker, person, book bag, clothes, etc. Your suspicion of "Well, she just looked guilty" will not cut it.	harmful, take the following precautions: Notify the school building administration immediately. If it is not an emergency, make sure to document and date everything that you notice.
Tinker v. Des Moines (1969) Issue: Do students have First Amendment protection at school? To protest the Vietnam War, Mary Beth Tinker and her brother wore black armbands to school. Fearing a disruption, the administration prohibited wearing such armbands. The Tinkers were removed from school when they failed to comply, but the Supreme Court ruled that their actions were protected by the First Amendment. The court's 7-to-2 decision held that the First Amendment applied to public schools, and that administrators have to demonstrate constitutionally valid reasons for any specific regulation of speech in the classroom. As Justice Fortas put it, "In order for school officials to justify censoring speech, they must be able to show that [their] action was caused by something more than a mere desire to avoid the discomfort and unpleasantness that always accompanies an unpopular viewpoint."	Yes, students do have rights that are protected under the Constitution! They have a right not only to think differently than you, but to voice their opinions as well. Moreover, it is your responsibility as a teacher to encourage your students to engage in conversation that is supportive of diverse viewpoints.	How can you support this decision in your classroom? Get to know your students and find out what makes them special. Offer multiple ways for students to share their thoughts and ideas (suggestion box, community meeting, webcast, etc.). Incorporate debate techniques as a regular part of your instruction.
Title IX of the Education Amendments (1972) Issue: Should institutions that limit gender equality receive federal funds?	If nothing else, this law should make you think twice about how you work toward gender equality in your classroom (and school).	Ask yourself these questions: Do I have any gender biases that I need to face and change in order to be a better teacher?

Landmark Case	Why It Matters to You	What You Should Do
Although Title IX is best known for its impact on high school and collegiate athletics, the original statute made no explicit mention of sports. Title IX of the Civil Rights Act of 1964 says that any institution receiving federal funding may not discriminate against anyone based on gender. The legislation covers all educational activities and complaints under Title IX alleging discrimination in fields such as science and math education and in other aspects of academic life, such as access to health care and dormitory facilities. It also applies to other extracurricular activities, including school band and clubs; however, social fraternities and sororities, sex-specific youth clubs (Girl Scouts and Boy Scouts) are specifically exempt from Title IX requirements.		Do I equally call on all of my students? Does my class/school offer academic opportunities for underrepresented populations?
The Child Abuse Prevention and Treatment Act (PL 93-247) (1974) Issue: Should states be mandated to provide funding for the prevention of the welfare of children? This key federal legislation addressing child abuse and neglect provides federal funding to states in support of prevention, assessment, investigation, prosecution, and treatment activities; it also provides grants to public agencies and nonprofit organizations for demonstration programs and projects. All 50 states have passed some type of mandatory legislation that requires certain professionals and institutions to report suspected child abuse. These include (but are not limited to) health care providers, mental health care providers, teachers and other school personnel, social workers, day care providers, and law enforcement personnel. The act, originally passed in 1974, has been amended several times and was most recently amended and reauthorized on June 25, 2003, by the Keeping Children and Families Safe Act of 2003 (P.L.108-36).	This one is a no-brainer—it is your legal and ethical responsibility as a teacher to report any suspected abuse of a child. This extends not only to children who are in your classroom but also to others who attend the school.	If you have a suspicion it is best to do the following: Take your concerns to your CT, administrator, school counselor, or school social worker. Document and date everything that you notice.

Source: United States Courts, http://www.uscourts.gov/EducationalResources/ConstitutionResources/LegalLandmarks/Landmark SupremeCourtCasesAboutStudents.aspx

WORKPLACE PROFESSIONALISM

So far in this chapter, we walked you through an overview of school culture and its importance to your role as a student teacher, unmasked the hidden roles of school professionals, and given you an overview (or maybe a review) of the major legal and ethical issues involved in teaching. Never is an understanding of these concepts more important than when it comes to professionalism. This term is defined as the ability to adhere to a set of values that are composed of standards, obligations, formally agreed on codes of conduct, and informal expectations. Think about your attire, how you carry yourself, your attitude, and how you interact with others. Typically, these issues revolve around a common understanding (sometimes unspoken, but if you're lucky, spoken) about expectations.

Workplace Rules

The teaching profession may appear to be a more relaxed environment than corporate America (think starched white collars, pearls, neckties, business suits, wing tips and high heels), however, it isn't as laid back as the constant images we see of workplace environments like Google, Amazon, and Yahoo. Sure, it would be nice to bring your dog to work every day, play Ping-Pong to relieve stress and encourage creativity, or not have to worry about leaving your Yoga class to be bothered by work (since you can work when you want to—and still get PAID); but this is the real world. It doesn't really matter whether or not these types of workplace environments really exist, because at the end of the day, that is not the reality of our profession (nor is it the reality of most professions). In the real world, the rules regarding what you can and cannot do at work (if you want to keep your job) are very clear. Conducted in 2013 by Polk-Lepson, a custom marketing research firm, a nationwide study on the state of professionalism in the workplace revealed nothing new, yet confirmed EVERYTHING that you probably already suspected. The study focused largely on employer's experiences with new college graduates and the professionalism (or lack thereof) that was exhibited by these employees. A nationwide sample of 401 human resource professionals was surveyed via an online questionnaire that also included open-ended response options. Now, it may seem as though this conversation is a bit premature (since you have yet to graduate); however, we know good information when we see it, and as your "School Culture Coaches" we feel compelled to give you the scoop in advance (you'll thank us later). Here are the highlights of that study:

Table 1.3 State of Professionalism

State of Professionalism		
Employers feel that . . .	Percentage (%)	What Can I Do to Be Successful?
Less than 50% of new employees exhibit professionalism in their first year. • The data trends show that no improvements were made during the four years of the survey administration.	48.9% (Strongly Agree/ Agree)	Define professionalism* While the percentage of respondents identifying each quality varies from year to year, the qualities that are consistently mentioned remain constant. To be a professional in the workplace, you should demonstrate the following qualities: • Work until a task is completed competently • Indicate interpersonal skills, including civility

Employers feel that . . .	Percentage (%)	What Can I Do to Be Successful?
There is a decrease in the number of new employees demonstrating professionalism. • This percentage is the highest it has been in the four years of data collection.	35.9% (Strongly Agree/ Agree)	• Reflect appropriate appearance • Exhibit punctuality and regular attendance • Evidence appropriate communication skills (written and oral) • Express honesty • Reveal focus/attentiveness *Interestingly, in this definition, few respondents mentioned expertise in one's field. Most likely, the assumption is that this is an expected quality of a professional.
There is an increase in the number of new employees exhibiting a sense of entitlement. • A recurring theme in the research is the sense of entitlement that new hires demonstrate. The way parents raised their children is most often seen as the reason for new employees feeling entitled (34.5%). Related to this, another 16.2% of the respondents believe new employees exhibiting a sense of entitlement were overly coddled and excessively praised. Lastly, some (15.8%) feel that the current education system may be the culprit. As one example offered, "Students have learned that they can receive acceptable grades without necessarily putting in the effort that should be required to earn those grades. Any teacher who has given a student the opportunity to get extra credit to improve a grade has contributed to a sense that anyone can receive a reward without putting in the effort."	52.9% (Strongly Agree/ Agree)	Demonstrate a sense of humility, not entitlement Respondents commented that new job applicants feel that they have paid their dues by graduating from college. While you certainly have the right to feel joyous about graduating from college, it is wise to remember that the undergraduate degree is only a start. It is a prerequisite for eligibility for many of today's jobs. The degree entitles you to the opportunity to compete with others for the same job. An attitude that works every time is "no one owes you anything; work hard to earn the reward."
• There is an increase in IT etiquette problems. Abuses of information technology continue to plague the workplace. IT abuses have increased over the past five years. It is estimated that, on the average, half of all new college graduate employees (48.8%) abuse IT in some way.	50.1% (Strongly Agree/ Agree)	Control your on-the-job use of technology Abuse of technology is now common in the workplace, and other studies validate that people feel lost without their cell phones. Nevertheless, it is time to be weaned from the addiction of constantly having to be in contact with others via technology. Twittering or checking Facebook are activities that do not belong on the job (especially when you have 20 to 25 eager children waiting for you). Additionally, with job-related activities, when you are sending an email or text, ask yourself if a direct conversation with the person isn't more appropriate. The convenience of technology often prompts us to use it when other means of communication are better or more effective.

(Continued)

Table 1.3 (Continued)

Employers feel that . . .	Percentage (%)	What Can I Do to Be Successful?
There has been a negative change in the work ethic. • On this measure, 44.6% of the respondents indicate the work ethic is worse. The decline in the work ethic is attributed to unprofessional characteristics and attire/appearance (keep reading for more information).	44.6% (Strongly Agree/ Agree)	Commit to producing quality work. Close to half of the respondents feel the work ethic in new employees has deteriorated. When asked why they believe this, respondents reply that employees take a casual attitude toward their work and are willing to do work that is less than professional quality. The education system may have to take some blame for this. Giving students extensions on deadlines for assignments and not taking the time and effort to demand quality work may promote the mistaken belief that this is acceptable behavior. When students receive good grades for mediocre work, they can develop an inflated image of their abilities and talents. It then becomes too easy to transfer these learned behaviors to the job. So, even though you want to be upset at your professors for holding true to deadlines and giving you the grades that you **EARN**, it really does help you in the long run. Remember that appearance DOES matter. It is important to recognize that what was acceptable or the norm in college does not necessarily apply to the workplace. The impact of appearance goes beyond affecting the likelihood of getting hired; the study also indicates that it has an impact on the perception of one's competence on the job.

Unprofessional Characteristics

These behaviors were rated high on the list of frequent offenses and were cited as the most common causes to "let go" or "not ask to return" (fire) new college graduates.

Indicator	Percentage (%)
Absenteeism/Punctuality	57.9%
Incompetent/poor performance/poor work quality: • Willingness to do work that is less than professional quality • Not self-driven or motivated • Not understanding the meaning/value of hard work	45.5%
IT Etiquette: • Text messaging at inappropriate times • Inappropriate use of Internet • Excessive Internet and cell phone usage for personal calls • Text messaging/email instead of face-to-face conversation	16.3%
Time Management/failure to meet deadlines	14.6%
Arrogant/lack of respect/rude to coworkers	14.3%

Impact of Attire/Appearance on Perception of Competence

Your appearance **CAN** (and most often **DOES**) have an effect on others' perceptions of an employee's ability to perform job requirements. Over half (58.9%) of the survey respondents noted that they Strongly Agree or Agree that your attire/appearance has an impact on perception of competence. Below are a few of the frequently mentioned issues that respondents feel impact perception of competence.

Indicator	Percentage (%)
Personal Hygiene	90.8%
Attire/dress	74.8%
Facial piercings (other than ears)	74.3%
Inappropriate footwear	70.8%
Visible tattoos	60.6%
Unnatural hair color	39.2%

Source: Adapted from Polk-Lepson Research Group. (2013). York: Center for Professional Excellence at York College of Pennsylvania.

We hope that by offering this overview, we have clarified the characteristics of professional and unprofessional behaviors. With the state of professionalism in the workplace not improving, candidates who understand and display professionalism have significant advantages over those who do not. The qualities that characterize a professional are straightforward. However, the challenge is that many of the behaviors and attitudes that epitomize unprofessionalism (as discussed above) are a part of our daily lives and in most cases are culturally accepted. Therefore, your job (along with all of the other things that you have to do) is to recognize the culture of your school and act accordingly.

Remember, culture in the workplace may have less to do with art, music, and literature than with shared belief systems, expected effort, and behavior expectations. This culture definitely includes such things as dress codes, socialization expectations, how the group feels about attendance, work output, problem solving, and so on.

Additionally, these expectations are also closely linked to *principles of professional ethics*, which are defined as "the norms, values and principles that should govern the professional conduct of a teacher" (Campbell, p. 29). Now, before you begin the internship, we have to make certain that you don't overlook some obvious details that, if not observed, might jeopardize the first impressions you make. We want to ensure that you don't risk making a negative impression that can hurt your career, but we certainly don't want this to turn into a boring review section of dos and don'ts; so, we'd like to offer a fresh perspective on the tried-and-true rules.

NEWS YOU CAN USE

What to Wear

It has been a long time since teachers dressed in their Sunday best to teach in a school. Nowadays, most schools are pretty casual, which can sometimes present a problem. With the freedom of being able to dress casually comes the responsibility of being able to maintain a professional work environment. Everything is not for everybody (even if it is the latest fad) and certain clothing is best left in your closet (even if your friend or mother tells you that you look fabulous in it). Let's be honest. Do your coworkers really need to see you in tight pants (yes, guys, this is for you, too), a miniskirt, or plunging neckline? Come on! Not only does it look unprofessional, it is inappropriate. Moreover, sweats or overly baggy pants and a T-shirt that says, "Where's the Party?" or "I Love Beer" also shouldn't be worn at your job. What you wear to work makes an individual statement about you that communicates your professionalism to others. Wearing

(Continued)

(Continued)

an outfit to work that you would wear to a nightclub on Friday night or for a weekend stroll at the beach suggests that your free time is more important than or indistinguishable from your job.

Be mindful of the dress code that the school culture dictates in the building. If one hasn't been presented to you, take your clues from the other teachers (or just ask). If your CT wears a suit every day, that doesn't necessarily mean you have to, but it most likely means that you should dress nicely. Now we're not saying that you need to go out and spend a lot of money on a new wardrobe. Some simple understated pieces can carry you through the semester. Add flair with your personality, not with your wardrobe. You always hear "Dress for success" and "Dress for the job you want, not the job you have." As cheesy as those adages may sound, they couldn't be truer. Save your casual dress for when you've got the job. Until that time—dress as if you are interviewing for a job.

Top 10 Rules of Conduct

These are statements you should *never* hear during your student teaching experience:

1. "You left your Facebook page up for the kids to read."

   Don't use the school day to advance your personal activities.

2. "Can you please take that cell phone call outside?"

   Put your phone on silent or vibrate when you come into the building.

3. "Are you dating my mom?"

   Keep your relationships with your students and their families on a professional level.

4. "Where is your lesson plan?"

   Always be prepared.

5. "You overslept again?"

   Always be punctual.

6. "Did you forget to proofread this before you sent it home?"

   Go beyond spell check when using written communication (proofread it yourself or ask your CT for help).

7. "Did you hear about Mr. Jones and Mrs. Kelly?"

   Don't feed into the rumor mill. This extends to verbalizing generalizations about children based on prior experiences with their siblings or family members.

8. "My husband heard your name on the police scanner on Saturday."

   Don't break any laws.

9. "My 10-year-old daughter has that shirt."

   Dress professionally.

10. "I'm sorry, I thought that you were the custodian."

   Know all of the players.

The Doctor Is In . . .

Dear Doc,

My CT's team member is so rude. It's gotten to the point that I just have stopped trying to be nice. My CT just seems to know how to deal. They plan and teach a lot together, so it's not like I can stay away from him. I don't want to blow my top, but I am on the edge.

Sincerely,
HELP!

Dear HELP,

I'm glad you sought out my advice before you lost your temper. It seems as though you need to take a page from your CT's book of cool. He obviously has some practice when it comes to working with lots of different people. While I can't tell you what to say, I can offer some tips to help you focus on what matters most.

- *Look for the positive*

- *Strive to understand and value other people's opinions and differences*
- *Listen carefully*
- *Try not to interrupt*
- *Don't overreact (much easier to say than to do)*
- *Know your boundaries/limits*
- *When in doubt . . . Smile*

Sincerely,

Doc

According to a Yahoo! Hot Jobs and Banana Republic survey (2007), 82% of Human Resources (HR) managers and directors agree that the way you dress directly affects the prospect of getting hired, retaining your position, and/or getting a promotion.

Transitioning Into Your New Environment

We know that you have a lot on your plate right now, but forgetting to **transition** (moving from one thing to another) into the school culture could be detrimental to your success as a student professional. Transitions are important. You never ask your students to move from one activity to another without planning for a transition, so why is it any different for you? You can make a successful transition by better understanding how all elements work together; this helps connect you to the school community. The alternative to this adaptation inevitably results in the impression that you really don't want to get to know (or care about) your new community—you stick out like a sore thumb! When you link transitioning ideas into the phase-in schedule dictated by your teacher licensing and/or certification program, also referred to as your **teacher education program (TEP)**, the ideas support your student teaching experience. We provide additional activities on this topic in the "Extra Credit" section below (these are most helpful if your internship site is unfamiliar or if you've had limited experience at your placement site).

FINAL THOUGHTS

You are now armed with important information to help you get started on your student teaching journey. As you begin your internship, consider how school culture and organizational structure work together. They really go hand in hand to make your placement unique. The outcome of the relationship between the school culture and the organization determines many spoken and unspoken rules regarding workplace professionalism. Yet some rules are the direct result of legal policies. Now that you understand the concepts, it's time to put your best foot forward. In the next chapter, we introduce you to your CT, so go out, take what you've learned, and make your first impression the best.

BULLETIN BOARD

Welcome to Student Teaching: The Open House

School Culture

School culture refers to a school's shared beliefs, customs, and behaviors. School cultures are typically exemplified by unspoken or unwritten rules. These unwritten rules often reflect the concerns and interests of the school and its members. The student teaching experience is unique, and it is important for you to understand a school's culture in order to be able to transition into a successful experience.

School culture is important.

Legal and Ethical Issues

Many landmark, historic cases helped to shape the way that we teach and interact with students, staff, and administration in schools. It is important for you as a teacher to know the difference between the legal and ethical responsibilities of the profession.

Organizational Structure

Every school has an organizational structure. Often the employees do much more than their job title indicates. It is important to understand the different school roles, how they work together, and how you can best adapt to those roles. Take the time in the beginning of your internship to transition into your new surroundings.

Workplace Professionalism

Always remember that professionalism is defined as a set of characteristics that are determined by a culture (in this case, your school's culture). Take this into account as you make appropriate etiquette choices, as the right decisions can make a great first (and last) impression.

EXTRA CREDIT

Read About It

School Culture

http://www.ksde.org/LinkClick.aspx?fileticket=e2aiFroKYFU%3D&tabid=4398

http://usca.edu/essays/vol122004/hinde.pdf

Legal and Ethical Issues

http://www.streetlaw.org/en/landmark.aspx

http://www.uscourts.gov/outreach/resources/landmark_studentcases.htm

http://everything2.com/title/Important+Landmark+Cases+in+Educational+Law

http://www.nea.org—National Education Association's (NEA) Code of Ethics for the Education Profession

Workplace Professionalism

http://www.ycp.edu/offices-and-services/academic-services/center-for-professional-excellence/2013-professionalism-study

http://investor.yahoo.net/releasedetail.cfm?ReleaseID=261265—Are You Primed for a Promotion? Check Your Wardrobe First

Think About It

Understanding School Culture

The following section includes an overview from a school that conscientiously connected its school culture and mission statements to its school activities. The artifact is from the Academy of the Pacific Rim charter school (http://www.pacrim.org), whose mission "is to empower urban students of all racial and ethnic backgrounds to achieve their full intellectual and social potential by combining the best of the East—high standards, discipline and character education—with the best of the West—a commitment to individualism, creativity and diversity." Review the following artifact and ask yourself the questions that are listed at the end:

Artifact:
A middle school begins each day by publicly honoring a student who has demonstrated a *gambatte* spirit. This word, taken from Japanese education, is used to explain when a person's opportunity is not due to luck or happenstance, but to their effort, diligence, and perseverance. In this school, students participate in daily community meetings, wear student uniforms, and enroll in Mandarin Chinese language classes beginning in the seventh grade. Students also participate in cleaning the school and their classrooms. Students and staff clean desks, sweep floors, take out the trash, sweep stairs, clean bathrooms, and pick up trash around the grounds of the school. In addition to the progress report, a journal is sent home with each student at the end of each week outlining major events that have gone on at the school. It also contains information about student achievement and reminders to parents of upcoming events. Parents/guardians must sign the Reply Form every week to indicate that they have read the journal and have seen their child's progress report. The Reply Form also provides space for comments or questions for teachers and/or advisors. Families are encouraged to call or email teachers or staff when questions or concerns arise.

Questions:

- What values and expectations are respected at this school?
- How has the school attempted to communicate these values and expectations to the community (students, staff, faculty, parents, etc.)?

Focus on the above artifact and relate this to your student teaching placement site in order to think about this question: How does your school use expectations, traditions, celebrations, scheduling, and physical space to support and reinforce the culture? Use Table 1.4 as a model to initiate your own school evaluation.

Table 1.4

School Culture Element	Evidence
Traditions and celebrations	My school recognizes each child's birthday by announcing his or her name over the PA system and by giving the child a pencil. The birthdays of teachers and staff are posted on the school calendar and are celebrated with a cake in the teachers' lounge at the end of the month. This shows that the school really values and sets aside time to recognize the kids and people who work in the building.

Legal and Ethical Issues

Read this case study and answer the questions that follow it.

Case Study

Gail is very excited about beginning her student teaching placement. She is hoping she will receive a job offer in the district (or school) where she is completing her student teaching internship. This also happens to be the same town that she grew up in, as well as the same district where she received her education. In fact, she knows most of the teachers and students in the building and even worked out a transportation schedule with a couple of the teachers in the building who are friends of her older sister. They bring her to school, and her boyfriend picks her up. Because she is saving money for a car and in spite of the long hours during the day, Gail decided that it makes sense for her to keep her job at a restaurant and just switch her shifts to the evenings. Her boss already agreed to the change, and she is confident that she has thought of everything and is prepared for her internship.

As the semester gets under way, Gail's cooperating teacher, Mr. Jones, notices that she doesn't seem to be available to meet as often as he would like. He wants to meet after school in order to plan for the following day or week, but Gail is always rushing out of the school to get to work. Additionally, Gail is observed yawning throughout the day and is constantly sending a student to the lounge to refill her coffee mug. Her lesson planning has dropped off considerably as well, and she just doesn't seem to be prepared to teach.

To add to these issues, Mr. Jones notices other behaviors that concern him. For example, Gail is typically seen talking to her friends (other teachers at the school) while the children are on the playground during recess rather than interacting with the children. When she takes the students to the computer lab, instead of instructing them, she surfs the web. She also has been overheard telling the children that if they don't complete their work, they will not have snack or recess, and she has been caught gossiping about students' families and other teachers at the school. Mr. Jones is very disappointed in her performance thus far. He sees that she has a lot of potential, but he is concerned by her lack of professional ethics.

Questions:

1. List some possible reasons to explain Gail's behavior.

2. After reading the National Education Association's Code of Ethics of the Education Profession listed in the "Read About It" section, answer the following question: Does Gail's behavior violate any of the principles? If so, which one(s)?

3. What would you say to Gail if you were Mr. Jones?

Source: Adapted from www.bigpicture.org. Reprinted from a 2010 article by Ron Wolk, "Education: The Case for Making It Personal." *Educational Leadership, 67*(7), 16–17.

Try It

What Are the Expectations?

Use Table 1.5 as a planning tool to outline and understand your CT's expectations and to develop strategies for addressing them during your student teaching internship. The worksheet lists one expectation example, and there are additional spaces for you and your CT to design expectations that may not be on the worksheet. This activity is particularly helpful to complete during the first week of the internship.

Table 1.5

Expectation	My CT expects me to . . .	I will do the following . . .
Dress attire	Dress in comfortable clothes that are not too tight or revealing and do not have suggestive language. Follow my CT's recommendation to not wear very high heels, as I will be responsible for taking the kids outside during recess and participating in games with them. Fridays are school spirit days and everyone wears the school colors or school T-shirts.	Make sure that I dress appropriately and wear low-heeled shoes (or clean sneakers). If necessary, purchase a school T-shirt or see what clothes I have that have the school colors.
Time management		
Planning		
Instructional strategies		
Classroom management		
Technology integration		
Exceptional children		
Family involvement		
Professional development		
Extra school duties (staff meetings, curriculum nights, PTA meetings, etc.)		

Transition Checklist

Sunday: Get ready for a walk around the block.

- Spend some time before your first day of work thinking about how you will transition into your new surroundings. Start by making a great first impression.
- Write a brief narrative about yourself. It should be four or five sentences. Include information about your interests outside of school, where you are from, your family, your pets, and so on. Make sure to end with how excited you are about being a part of the school community.

Monday: Meet the neighbors (school and clerical staff).

- This is no time to be shy. Begin your first week with a smile and a firm handshake.
- Make a special trip to the front office and introduce yourself to all of the office staff.
- Deliver your narrative (via mailboxes) to every staff, faculty, and PTA member.
- Stop by the office of the principal or assistant principal to set up an appointment for Friday.

Tuesday: Meet the neighbors (teachers).

- Find out more about the school's mission and professionalism policies and what is valued at the school.
- Ask your CT how the school engages the community, families, and businesses in the goals and objectives of the school.
- Ask a teacher at your grade level the following question: "If testing were not an issue, what would you spend most of your time teaching?"
- Talk to your CT about the school's dress policy. Ask specifically about any dos and don'ts.

Wednesday: Meet the neighbors (custodial and cafeteria staff).

- Take the time to celebrate and show your new neighbors that you value their daily contributions.
- Buy a few cards or have your class make a special card or picture for the custodial and cafeteria staff to show your appreciation for all that they do (clear this with your CT first). Present it to them personally (you may have to reintroduce yourself).

Thursday: Meet the neighbors (the community).

- With the support of your CT, prepare a letter of introduction to send home with your new students. Don't forget to proofread it before you send it home—better yet, let someone else read it.

Friday: Meet the neighbors (administrator/s).

- Ask the following questions during your meeting with the school building administrator/s. This helps you to gain a more substantive understanding about the school culture.
  - What is the mission of the school/district?
  - What type of decision-making structure is valued at the school?
  - How does the school recognize celebrations and traditions?
  - What advice can they offer you?

Saturday: R&R (rest and reflect).

- Think about all of the new information that you learned. How does it support your student teaching experience? Are there additional questions that you want to ask? Who has the answers?

Meeting Your Cooperating Teacher

The Teacher Conference

Dear Student Teacher:

We know how excited you are about meeting and getting to know your CT. This could potentially be a long-lasting mentoring relationship and friendship. By this point, I imagine you have spent a lot of time visualizing the student internship from your perspective. But have you ever stopped to think about this experience from your CT's position? We are lucky to have experiences on both sides of this fence, and it is really true what they say—you never know people until you walk a mile in their shoes. As student teachers, we had experiences that made us want to laugh and cry. However, we also
had many "aha" moments after we became supervisors. The opportunities to mentor, coach, and facilitate learning for new student teachers is never ending. We haven't yet decided unanimously on which role is more difficult—being a student teacher or a cooperating teacher.

Understanding your CT's role in this internship helps you to gain a better perspective on the time and effort that goes into the job (and don't forget—your CT still has to teach during this process).

Your cooperating teacher is one of the most important participants in your internship. In order to start things off right, there must be mutual understanding and respect. Get ready to thank your CT in advance for the guidance and direction that he or she unselfishly offers you during your last phase of this incredible journey.

Sincerely,

Your Merry Matchmakers

CHAPTER OBJECTIVES

After reading this chapter, you will be able to

- recognize the factors involved in matching student teachers with cooperating teachers;
- identify how the relationship between student teacher and cooperating teacher supports the transition into the teaching profession;
- define the difference between *change* and *growth* and understand how both are essential to a successful internship;
- compare and contrast the three different types of leadership models; and
- describe how the supervisory process changes during the course of the internship.

IT'S NICE TO MEET YOU

Have you ever been on a blind date? Perhaps a friend or coworker thought you might really hit it off with someone they knew. Or, perhaps your blind date was the result of an online dating service that matches people based on their personality profiles. Regardless of the method, once a date is confirmed, you anxiously anticipate the meeting, hoping to make a love connection. If you recall this blind date scenario, you certainly remember those anxious feelings where you hoped the person would be funny and attractive—and would think you were the perfect date.

For many of you, meeting your cooperating teacher is going to feel like a blind date. The ideal situation is when someone who knows you (preferably a **university supervisor (US)**—the person who is employed by the university to supervise you)—thinks you would be a good match for someone he or she knows well. As you prepare for that first meeting, you hope the person is a great teacher, but also kind, funny, and helpful. You also hope he or she will like you and think you were a well-prepared, natural-born teacher.

However, just like a blind date, the meeting can turn out to be the start of a wonderful, long relationship, or it also has the potential to go awry (sometimes the match just isn't what you envisioned). It doesn't happen often, but when it does (and everyone survives the experiences with smiles), it is always worth sharing the funny tales. This was actually the case for us during our student teaching. As you read on, we want to note that no cooperating teacher's feelings were hurt during the writing of this chapter. All the names were changed to protect the innocent and for the sake of anonymity, we refer to the student teachers (STs) as Larry, Curly, and Moe. Do you remember *The Three Stooges* (www.threestooges.com)? You may be thinking that these names are odd choices, but the definition of a *stooge* is "one who plays a compliant role," so the names actually fit quite well.

Larry had a cooperating teacher who handed over a class of first graders to him during the first week of the internship. The CT was present and supportive and didn't hover; he encouraged Larry to think of and implement his own ideas for teaching and classroom management—quite a different approach for Larry, who typically preferred to be told exactly what he should be doing all of the time. Larry was in a split internship, which meant that midway through the semester he moved to a different class, in a different grade level, with a different CT—who also "allowed" him to figure out what to do on his own.

Curly's cooperating teacher was the ultimate warm fuzzy teacher. Like a fairy godmother, she was always positive, in a perpetual good mood, and syrupy sweet. Even when Curly's efforts required constructive criticism, his CT kindly flipped the advice into positive (and from Curly's perspective, less than useful) feedback. This CT was quite the overachiever, as well. She didn't allow Curly to use "store bought" resources—he had to create all of his supplemental material from scratch. He wasn't even allowed to show a video, unless of course he'd made it himself. This posed a bit of a problem for Curly, who would have happily stocked up on Carson-Dellosa materials in order to have a life outside of student teaching. (For those of you who are unfamiliar with Carson-Dellosa, they are one of the leading publishers of affordable supplemental educational materials in the United States [see www .Carson-Dellosa.com].)

Moe's cooperating teacher required him to wear a suit or dress coat and pants (and this was during his surfer phase), asked that he cut his hair super short, and required him to refer to all students by their last names. The CT said that Moe's youthful appearance (along with his California good looks) wouldn't allow the kids to take him seriously. Not wanting to make waves (no pun intended), Moe called his mom for money, went to the local department store, and bought three pairs of dress pants, two jackets, two shirts, and a couple of extra ties—which he rotated for 15 weeks. Once the semester was over, he tossed them to the back of his closet and pulled out his swim trunks and Vans.

Even though these relationships were challenging for each of the stooges, they also learned many valuable lessons. Larry discovered that he had the content knowledge and pedagogical skills to be an effective teacher and that he *could* teach with minimal guidance. Curly learned how to create engaging materials and activities to address the needs of specific students rather than relying on purchased supplements that appeal to the mass market. Moe learned how appearance can hinder or help in creating a professional, authoritative demeanor in the classroom. (He eventually traded the shorts and T-shirts for the more appropriate khakis and oxford shirts, at least while teaching in the classroom.)

We all learned something from our relationships with our CTs, even though they clearly were not perfect matches (we are your Merry Matchmakers, not your Perfect Matchmakers). Although we offer you many tips throughout this chapter, two essentials that we learned from our student teaching experiences are (1) it is important to stay focused, and (2) continue to look for the positives.

DO I HAVE TO?

You're probably wondering why you even need a cooperating teacher. You know your content, you've taken all of your education classes, and you've spent a great deal of time observing, tutoring, and volunteering in the schools. You're ready to use what you know. But let's be honest. Even though you're pretty confident that you have what it takes (you wouldn't have made it through your teacher education program if you didn't), you're probably a little nervous about tackling all of the responsibilities that come with teaching. The truth is, you should be nervous. You are working with real children. Would you want a pilot to fly your plane who never trained with an experienced pilot or flew a real plane? Would you want a doctor to operate on you who hadn't practiced with an experienced surgeon? Would you want a hairstylist to cut your hair who had only cut doll's hair? Do you get the idea? Tackling the daily demands that come along with teaching is a daunting task for even the most seasoned of teachers. Educational policy makers and teacher education programs know this reality, so the **student teaching internship**, which is characterized by a specific number of weeks spent teaching under the supervision of a certified teacher and university supervisor, is designed as a built-in checks and balances system. This structure ensures that you have the proper guidance to help you successfully navigate the challenges that inevitably arise. This checks and balances system is known to most as **standards**; this is important as these standards serve as the basis for comparison and evaluation within program elements.

In the world of education, standards and CAEP are synonymous. **CAEP**, or the **Council for the Accreditation of Educator Preparation,** is the newest agency created to ensure the quality of teacher preparation and teacher certification programs of U.S. colleges and universities. CAEP is a consolidation of NCATE (the National Council for the Accreditation of Teacher

Education) and TEAC (the Teacher Education Accreditation Council), with a commitment to establishing rigorous standards for teacher preparation programs and elevating the stature of the education profession overall. By uniting these two major accrediting bodies, the profession is now able to speak with a unified voice about educator preparation. Additionally, this merging of councils ensures that stature and rigor are maintained as similar recommendations for accreditation are made on the basis of similar evidence that the CAEP standards are being met. (In other words, everyone is on the same page and singing in the same key.) So, what are the new CAEP standards? At the printing of this edition, the Draft Standards include the following:

- Standard 1: Content and Pedagogical Knowledge (what you need to know and be able to do to work effectively in today's school environments)
- Standard 2: Clinical Partnerships and Practice (your opportunities for nurturing and application of your developing knowledge and skills—e.g., field experiences and student teaching internships)
- Standard 3: Candidate Quality, Recruitment, and Selectivity (your demonstration of readiness upon admission and proficiency at different checkpoints along the road to program completion)
- Standard 4: Program Impact (your impact on P–12 student learning and development and how your program preparation played a role in that impact)
- Standard 5: Provider Quality, Continuous Improvement, and Capacity (your school's system for collecting and analyzing data on its program completers in an effort to support continuous improvement) (http://caepnet.org/commission/standards/, 2010)

We're not going to bore you with more than you need to know about accreditation and standards. (If you want the details on accreditation and CAEP's role in teacher education, visit www.caepsite.org, http://caepnet.org/commission/standards/, and http://caepnet.org/commission/standards/introduction/.) Just know that reputable teacher education programs seek and obtain accreditation. This is just a fancy way of saying they regularly provide multiple forms of evidence to document effective teacher preparation and can publicly verify that they have a good program. Therefore, both in the short term and the long term, you will be very happy you attended a program that took the time to jump through all of the accreditation hoops.

While all of the CAEP standards deal with the quality of your teacher education program, the one that explains why you have a cooperating teacher is Standard 2: Clinical Partnerships and Practice. The unit and its school partners design, implement, and evaluate field experiences and clinical practice so that teacher candidates and other school professionals develop and demonstrate the knowledge, skills, and professional **disposition** (a tendency or inclination to act or behave a certain way under given circumstances) necessary to help all students learn. Basically, this standard requires teacher education programs to create a student teaching internship that allows you to grow in the profession and demonstrate your knowledge. Part of what this means is that you have partners during student teaching—a university supervisor and a cooperating teacher. Remember that checks and balances system mentioned earlier? The university supervisor and cooperating teacher work together to ensure that you get exactly what you need from the student teaching internship. We discuss the university supervisor's role in depth in Chapter 8, but for now, let's explore cooperating teachers and what makes them tick.

YOUR CT ISN'T IN IT FOR THE MONEY (AND OTHER TIDBITS)

Here's some straight talk about finding cooperating teachers. The truth is that in some areas the pool of ST candidates is extremely small, and there are many, many wonderful CTs available to take a fresh, new teacher-to-be under their wings. By contrast, in other areas, there are several universities within miles of each other, and they are all looking for qualified willing CTs. One thing you need to realize is that CTs are paid very little money (if any) to guide the student teacher through the internship. When you factor in that reality along with asking them to relinquish control in their own classrooms, turn over the students, model effective teaching, serve as your advocate in the building, yet still remain responsible for the final outcome—it is a tough job. In spite of those issues, teachers continue to agree to serve as CTs for a variety of reasons, including opportunities to give back to the teaching profession and the prospect of gaining new knowledge and teaching techniques (Kitchel & White, 2007).

For whatever reason, your CT has agreed to do the job. Now, her primary task is to help you develop professionally by hosting you in her classroom during your internship. She provides the environment for you to grow as a teacher, to demonstrate the content knowledge, pedagogical skills, and professional disposition necessary to assist students in learning. You teach the CT's students, typically cover the content she scheduled, and usually incorporate her management strategies. That doesn't sound very difficult, does it? Keep reading.

To make this work, you must keep in mind that you are a *guest* in her room. She was there before you arrived, and she will be there after you leave. Similarly, the students in her classroom belong to her, and she is ultimately responsible for their academic, social, and emotional growth—even though you are "borrowing" them for several weeks. Try to imagine how this must feel by looking at a similar situation. Let's say that you have been living on your own in an awesome apartment for a few years, and you have organized your living space just the way you like it. You're used to a clean kitchen, your poodle or Labrador has been trained to stay off the couch, and you like to fall asleep around 10:00 p.m. in pure silence. Now, your younger brother asks if he can stay with you for a few weeks, which you know will actually mean three months or more. Of course, you really want to help him, but in your mind you are picturing an all-out disaster area, a dog that's now encouraged to lounge on the couch, and the need for ear plugs after 10:00 p.m. You agree to allow him to stay, but you know it will get tense if you have to keep reminding him that he is a guest in your home. In an ideal world, he would realize he is a guest, pick up his dirty socks, and make sure he respects your need for peace and quiet. Additionally, he would bring you mocha lattes every evening to remind you what a wonderful host you are. Since we don't live in an ideal world, and because he's family, you probably spritz the couch with fabric refresher, kick his dirty socks out of the way, and grit your teeth when you can still hear the sound of a TV in the distance after 10:00 p.m.

Now, imagine how a CT feels with another *teacher* in the room—someone who is not a relative, someone she has to nurture, talk to, and physically share a space with. She has to entrust her students into your care—knowing that the end-of-year test scores will reflect on *her* rather than on *you*. If there's a problem in the class, the principal is going to address *her* rather than *you*. It's no wonder that this relationship has the potential to be a bit of a challenge for both of you. So, never forget that you are a guest in the CT's room, and unless some other agreement is reached, do your best to follow her example and instructions. She takes the heat, so she calls the shots. Although you may not have complete and total control during the internship, you and your CT still need to work together to get you ready to teach in your own classroom. She is the instructional leader of the classroom and will use different leadership styles to guide you to success. The outcome will cause you to change and grow as a person and teacher. Before we cue you into the different leadership styles your CT may employ, we want to further discuss these ideas and share why they are important to a successful experience.

CHANGE VERSUS GROWTH

During the internship, you may hear references to **change** and **growth**. Examples include the following:

- "This is a growing experience."
- "How have you grown during this experience?"

- "You will go through many changes during student teaching."
- "Please reflect on the changes you made in this growing experience."

We could go on, but we think you get the point. Your college instructors or professors spent a lot of time getting you to reflect on your early and clinical field experiences. For good reason too, as reflection is critical to professional *growth* and it encourages you to *change* things that aren't working (we talk more about the importance of reflection in Chapter 8). Appreciate that it just can't be avoided; teaching goes hand in hand with change and growth. Likewise, two major outcomes of your student teaching experience are for you to change and grow. It is very common for these two words to be used interchangeably, but they are in fact distinctly different terms.

What Is Change?

Take a moment to think about how many different phrases you can come up with that start, end, or have the word *change* in them. We'll start you off: *change* agent, have a *change* of heart, *change* of scenery, and *change* the channel. . . . Okay, now it's your turn. How many additional *change* idioms did you come up with? The concept of change is certainly not new, but have you ever really stopped to think about what it means and, more important, what it means for you as you embark on this journey? We've listed a few definitions for the word *change* as offered by *Webster's Dictionary*:

- To become different in some particular way
- To switch, lay aside, abandon, or leave for another
- The result of alteration or modification
- To exchange or replace with another, usually of the same kind or category
- A thing that is different

Additionally, *change* can be categorized as a one-time event or a series of one-time events that are either internally or externally imposed. For example, the internally imposed decision to start a family is a one-time event that changes a person's life for a long time after the decision is made. The one-time event of losing a job may have been externally imposed, prompting the person to follow her heart's desire and enroll in a teacher education program. This one event likely spiraled into a series of other changes (selecting a school, maybe moving, learning new skills, finding time to study, etc.). Whatever changes come your way, it's how you respond to them that either encourages or stifles growth.

What Is Growth?

The spring season always ushers in massive growth spurts. Every time you turn around, it seems as though some new plant sprouted in a place where there was nothing before. In some cases, there was something very small there (like a stem and a leaf), and by the end of the day there is a bloom. Or, you might already have a green lawn, but a week of showers turns it into a lush, dark green carpet. These scenarios paint a picture of growth. *Webster's* gives us the following definitions:

- A progression from simpler to more complex forms
- An emergence
- An increase (whether planned or not)

While it is typically easy to see growth occurring, the progression of the growth is still a bit of a mystery. And although the process is different for everyone, the experts tell us that there are common themes involved.

1. *Growth takes time.* Teachers do not become great overnight. Neither do doctors, lawyers, singers, or athletes, for that matter. It takes time to understand the theories, become skilled in the methods, and practice effective dispositions. You have to consistently work on growing.

2. *Growth is gradual.* Baby steps, baby steps. Set your course in the right direction and forge ahead. You may have setbacks, but knowing where you are trying to go makes it easier to get back on track. This might mean trying a new classroom management strategy, especially when it seems as though none of the others have worked.

3. *Growth requires inspiration.* Are you up for the challenge? Growth does not occur unless you really want it. You can take all of the exams, read all of the books, tutor all of the children, but if you haven't made the commitment to grow from your experiences, not only is student teaching hard, but keeping up with the profession is even harder.

Do You Need to Change or Just to Grow?

We think it is fair to say that most people need both change and growth. Honestly, entire theories are built on this premise. Forced change (whether internal or external) imparts some type of growth; is your growth causing you to make a radical change? Either way, the two are connected. This is important to acknowledge, especially since you selected a profession that relies on your ability to change and grow at the drop of a hat. The good thing to remember is that there is no single prescription for *change* and *growth.* Your fellow classmate might need to grow a better understanding of algebraic content knowledge, and you might need to work on your instructional presentation. One person's baby step is another person's giant leap. Changes may come from the outside, but growth always comes from within. Ultimately, the decision to grow is a deliberate, personal choice.

Although we don't know you personally, we can assume that because you are reading this book and are getting ready to be (or are) a student teacher, you have done your fair share of changing and growing. It may have been easy for some and challenging for others, but you're here. You are ready and willing to put in the time and effort it takes to grow and change a little bit more, and luckily, you have a willing participant (your CT) who is going to help you every step of the way.

ON TIME SUPERVISION

Let's cut to the chase: The CT has a real job to do—teach the students in her room—and you are to (somehow) learn to do that within her environment. That "somehow" is evidenced by the level of guidance and support she provides for you; it varies depending on her perception of your role, and how willing, ready, and able you appear to be to jump in and do the job.

First, cooperating teachers view themselves in a variety of roles, which impact the type of leadership they provide (Russell & Russell, 2011). Your CT may emulate one of the following roles:

- *Model.* This CT *shows the student teacher how the job is done* by demonstrating what she believes are effective practices. The student teacher's job is to *observe and replicate* the CT's instructional strategies and techniques for interacting with students and others in the school community.

- *Mentor.* This CT *allows the student teacher to try out strategies and techniques,* then later sets up conferences to discuss strengths and areas for growth. Additionally, the student teacher is encouraged to ask questions for clarity.
- *Guide.* This CT *promotes dialogue about activities or strategies the student teacher wants to implement.* This way, the student teacher gets an expert's opinion about whether a so-called great idea will work or not—before actually trying it. As an expert guide, this type of CT may also intervene mid-lesson when she believes the student teacher has gone off track (e.g., providing misinformation or using a blatantly ineffective management strategy).

It may help to think of these styles as cyclical processes. Figure 2.1 provides a visual of the process.

Figure 2.1   Three Types of Cooperating Teacher Roles

CT as Model   **CT as Mentor**   **CT as Guide**

Additionally, Russell and Russell (2011) found that cooperating teachers saw themselves in one, two, or all three of these roles at different points during the internship. Perhaps this fluctuation by the CTs in their perceived role is impacted by how prepared the student teacher appears to be for the job. Robert Rando (2000) studied this connection between preparedness and level of supervision when observing participants in a counselor training program. In his model, Rando found that supervisors could consciously select the appropriate level of direction and support a particular supervisee required in order to grow, based on the supervisee's readiness for the task at hand. Critical to the model is the concept of match and move—meaning supervisors *match* the support provided to the supervisee's readiness (defined in terms of willingness, ability, and self-confidence) for the task, and then *move* the supervisee to increased readiness for dealing with that task in the future. Another way to think of this is like a scaffold or a support system in a work-related environment. The supervisor (teacher) provides the supervisee (student) with the support needed to be able to independently perform the task in the future.

Supervisory Leadership Roles

Rando (2000) developed a continuum for understanding how supervision varied with readiness. Supervisory style was presented in terms of high/low direction, high/low support, and high/low supervisee readiness. Table 2.1 highlights the four different supervisory styles.

So, how does this research translate to the world of student teaching? Well, it means that your cooperating teacher may actually be quite deliberate rather than haphazard or irrational, when it comes to her interactions with you. Her choices may be based on how she views her role (model, mentor, or guide), as well as her perception of your readiness for the job (willingness, ability, and confidence). But don't forget—just as your preparedness and confidence evolve during the course of the internship, your cooperating teacher's perceived role (and, consequently, level of direction and support provided) changes as well.

There is a great deal of literature documenting how important the cooperating teacher's role is in the professional development of student teachers. We offer additional resources at the end of the chapter, but if you just have to check right now, conduct an online search for Russell and Russell, 2011 (http://www.questia.com/library/1P3-2477422431/mentoring-relationships-cooperating-teachers-perspectives). This website offers further reading about CTs helping student teachers prepare for the realities of teaching.

Table 2.1   Supervisory Leadership Styles

Supervisory Style	Degree of Supervisee Readiness	Degree of Supervisor Direction	Degree of Supervisor Support	What Does It Mean?
Technical director	Low	High	Low	You are really new at this component. You're unfamiliar with the fundamentals of the job. I can provide you with the basics, and in time, your readiness will improve.
Teaching mentor	Moderately low	High	High	You are still new to this job. I can provide you with resources, strategies, and support. As you learn more, your confidence in your abilities will grow.
Supportive mentor	Moderately high	Low	High	You know what to do, but you still need me to boost your confidence. Make some decisions on your own. I'll offer feedback for your choices.
Delegating colleague	High	Low	Low	You're ready for this task. I don't need to tell you what to do, how to do it, or to boost your confidence. I can stand back and let you handle this on your own.

Source: Adapted from Rando, R. A. (2000). *Adaptive supervision in counselor training.* Retrieved from http://ccvillage .buffalo.edu/ Village/ElecProj/Rando.htm

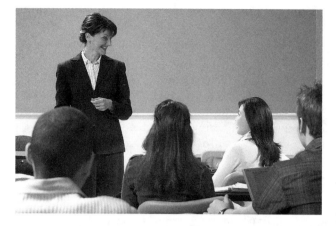

Your relationship with your cooperating teacher can make or break your internship. Remember, you will be spending on average 8 hours a day, 5 days a week, for 15 weeks with your CT. You want to make sure that you enjoy that time in the classroom. There will be plenty of challenges to come during the internship (and we offer help for those throughout the text) without adding the challenge of managing a difficult relationship with your CT. Also, do not forget that you require your CT's verification on various forms to document that you successfully completed the internship. The CT is also the person that potential employers will most likely call for a detailed reference on your teaching performance, ability to work with others, and content knowledge. You need this relationship to work, and we are dedicated to showing you how to do just that—make it work!

Guidelines for the Relationship

There are some very basic guidelines that you can follow to create a great relationship with your CT. These guidelines apply to all student teachers, regardless of the specifics of your placement. The following chart offers a few helpful hints to get you started.

BASIC GUIDELINES FOR MAKING THE ST/CT RELATIONSHIP WORK

☐ *Make a good first impression.* We don't care what anyone tells you.... First impressions matter. You only get one shot at this, so make it a good one.

☐ *Be a respectful guest.* Observe how your CT manages the entire school day, and try to figure out when and how you fit in. If you want to make changes (e.g., to the schedule, the room layout, the classroom management system), ask first, and don't be offended if the answer is no. Relax.... You will have your own class before you know it.

☐ *Do your research.* If you discover you don't know enough about what you are expected to do (e.g., content, pedagogy, management, school policies), take the initiative to find the answers on your own. Revisit textbooks, talk to other student teachers or teachers, and/or try an Internet search.

☐ *Don't be afraid to ask questions.* This is no time to be timid. It helps to begin with, "I've already looked into this, but I am not finding the answers I need. Can you help me?" Your CT may be more willing to help you if she believes you have been trying to help yourself.

☐ *If you think you're ready, ask for more responsibilities.* CTs may not realize that you're up for a challenge. Be specific about what you want to do (e.g., write the weekly newsletter, lead a parent-teacher conference, or pick up third period) and the level of support you think you will need. Be realistic, and follow through.

☐ *If you think you're not ready yet, ask to scale back a bit.* Sometimes CTs give you too much too soon. Develop a plan for eventually moving forward in a timely manner. For example, you might say, "I don't think I'm ready to take on third period, but I would like to start by team teaching with you. Maybe by the end of the week, I'll be ready to teach it on my own."

☐ *Give it time.* The relationship with your CT may not be roses and rainbows from Day 1. You will have to allow time to figure out what each other's quirks are and how to work together in harmony. Even if you have a less than perfect beginning, you can use the strategies listed here to try to make positive changes in how your CT views you, which consequently impacts the types of interactions you have with your CT.

☐ *If the relationship is exceptionally unpleasant, speak with your university supervisor.* At times, a case may arise when the student teacher–cooperating teacher relationship is not conducive to a positive student teaching experience. If this is your situation, you need to inform your supervisor. We recommend keeping a written (and dated) log of concerns that are specific and factual. We also recommend that you ask your supervisor to come in to purposefully observe what may be a tense or hostile relationship. If it is warranted, your supervisor may even schedule a meeting involving all three of you, where you can share your concerns with the support of the university. What happens after this meeting varies by university, but options may include a plan for remaining in the classroom, moving to another classroom, or moving to a new school.

FINAL THOUGHTS

Cooperating teachers work diligently to guide you through the internship by serving as a resource and sounding board. CTs are an essential component of your experience, and they are mandated by CAEP. Additionally, a major role they fulfill is providing you with guidance to help you extend your knowledge, skills, and teaching dispositions (remember our discussion of *change* and *growth*). A CT's supervisory style is based on the CT's perceptions of his or her role and your readiness for teaching. This style may be one of the three styles of model, mentor, and guide, or it may be a combination of the three.

Your CT can help you avoid pitfalls, give you advice on creating relationships with students and parents, and serve as your advocate within the school. If this describes your cooperating teacher, that's great. Feel free to skim the next chapter and refer to it later if you need to remind yourself of all of the work that your CT does behind the scenes. We don't want to waste your valuable time when you could be planning a lesson, organizing your files, or just taking a much-needed break. If, however, you've had a few tense moments with your cooperating teacher, or if his or her style is not compatible with yours, Chapter 3 is a great resource for you.

BULLETIN BOARD

Meeting Your Cooperating Teacher: The Teacher Conference

Greetings and Salutations

You must have a CT, so you may as well do everything in your power to make the relationship, as well as the overall student teaching experience, a positive one.

Strive to work together.

Do I Have To?

As a guest in your CT's classroom, your first task is to determine how you fit into the picture rather than how to modify the picture to fit you. (That may come later, but there is no guarantee.)

On Time Supervision

Your CT wants you to be successful. Each CT views his or her role differently (model, mentor, guide, or a combination of these), and each student teacher comes to the internship with varying degrees of readiness. These factors may impact the type of supervision the CT provides.

Change vs. Growth

You will change and grow as a result of this experience. These two concepts are distinct yet interrelated. Being successful in the teaching profession relies on an understanding of how they work together. Change can be an internal or external act. Growth is always an internal choice.

EXTRA CREDIT

Read About It

Working With Your Cooperating Teacher

http://roadtoteaching.com/2009/08/08/working-with-your-cooperating-teacher

Leadership Styles

http://www.buzzle.com/articles/types-of-leadership-styles-in-education.html

http://psychology.about.com/od/leadership/a/leadstyles.htm

Thinking About the Process of Change

http://www.ocfs.state.ny.us/ohrd/materials/30370.pdf

Teacher Blogs

http://www.gwu.edu/~cooptchr

http://www.tooter4kids.com/classroom/tips_for_cooperating_teachers.htm

Think About It

Dealing With Unique Supervisory Issues

Read the case study and complete the activities that follow.

"HELP! I'M OLDER THAN MY COOPERATING TEACHER"

Dear Merry Matchmakers:

I have just returned from meeting my cooperating teacher, and I'm not sure whether I want to laugh or cry. I walked into my CT's classroom and was greeted by a young woman who looked to be about 30 years old. Well, you could have knocked me over with a feather when I found out that she is actually 25. I mean, gosh—I have grandchildren who are older than she is. To add insult to injury, she is cute and perky and has an actual bounce in her step when she walks (rumor has it that she was captain of her college cheerleading team). I'm not sure that I am going to be able to take feedback from her, whether it's good or bad. Since I don't think it appropriate to share my age with the world, let's just say that I am a mature student. I've had a career and raised a family, and I didn't want to sit around the house all day. I love children and have done really well in all of my teacher education classes. I'm excited about student teaching, but this really feels like a setback. I don't want to ask for a change in placement so soon, but I know myself and I don't think that I will be able to deal with this all semester. What should I do?

Sincerely,

Doomed From Day One

1. Write a response to Doomed From Day One. Be sure to include a discussion about change and growth in your letter. What does "Doomed" need to hear about these concepts that might help? We've also written a response, but don't take a look at it until you have completed your letter. Who knows, yours might just be better.

2. If you were in charge of making student teaching placements, what type of leadership style do you think would match well with Doomed From Day One? Explain your answer.

3. What type of leadership style do you prefer? Why? Explain your answer.

4. Write a one-page letter introducing yourself to your cooperating teacher. Make sure to highlight things that may not have to do with school (e.g., your hobbies, interests, family). You are one of a kind—make sure that this comes across in your letter.

THE MERRY MATCHMAKERS' RESPONSE

Dear Doomed From Day One,

We're going to have to be blunt here and just tell it like it is. We actually think that you are being too hard on yourself and on the Perky Princess. First of all, you sound as if you are selling yourself short by not giving your CT a chance. If you opened yourself up to the experience, you might learn something from her and conversely offer her some of your infinite wisdom. She might be a teaching superstar, but we're sure that you've got something in your "toolbox" to help in the classroom.

Before you try to jump ship, think about all of the hard work that you have put into getting here. It is unlikely that your university supervisor will give you a new placement without first assessing if there is an instructional issue with your current placement, so what's the harm in trying to make it work? We sense that the real issue may have more to do with your pride and ego than you realize. If she is an excellent teacher, it shouldn't matter that she's younger. But, if you're concerned with not being able to connect with her due to your age difference, then be up front about it and invite your US to sit down with both of you to see how you might be able to connect. Remember, the university matched you two together for a reason; it might be because of your calm temperament to balance her drill sergeant organizational skills. Or, maybe you have strengths in math and science and her strengths are in language arts and social studies. Either way, you may make a winning team. We want to see you give it a try. Like Mom always says, "Try it; you just might like it."

Good luck, and keep us posted.

Sincerely,

Your Merry Matchmakers

Try It

Getting to Know You

You spend a considerable amount of time with your CT during the student teaching internship. It might be helpful to connect with him or her on subjects other than teaching. Use these fun questions to get to know your CT better. Feel free to create other questions (but don't make them about work). Try asking your CT a couple of questions a week, and don't forget to offer some information about yourself as well. Here are some examples:

- If you knew you could try anything and not fail, what would you attempt?
- What superpower would you most like to have, and why?

- Would you rather take pictures or be in pictures?
- Are you a beach, country, or city person?
- Do you live in a house or an apartment?
- Have you ever lived in another country?
- Have you ever met a famous person?
- How do you spend your free time?
- Tell me about a favorite event of your adulthood.
- Tell me about a favorite event of your childhood.
- What are your hobbies?
- What countries have you visited?
- Which country are you from?
- What do you do on Sundays?
- What is your motto in life?
- What kind of food do you like?
- Which languages do you speak?
- What cartoon character best describes you?
- If you could live anywhere in the world for a year, where would it be?
- What do you think is your best talent?
- Whom do you respect the most?
- Who has had the most influence in your life?
- Would you like to be famous?

Be creative and write three additional questions.

Part II

Politics

3

Understanding Your Cooperating Teacher

The Rules

Dear Student Teacher:

When it comes to cooperating teachers, we've seen it all. Whether looking back on our own experiences as student teachers (back in the Stone Age), through watching the experiences of student teachers in the schools where we worked, or when serving as supervisors and liaisons for student teachers at the university level, we have observed a variety of different types of student teacher–cooperating teacher relationships. Based on our extensive experience in this area, we feel well qualified to recommend the information you need to have a positive professional relationship with your cooperating teacher. In our experience, most cooperating teachers have excellent content knowledge (they know what to teach), are skilled in pedagogy (they know how to teach), and are kind, caring, understanding, and enthusiastic educational leaders (they know how to act). Most of them are great (really, they just want to help you), but if you happen to encounter conflicts based on differing personality traits, after reading this chapter, you'll walk away with practical strategies for turning lemons into lemonade (along with a few very funny stories).

Aside from entertaining you with stories from our own experiences, our ultimate goal is to provide you with the secrets to a successful relationship with your cooperating teacher—no matter what.

Sincerely,

Your Relationship Therapists

PERSONALITY THEORY

An important factor in any relationship is to understand the **traits** or characteristics that each person brings to the table. In short, what specific personality traits do you and your CT possess? The answers are important for three reasons:

- Understanding personality traits may give you insight into behavior—both yours and your CT's.
- Understanding the traits behind the behaviors allows you to select appropriate strategies to handle almost any situation (we refer to this as strategic problem solving).
- Understanding the art of strategic problem solving (with a win-win attitude) often leads to a positive outcome (i.e., a better student teacher–cooperating teacher relationship). Initially, as we start this chapter you may feel as though you are back in Psych 101, but bear with us. There's a lot of information presented that you might want to use in other relationships. But if you're having trouble retaining all the valuable information in this chapter, then focus on the charts, which provide you with the same valuable information in an easy-to-read visual format. So, there you have it; now let's get started.

Getting the Cold Shoulder

To set the scene for this section, we have to go back to the '70s (key the wacky music, and think cheesy sitcom flashback scenes).

Has this ever happened to you? You are in your favorite coffee shop and you see someone you know (not a particularly good friend, but you know her nonetheless). You acknowledge her and say "Hi." Of course she is equally happy to see you, and she responds by smiling and saying "Hi" back to you. You don't slow down to engage in trivial chitchat, and you go along your merry way. The act of saying "Hi" was enough to solidify the fact that there is mutual respect on both of your parts. Now, let's fast-forward—different day, similar scenario with a much different outcome. You are in the same coffee shop and you see the same person you know. But this time when you smile and say "Hi," the person looks right through you, doesn't smile, doesn't say hello and just keeps on walking. "Wait," you say to yourself. "Did that just happen?" Clearly you were still being your ever-polite (dare you say charming) self. What could have happened to make this person not respond? Who would do something like that, and what should you do as a result of the person's actions?

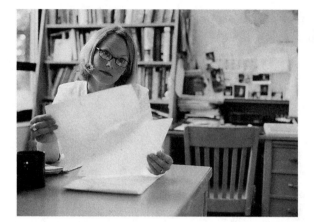

By channeling your inner Oprah or Dr. Phil, you've probably come up with the following solutions:

- You decide that she has a major character flaw and her behavior is a recurring interaction—in which case you decide to ignore it forever (or until she decides to speak again).
- You decide that she was just having a really bad day and was so preoccupied that she didn't even notice you—in which case you secretly forgive and forget (because we've all been there at least once in our lives—right?).
- You decide that even if the rude behavior continues, you are a better person and you will still continue to say hello every time—in spite of the apparent flaw in her disposition.

Whatever course you decide on, you are inherently making judgments about a personality and basing your response on this opinion. In order to level the playing field, here is some basic information along with other interesting facts about personality traits. This information is not intended to fast-track you to a psychology degree, but it should be used to gather additional information in order to understand different behaviors.

PERSONALITY TRAITS

Gordon Allport (1897–1967) is considered by many the father of **personality theory**. This branch of psychology studies personality and individual differences. Among his various contributions to the field, he believed that people have consistent personalities, that individuals are unique, and that personality traits could be better understood through careful review of autobiographies, diaries, and letters. Needless to say, he did a lot of reading and writing in his lifetime. In one classic study, he read over 300 letters written by the same person (a girl named Jenny) and after it was all said and done, he was able to describe her in eight distinct personality traits (Cattell, 1965).

Many Traits Theory

Personality traits are distinguishing qualities or characteristics. Think back to the coffee shop "cold shoulder" incident. Is there a personality trait that can be used to describe behavior that some might call "fickle" and others might call "snobbish"? The answer is a resounding "yes." What is most important to note is that many personality traits work together to make you and your CT unique people. You have specific traits, and your CT also has specific traits. Basically, personality development is an ongoing process. How a trait is displayed (as behavior or action) is dependent on more than one factor. All of your traits work together in different situations to give you your unique personality. Figure 3.1 illustrates how seven important factors represent this complex idea of personality as an ongoing process.

Think about it like this: You may be extremely outgoing (Common and Cardinal traits) with people you know well, but when you are in a new situation with strangers, you become shy, sensitive, and intimidated (Central traits). However, you feel strongly that it is rude not to converse (Motivational trait), so you force yourself to say hello when someone looks your way. Some theorists believe that looking at many personality traits at once can help determine which traits can be linked to certain behaviors. This is an interesting idea because it could

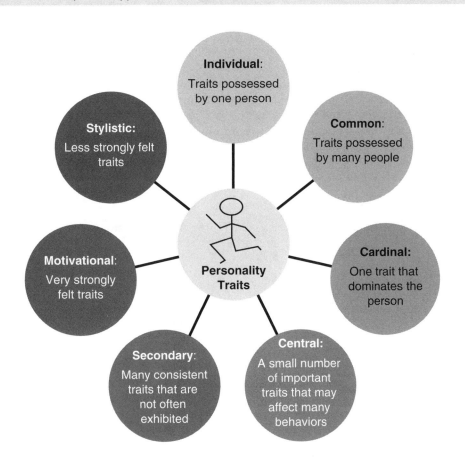

Source: Adapted from Cattell, R. B. (1965). *The scientific analysis of personality.* Baltimore, MD: Penguin.

provide a better understanding of what sustains conduct and actions and how they should be handled. Would you like to know which personality traits are linked to getting straight A's? What about a more serious issue, such as which personality traits are linked to a person's propensity to take drugs? Believe it or not, there was actually a study done that found that four-year-olds rated as aggressive, fidgety, restless, and disobedient were more likely to use illegal drugs nearly a decade later (Carver & Scheier, 2013, p. 176). But more important, let's go back to the reason you are reading this chapter. Would a better understanding of your unique personality traits and those of your cooperating teacher influence how you might handle **conflict** (an actual or perceived opposition of needs, values, and/or interests)?

PERSONALITY TRAITS AND THE STUDENT/COOPERATING TEACHER RELATIONSHIP

There are an unlimited number of potential traits used to describe personality. For the sake of time, we condensed the work of Cattell (1965), who came up with 16 primary personality factors and their corresponding traits. Raymond Cattell was a smart man (he went to college at 16 and earned a doctorate at age 20), and his theory is useful, but his findings were criticized and never replicated with similar results, which is frowned on in research. His work was later revised by Conn and Rieke in 1994. Table 3.1 presents a condensed version of Cattell's work. It introduces some factors and personality descriptors. If you want to see all of the factors, check the Further Readings section at the end of this book or conduct an online search of "Raymond Cattell" or "16 Personality Factors." Some important points to keep in mind as you are reading the table include the following:

- The primary factor (first column) represents the overall personality, and the traits (second column) represent the characteristics or behaviors that you might observe.
- Each factor is connected to a cluster of specific traits that typically go together, and Cattell labeled these low range (LR) traits and high range (HR) traits.
- The traits should be viewed as a range of behaviors that create your individuality. For example, warmth (in the high range) includes such related qualities as kind, easygoing, participatory, and friendly. However, exceptions and situational influences exist (e.g., even the most easygoing among us may get their feathers ruffled at times).

Take a look and see if the characteristics in Table 3.1 describe either you or your CT.

Table 3.1 Personality Factors and Descriptors

Personality Factor	Personality Traits (i.e., observed behaviors)	
	Low Range (LR)	High Range (HR)
Warmth	Reserved, distant, cool, impersonal, detached, formal, aloof	Outgoing, attentive to others, kind, easygoing, participating, people person
Dominance	Cooperative, avoids conflict, submissive, humble, obedient, easily led, docile, accommodating	Dominant, forceful, assertive, aggressive, competitive, stubborn, bossy
Liveliness	Serious, restrained, prudent, taciturn, introspective, silent	Lively, animated, spontaneous, enthusiastic, happy-go-lucky, cheerful, expressive, impulsive
Rule-Consciousness	Expedient, nonconforming, disregards rules, self-indulgent	Rule-conscious, dutiful, conscientious, conforming, moralistic, staid, rule bound
Sensitivity	Utilitarian, objective, unsentimental, tough minded, self-reliant, no-nonsense, rough	Sensitive, aesthetic, sentimental, tender-minded, intuitive, refined
Vigilance	Trusting, unsuspecting, accepting, unconditional, easy	Vigilant, suspicious, skeptical, distrustful, oppositional
Abstractedness	Grounded, practical, solution oriented, steady, conventional	Abstract, imaginative, absentminded, impractical, absorbed
Apprehension	Self-assured, unworried, complacent, secure, free of guilt, confident, self-satisfied, untroubled	Apprehensive, self-doubting, worried, guilt prone, insecure, worrying, self-blaming
Openness to Change	Traditional, attached to familiar, conservative, respecting traditional ideas	Open to change, experimental, liberal, analytical, critical, free thinking, flexibility
Self-Reliance	Group-oriented, a joiner and follower dependent	Self-reliant, solitary, resourceful, individualistic, self-sufficient

	Personality Traits (i.e., observed behaviors)	
Personality Factor	Low Range (LR)	High Range (HR)
Perfectionism	Disorder, flexible, undisciplined, lax, self-conflict, impulsive, careless of social rules, uncontrolled	Perfectionist, organized, compulsive, self-disciplined, socially precise, exacting will power, control, self-sentimental
Tension	Relaxed, placid, tranquil, patient	Tense, high energy, impatient, driven, overwrought, time driven

Source: Adapted from Cattell, R. B. (1970). Advances in Cattellian personality theory. In L. A. Pervin (Ed.), *Handbook of personality: Theory and research* (pp. 101–110). New York: Guilford Press.

Did you notice yourself in any of the descriptors? Better yet, did you notice your cooperating teacher? Of course you did. This list of characteristics is extensive, and personality is always an interesting topic. You and your CT (and the rest of the world) are individuals who bring unique personalities to every situation. So how does all of this information about personality traits help you? You want to work positively with your CT. Let's be honest; you wouldn't really be as interested in this chapter if you and your CT weren't butting heads on at least one important issue. Or, you might not disagree with your CT on anything and want to know how it is that you are so alike. You want to have a positive student teaching experience, and understanding your CT's unique personality is important to this goal. The idea is to recognize how your traits and the traits of your CT can work together to foster a positive relationship.

A Day in the Life

As we mentioned earlier, over the years we've helped a lot of student teachers and CTs. So, you can imagine that we have a lot of stories to share. Fortunately for you, many of our former student teachers don't mind sharing. Consequently, we are now going to give you an unprecedented opportunity to be a fly on the wall during an email "gripe" session and eavesdrop on the conversation of three student teachers who are discussing their relationships with their CTs. These are real experiences, and only the names have been changed.

THE DAILY NEWS

Day 15

Luis: Is anybody out there? I really need to get something off of my chest or I might just quit.

Jane3:   Hey I'm here. You must have been reading my mind. I'm not even going to the gym tonight, I'm so exhausted. What's up?

(Continued)

(Continued)

iteach105: Wait, I'm here too. Don't start without me. I know that I can contribute to this conversation. ☺

Luis: I don't think that I can take it another day. He is driving me crazy. . . . I have secretly renamed him "Lazy Larry." He just gave me all of his teaching manuals, pacing guides, courses of study for English. I mean, I haven't even learned all of the kids' names yet, not to mention that some of them really scare me >-).

He's never in the room. He gets here in the morning and posts the schedule and disappears to get coffee, but there is no way that it takes four periods to get coffee. Where is he going—Starbucks?

Jane3: LOLH, can't respond right now.

Luis: But wait—he even wants me to take over his elective courses. I don't know a thing about editing the school newspaper. I don't even like to read the newspaper. . . . Okay, this is the last thing, and then I want someone to tell me why I should stay. Every time I ask him a question, guess what he says—"I know you can figure that out. I'm sure that 'Top Notch U' has totally prepared you for this, so I trust your judgment. If you have any questions, I'm in the lounge." He's got no real advice, except what not to eat from the cafeteria—my all-time favorite advice, "By the way, don't eat school lunch on Taco Day."

iteach105: ?4U. Why would you go back? It doesn't sound like you're learning anything except how to have a stressful senior year.

Luis: I have to graduate. I have about 50 people coming to see me walk. ☺

Jane3: Tell me about it. Everyone in my family is a teacher. Ha! Ha!

iteach105: But you think you've got it bad, I call my CT "the Killjoy." I've learned all of this stuff in my classes, but she won't let me try any of it. She says that teacher ed programs teach you how to teach in "perfect" schools, but that if I just follow her advice, I'll learn how to teach in a "real" school. So, do you know what that means for me? It means that she wants me to do everything she does. She wants me to plan my lessons exactly like hers, using only her resources and the activities she used in the past. She has totally killed all of my ideas and taken the joy out of teaching.

Jane3: Sounds good to me. You don't have to plan much.

iteach105: On my last lesson plan, she wrote down the exact words she wanted me to say and suggested that I model her clothing style because she thought mine was a distraction for the students.

Luis: Is she talking about your tongue ring?

Jane3: OMG, you did take that thing out, didn't you?

iteach105: I have absolutely no room to be myself. I can't go to the teachers' lounge because she believes it will taint my enthusiasm. I think it's because she doesn't want me to get to know other teachers. I stand with her during cafeteria duty and bus duty, and if I leave the room I have to tell her where I'm going. I sit with her at every meeting and have lunch with her every day. She even suggested that we take our bathroom breaks together. I'm fed up, and I have no idea of how I'll make it through the internship.

Luis: Wow. I'm not sure which one is worse, yours or mine %-(.

Jane3:   Okay, just when I thought I got myself together from laughing myself silly from Luis's problems, you come along with another one. Geez.

iteach105:   RU saying that things R GR8 with your CT?

Jane3:   No way! I just don't have much advice since I've got my own problems. Let me tell U what my CT did today. She is over the top. I've been trying to make a good impression by getting to school earlier than normal; I mean, I'm even coming before the other student teachers, and that is saying a lot. Anyway, I get to school at 7:15 a.m. and I walk in to find that she is already organizing the morning work (this is supposed to be my job), she has reshelved all of the take-home books (my job too), cut out all of the bulletin board shapes (my job—again) and written the parent newsletter (not my job, but she said that she would show me). And you know what's the worst part? I think she did it this morning before I got here. I know this woman slept in the classroom (LOL).

iteach105:   LHO and picking my jaw up off the floor.

Jane3:   Wait, there's more. She is always telling me that she gets here early, but I stay pretty late (7:00 p.m.), and she is here when I leave and she is here when I come in. I really like her, but she is so impatient sometimes like she can't take the time to teach me or she thinks I won't do it exactly like she does it, so she just goes ahead and does it herself. I wonder if that is why she tends to work alone on a lot of projects. She is an awesome teacher— too bad I'm being left in the dust. Either she is treating me like an errand girl, or she is watching over my every move, so either way I feel like I don't have room to breathe. Do you know that she makes up songs for everything? She's written at least 25 since I've been here. She takes common melodies (think "Twinkle Twinkle") and changes the words to fit the theme (like spiders). She also did a unit on baskets and actually went out into the woods, gathered up sticks, put them in water (so that they'd get flexible) and made a basket from scratch.

Who does that kind of stuff? She is obviously the real deal, but I don't know how much I'm getting out of this experience because I am not like her at all. I didn't think ST was supposed to be like this. I think she is setting herself up to burn out, really fast. Are you guys still out there?

iteach105:   Okay, that was worth every long-winded moment. I'm too tired to offer you any help.

(Continued)

(Continued)

Luis: I guess @TEOTD, life is just going to have to get better.

Legend:

  LOLH = Laugh out loud hard

  %-(= Puzzled Face

  ?4U = Question for you

  *GR8 = Great

  >-) = Scary face

  LHO = Laughing my Head Off

  OMG = Oh My Gosh, God, Goodness

  @TEOTD = At The End Of The Day

Could you feel their pain (or can you empathize because of your own pain)? In no way are we saying that all cooperating teachers fit into one or more of these categories. Remember, we've said that most cooperating teachers are awesome mentors. Schools of education take great care to avoid placing student teachers with cooperating teachers who are not prepared to mentor. However, even with all of the policies and systems in place to ensure that you are placed with an excellent cooperating teacher, there are inevitably times when conflicts arise in this very important relationship.

If you noticed, the behaviors of the CTs who participated in the conversation can be found in many of the descriptions of personality traits in Table 3.1, Personality Factors and Descriptors. The CT's personality traits come from both the low range and the high range in the table. This further solidifies the theory that personalities should be thought of as a range of behaviors with many possible combinations. Figure 3.2 shows you how the behaviors of each CT stack up. The way a person (your CT) acts is fluid. It may change based on the situation, day of the week, or person with whom he or she is interacting. When you see your CT demonstrate a trait that conflicts with yours, remember that each of us has many traits. The point is that even the traits that frustrate you can be viewed from a positive perspective. We talk more about the steps that you can use to guide you through this process, but right now, take a moment to note the following example. Table 3.2 illustrates a few common experiences that when viewed in a positive light, don't really look so bad after all.

STRATEGIC PROBLEM SOLVING

So where are we now? Even though you just learned a lot about personality traits, you might still be frustrated and unsure as to how you're going to deal with your current conflict with your CT (or one that may be brewing). We want to suggest that the answer lies in looking at your situation through a different lens. This is the beginning of a three-step process that we referred to earlier as **strategic problem solving**. In essence, this higher-order cognitive process facilitates progress toward a desired goal. It outlines the steps you can take to build a positive relationship with your cooperating teacher. Here's what you need to do:

1. Think about the traits that drive you the craziest and look at them in a positive light. You just might have to work a bit to see them as positives, so we'll help you. Personality traits influence your actions. If the interaction between your traits and

actions and those of your CT leads to a conflict, you must select the appropriate lens for the conflict and a problem-solving strategy to solve it that will lead to a positive outcome.

Figure 3.2 Cooperating Teacher's Personality Traits

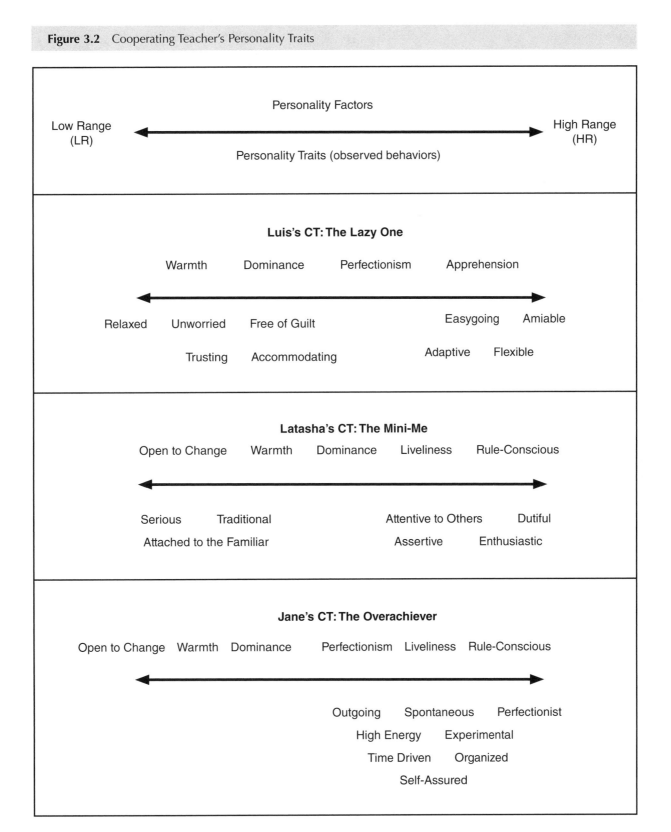

Table 3.2 The Win-Win Attitude

Negative Trait	Transform	Positive Trait
Rule Conscious "Mini-Me" wanted to make sure that the ST followed all of the same rules.		In the new light, this behavior helps you understand the importance of policies and procedures in the educational environment.
Overly Relaxed or Laid-Back "Lazy Gunther" made his ST do all of the work, while he chilled out. Nothing seemed to faze him.		In the new light, this behavior can give you the opportunity to get creative and design your own organizational system.
Perfectionist "The Overachiever" insisted her ST complete everything to perfection.		In the new light, this behavior can help you learn how to pay attention to details.
Forceful, Bossy or Assertive This could be anyone's CT. She or he needs to be heard on every topic that is brought up at the faculty meeting, or in the hallway, or in the front office, or at carpool, or . . . you get the point.		In the new light, this behavior can teach you how to have confidence in your abilities and to speak up for your strongly held beliefs.

2. Commit to having a win-win attitude (this is the strategic part). This is an effective form of problem solving where you pledge to work cooperatively so that all parties can win. In this case, *win* doesn't have to mean making a friend for life, but it definitely means keeping the peace, learning from your experience, and successfully completing your internship. First, you must be willing to set aside any attitudes that may undermine positive results, and resist your human urge to be right, look good, or teach a lesson. We provided an activity in the "Try It" section at the end of the chapter to help you practice the art of turning lemons into lemonade, or taking a perceived negative and turning it into a positive. This is not always easy, but for the student teacher–coordinating teacher relationship to work, someone has to start the process of communicating effectively, and it might as well be you.

3. Select a strategy (this is the problem-solving part of the equation) and "Just Do It" (we know that Nike coined this phrase first, but it works well here). We offer you 10 tried-and-true strategies to get you started. You may need to try a couple (or many) before you find the one that works the best (this is why we gave you so many options). Figure 3.3 gives you a visual depiction of how this works.

Strategies That Work

One of the most important steps in using the strategic problem-solving model is the selection of a strategy. After you have switched your view of the once negative conflict into a positive, you are ready to select a strategy and resolve the conflict. How you handle the situation

Figure 3.3   Strategic Problem-Solving Flow Chart

and the outcome will directly result from your strategy selection. Alan Fairweather is the author of four eBooks in the "How to Get More Sales" series. He describes many practical actions you can take to build your business and motivate your team. Here he outlines ways to deal with difficult people.

1. *Don't get hooked.* When people behave toward you in a manner that makes you feel angry, frustrated, or annoyed—this is known as a *hook*. We have a choice of whether we decide to get hooked or stay unhooked.

2. *Don't let them get to you.* We often allow the other person's attitude to irritate or annoy us. This becomes obvious to the other person through our tone of voice and our body language. This only fuels a difficult situation.

   When dealing with difficult people, stay out of it emotionally and concentrate on listening non-defensively and actively. People may make disparaging and emotional remarks—don't rise to the bait!

3. *Listen, listen, listen—and then listen some more.* Look and sound like you're listening. When face-to-face, you need to look interested. Nod your head, and keep good eye contact. If the other person senses that you care and that you're interested in the problem, then she is likely to become more reasonable.

4. *Get all the facts, and write them down.* Repeat (paraphrase) the problem to ensure your understanding and to let the other person know that you are listening. Keep a complete paper trail of the things that were discussed. This record is not to be used as a "gotcha"—but instead to validate and confirm your next step.

5. *Use names.* A person's name is one of the warmest sounds they hear. It says that you recognize them as an individual. It is important not to overdo it as it may come across as patronizing to the other person. Make sure they know your name and that you'll take ownership for the problem.

6. *Don't blame someone or something else.* Self-explanatory.

7. *Watch out for people's egos.* Here is a list of things for you to remember not to say or do:
   - Don't interrupt.
   - Don't argue.

- Don't jump in with solutions.
- Allow them to let off steam.
- Don't say, "Calm down."

8. *See the situation from the other person's point of view.* Too often we think the "difficult" person is making too much of a fuss. We think, "What's the big deal? I'll fix it right away." When it's a big deal for others, they want you to acknowledge it.

9. *Be very aware of your body language and tone of voice.* We often make a situation worse without even realizing it. Our tone of voice and body language frequently contradict what we're saying. We may be saying, "I'm sorry" while our tone of voice and body language (rolling eyes, sighing, chewing gum, crossing arms, etc.) are communicating our frustration and annoyance. Thus, people are actually listening with their eyes and notice more *how* you say something than *what* you say. In addition, it's important to use a warm tone of voice when dealing with a difficult situation. This doesn't mean being disingenuous or fake.

10. *Words to avoid.* There are certain trigger words that cause people to become more difficult, especially in emotionally charged situations. These include the following

   - "You have to"
   - "But"
   - "I want you to"
   - "I need you to"
   - "It's company policy"
   - "I can't" or "You can't"
   - "Sorry"
   - "I'll try"

11. *Stop saying sorry.* "Sorry" is an overused word. Everyone says it when something goes wrong and it has lost its value.

   How often have you heard someone say, "Sorry about that. Give me the details and I'll sort this out for you." It is far better to begin the conversation with, "I apologize for . . . ." If you really need to use the words "I'm sorry," always include it as part of a full sentence. "I'm sorry you haven't received that information as promised, Mr. Smith." (Again, it's good practice to use the person's name.)

   There are many other ways to say "I'm sorry."

12. *Empathize.* The important thing to realize when dealing with a difficult person is to

   - Deal with the person's feelings first and then deal with his or her problem.
   - Use empathy as an effective way to deal with a person's feelings. Empathy isn't about agreement, only acceptance of what the person is saying and feeling. Basically, the message is "I understand how you feel."

   "I can understand that you're angry" or "I see what you mean" are examples of an empathetic response. Again, these responses need to be genuine.

13. *Build rapport.* Sometimes, it's useful to add another phrase to the empathy response, including yourself in the picture. Try saying, "I can understand how you feel, I don't like it either when that happens to me." This has the effect of getting on the other person's side and helps build rapport.

   Some people get concerned when using this response, as they believe it'll lead to "Well, why don't you do something about it then?" The majority of people won't respond this way if they think you are a reasonable and caring person. If they do, then continue empathizing and tell the person what you'll do to try to resolve the situation.

14. *Underpromise and overdeliver.* Whatever you say to resolve a situation, don't make a rod for your own back. We are often tempted in a difficult situation to make promises

that are difficult to keep. We say things like, "I'll get this sorted this afternoon and phone you back." It may be difficult to get it sorted "this afternoon." Far better to say, "I'll get this sorted by tomorrow lunchtime." And then phone them back that afternoon or early the next morning, and they'll think you've done a great job.

15. *You don't win them all.* Remember that everyone gets a little mad from time to time, and you won't always be able to placate everyone. There's no magic formula. However, the majority of people in this world are reasonable people, and if you treat them as such, then they're more likely to respond in a positive manner.

16. *Some more thoughts to consider.* These notes are primarily designed to help deal with difficult people when we have made a mistake. We often have to deal with other people in a situation where we have not made a mistake. Occasionally, however, people will prove to be difficult and unwilling to accept what we say.

Therefore, demonstrating assertive behavior helps to communicate clearly and confidently what our needs, wants, and feelings are to other people without abusing their human rights.

17. *Some books to read*:

- *A Woman in Your Own Right* by Anne Dickson
- *Feel the Fear and Do It Anyway* by Susan Jeffers
- *Irresistibility by* Philippa Davis
- *Why Men Don't Listen and Women Can't Read Maps* by Allan and Barbara Pease

Source: Copyright © Alan Fairweather 2010. *What makes good managers good?* Retrieved September 7, 2010, from http://EzineArticles.com/?expert =Alan_Fairweather

The strategic problem-solving model is an excellent tool, but we know that nothing is infallible. This method works best when you allow yourself to be open to the process. If you go into a difficult situation armed with a constructive attitude and positive goals, you will more than likely to be pleased with the results. We also realize that some of you may have student teacher placements that include special circumstances, and you may even be thinking that the strategic problem-solving model only works for your classmates who have those "perfect" placements. A word of caution (in case we haven't yet made it clear): Nothing is perfect. Let us take a moment to share with you some unique situations and how you might handle them.

Unique Situations

If you are an instructional assistant or a lateral entry teacher, or if you think there is a factor (such as gender, race, or sexual orientation) that might pose a bit of a challenge for you in the internship, the following section is for you. Be forewarned: If you think we are going to tell you that you get a free pass on the "Let's Make This Relationship Work" train, you are sadly mistaken. We're going to require you to see things from a different perspective and to choose a strategy that brings about a positive outcome: a successful internship. Consistency is a wonderful thing. Table 3.3 explains a variety of responses that you can use in unique situations.

The Win-Win Attitude

The art of achieving positive results through strategic problem solving requires using all three steps together. We assure you, if you pick a strategy and try to implement it but don't adopt a Win-Win attitude, you won't get the same results. You must engage in all of the steps:

1. Think about the trait,

2. Think about the win-win, and

3. Think about the strategy.

The strategic problem-solving steps are dependent on each other, but even then it is not an exact science. You may still have conflicts, still want to scream, still beg your university supervisor to change your placement, but this probably signals that you need to select a different strategy.

Table 3.3   Dealing With Unique Situations

If you are . . .	Keep this in mind
A lateral entry teacher completing your student teaching while teaching	*Your CT/mentor will not be around as often as you would like, or able to offer immediate and regular feedback.* It's up to you to make sure that the two of you are communicating and that you are being observed and provided with enough pointers and praise. Additionally, it might be a good idea to find a peer on your grade level or team whom you can go to for advice or to blow off some steam.
	Because you're a full-time paid teacher, others around you may not always remember that you are involved in some serious on-the-job training. It may be hard for others to relate to your newness, and you may sense that they are being less than supportive. In this case, our advice to you is to locate a first-year teacher who is probably going through many of the same experiences you are (minus the portfolio and reflection journal entries). This way, you'll be able to ask those questions you may be apprehensive about asking of the more seasoned teachers in your building.
A teaching assistant working as a student teacher in your own classroom or school	*It may be difficult for others around you to see you in your new role.* Be sure to emphasize your student teaching role by playing the part. That may mean dressing a little more professionally or spending time with student teachers and teachers. Remember that you are transitioning into the role of teacher, and it may be awkward (for you as well as others) as you discover how you fit in.
	Your CT (and even the administration at your school) may continue to expect you to perform your TA duties in addition to your student teaching duties. This issue must be addressed early in the internship. Your CT, supervisor, and possibly even the school principal need to be in on this important conversation, because even though the university expects you to be on campus for weekly seminars, your school still needs someone to handle bus duty. These issues have to be worked out. Once your responsibilities have been defined and an agreement for meeting them has been reached, put it in writing and sign it. But don't be surprised if situations arise where you must fulfill a duty that wasn't on the list. On occasion, this is okay; however, if it becomes a recurring request, it begins to detract from your student teaching responsibilities. At that time, all involved parties need to revisit the original agreement.
	It may be a little uncomfortable for your CT (who was providing directions for you just a few weeks ago) as you assume full responsibility and provide directions. It is certainly normal for you to feel weird about asking your CT to make copies for you, manage a small group, or to take the kids to PE while you meet with your university supervisor. Sure, you can try to do it all, but let's be realistic: You are only expected to do on your own what a regular classroom teacher is expected to do on her own. In fact, one of your responsibilities as a student teacher is to use available resources—both material and human—effectively. The role reversal period is brief, and if your CT isn't okay with you giving her responsibilities, she will let you know. In that case, you will have to do it all. But again, it is only for a brief period.
Considerably older or younger than your CT	*Don't make assumptions or generalizations about younger or older teachers.* Get to know your CT as an individual, and make a point of learning something from him or her every day. You might discover some refreshingly insightful ideas. You never know. Your task is to absorb everything as data—use the information as a guide for what you do and choose not to do

If you are . . .	Keep this in mind
	once you get your own classroom of students. Additionally, be willing to look at issues from your CT's perspective. You may find yourself mirroring a classroom management tactic or an instructional strategy that you never thought you would try.
	Your CT may have expectations that are either too high or too low, entirely based on your age. Present yourself as a professional who is well prepared for the internship but who is also willing to learn and grow. Be teachable, but not needy. If you have great ideas, share them. If you have questions, ask them. But you will need to find a balance between the know-it-all and the doe-eyed newbie. Really, no one wants to work with either of those student teachers.
A different race, gender, or sexual orientation than your CT	*Don't rush to conclusions about the type of relationship you will have with your CT based on these factors.* Remember that teachers are individuals. Instead of assuming that you have everything (or nothing) in common based on these characteristics, get to know your CT as a person. You have to do this without getting too personal, though. A little too much information (TMI) from either party can cross the boundaries of professionalism and negatively impact a relationship. Each day, try to discover something the two of you have in common. Start with an easy one—you both chose teaching as a career.
	Refrain from attributing your CT's behavior to these factors. You wouldn't want someone accusing you of "just being an irrational female" or "a typical insensitive male." We all know that rationality and sensitivity are not gender-specific. Our traits and behaviors are not bound by race, culture, religion, and/or sexual orientation. There are many other factors that impact how we act and respond. These factors change daily, if not hourly—or sometimes even more frequently. Try to think of what else might be causing your CT to behave in a particular way. Even if you're wrong, at least you are considering a multiple perspectives point of view rather than stereotyping.
Contemplating a more personal relationship with your CT	*Keep it professional.* We've all heard of people finding love in the workplace. However, as long as you are functioning as a student teacher, it is not okay to develop a relationship with your CT (or for that matter, another person at your school) that involves or even resembles intimacy. Your CT is in a supervisory role, and while an intimate relationship is not illegal, it could cause problems if your CT doesn't have the same feelings for you or if the relationship goes sour before your internship ends. To prevent a catastrophic chain of events, we suggest that you refrain from doing or saying anything that could be misconstrued or possibly blur the lines of a professional working relationship.

FINAL THOUGHTS

Understanding how personality theory and traits fits into the student teaching experience can be challenging. Keep in mind the basics. You and your CT have a wide range of personality characteristics, and these traits (behaviors) are fluid (they change often) and are dependent on the situation. These situations vary, as not all internships are traditional, although we expect that they all will be successful. However, there may be a time when you have to deal with a conflict. If this happens, our advice is that you use strategic problem solving as a means of resolution. This model encourages you to view conflict through a positive lens and then select and utilize a strategy to solve the conflict. Remember, in the end, you and your CT are both striving for success. In order to do this, you must be organized. Chapter 4 gives you the tools to manage your increasing workload.

BULLETIN BOARD

Understanding Your Cooperating Teacher: The Rules

Personality Traits

Both you and your CT exhibit many traits that give each of you a unique personality. Furthermore, your actions (which are by-products of your personality) vary depending on the situation, people involved, mood, and so forth.

Personality Theory

Personality is designed by a blueprint of thoughts, feelings, and behaviors that make a person unique. Personality designs can be flexible, but remain fairly consistent throughout life.

Always try to have a win-win attitude.

Strategic Problem Solving

Conflicts may arise when you and your CT exhibit contrasting personality traits and their related actions or behaviors. Engaging in strategic problem solving allows you to view the conflict through a different lens so that you can reach a positive outcome. Remember to begin and end the day with a win-win attitude.

Students benefit when teachers work together.

EXTRA CREDIT

Read About It

Personality

What's Your Teacher Personality?

http://712educators.about.com/library/quizzes/blteacher_personality.htm

http://www.personalityquiz.net

http://www.gotoquiz.com/personality_quiz_1

http://www.outofservice.com/bigfive

http://www.humanmetrics.com/cgi-win/JTypes2.asp

The Student Teacher/Cooperating Teacher Relationship

Glenn, W. J. (2006, Winter). Model versus mentor: Defining the necessary qualities of the effective cooperating teacher. *Teacher Education Quarterly.* Retrieved from www.teqjournal.org/backvols/2006/33_1/12glenn.pdf

Lawley, J. A. (2012). *Pairing of pre-service and cooperating teachers during student internship: Opinions of collaborative relationships* (Doctoral dissertation). The University of Alabama, Tuscaloosa, AL.

Schauffele, R. (2008, April 22). *A student-teacher's reflection on school relationships.* Retrieved from http://ezinearticles.com/?A-Student-Teachers-Reflection-on-School-Relationships&id=689753

Think About It

Understanding Personality Traits

Grab a highlighter and get ready to think. Using the information from Table 3.1, Personality Factors and Descriptors, complete the following exercises.

Select the top five traits that best describe you, and in a brief statement (or list) explain how you effectively use each trait in the following situations (you may select the same or different traits for each situation, but pick only five):

I effectively use the following traits with my friends and family:

I effectively use the following traits in my university/college classes:

I effectively use the following traits in my student teaching internship:

The Student Teacher–Cooperating Teacher Relationship

Table 3.4 helps you plan for how you might handle tough situations with your CT. Think about some experiences that you had with your CT and consult the Personality Factors and Descriptors chart (Table 3.1) to complete this activity. Be honest.

Table 3.4 Critical Incident Chart

Your CT is . . .	You want to . . .	Instead, you should . . .
forceful and asks you to begin teaching sooner that you are ready.	say "Sure, no problem" to show him that you are well prepared for this job.	say "Thank you for the vote of confidence, but I think I need some more time observing before I jump in. Would you work with me to develop a plan for gradually assuming responsibility?"
a risk taker and expects you to teach, but does not provide sufficient information about what to teach or how to teach it.	whine about the lack of support you are receiving. You might even suggest to others that your CT is trying to sabotage your grade in the internship.	see this as an opportunity to take on a true professional role—complete with mistakes and growth. Hey, this person actually trusts your judgment.
lax and does not offer guidance for classroom management.	say, "Well, if my CT doesn't do anything about it, why should I be expected to?"	remember that management is your responsibility. Dig back into your notes from courses dealing with classroom management. Search websites. Talk to your peers. Find and try new ways to manage the class. Like every other teacher, you will have students who misbehave at some point. Your effectiveness depends on whether or not and how you address the behavior.

Try It

Strategic Problem Solving

Avoid trigger words. There are certain trigger words that cause people to become more upset, especially in emotionally charged situations. Can you think of some trigger words and/or phrases that cause you to shut down? These are probably the same words and phrases that other people don't like to hear.

List five words or phrases that you vow not to use in conversations with your CT, students, friends, and others. And while you are at it, also list what you can say in place of that word or phrase. We completed the first example for you.

Trigger Word or Phrase	What You Can Try Instead
"You did it wrong."	"I see where you got confused. Can I help you fix it?"

Trigger Word or Phrase	What You Can Try Instead

Source: Adapted from Fairweather, A. (2005, January 29). *Dealing with difficult people.* Retrieved May 19, 2010, from http://ezinearticles.com/? Dealing-with-Difficult-People&id=12110

Personality Quiz

How well do you really know yourself? If someone stopped you on the street and asked you to identify your personality traits, could you do it? Could you answer with 100% accuracy? Why don't you test yourself just to be sure? You might actually find out something new about yourself. In the "Read About It" section above, we provided you with links to a variety of different online personality quizzes in order to help you gain insight into the wonderful world of trait theory. Here are some helpful hints:

1. Take more than one quiz, if possible. This helps you to compare and contrast the outcomes. Take all of them if you have the time.

2. Compare and contrast various aspects of the quizzes. Were the answers similar? Did you prefer one quiz over the other? Were you in the same mood when you took each quiz?

3. Think about the outcome. Do you agree or disagree with the traits? If not, why not? If so, why? Can you think of specific examples that support or negate your explanations?

4. Share your results with a loved one or close friend and see if that person agrees or disagrees with the outcome.

5. Remember to have fun and try not to take the outcome too seriously, as we cannot guarantee the reliability or validity of the results.

Managing the Workload

The Late Bell

Dear Student Teacher:

By now, you've figured out and understand who the key players are in this next stage of your quest to become a teacher. No doubt it is challenging in the beginning, as you try to remember the names, roles, and personality traits of all of these new people. But it's not enough to learn titles, office or classroom locations, and personal quirks. There are many, many more balls you need to keep in the air to maintain this juggling act. For example, what do you do with all of the papers that continue to collect on your desk? Whom do you talk to about filling out paperwork for licensure? How can you manage the internship along with a part-time job?

Year after year, student teachers tell us that no one ever prepared them for the number of new responsibilities—essentially, a three-ring circus of new duties—which must all be handled concurrently and (seemingly) effortlessly. In all honesty, it can be a bit overwhelming. This chapter serves as a warning—a "heads up" about the new mountain of work you'll be expected to handle. And we'll do our best to help you tame the three-ring circus known as student teaching.

Sincerely,

Your Workload Warriors

After reading this chapter, you will be able to

- identify strategies for dealing with the stress that is a natural part of nearly any job, but particularly challenging during student teaching;
- acknowledge that successful student teaching is dependent on careful management of responsibilities in the classroom, at the university, and in your home;
- categorize and effectively handle the complexities of classroom demands during the internship, including instruction, classroom management, and communication;
- develop a plan to fulfill your university requirements, such as maintaining contact with university faculty, keeping up with assignments, and finishing your program; and
- develop a plan for taking care of yourself during the internship and staying connected with family and friends.

STUDENT TEACHING IS A JUGGLING ACT

The student teaching internship is a tremendous undertaking. In order for it (and you) to be successful, you have to manage some very important responsibilities. Let's compare the experience to a juggling act, with the following instructions:

1. You must manage multiple things (keep track of several balls) while only being able to do one thing (toss one ball) at a time.

2. You must keep more items in the air than you can hold in your hands. (Two hands means at least 3 balls.)

3. You can't let any of the balls hit the ground. (This is the critical part.)

To relate this to student teaching, imagine your juggling act with these three balls—*classroom, university,* and *home.* You've got to be in control—as much as possible—of all three responsibilities at all times. However, you can focus on only one of them at a time. In other words, you can't let issues from one area overflow into another area, such as arriving habitually late to school because of child care issues, or opting out of writing lesson plans in order to put final touches on your teaching portfolio. Additionally, when there's a problem with any of the balls, it prevents you from successfully managing the remaining balls. In the internship, if you are having trouble with outside issues, this may affect your experience in many ways—you may be late or physically absent, unable to focus, and/or feeling rushed or stressed.

We know it's humanly impossible to fully compartmentalize all of your responsibilities, but we do want you to work toward maintaining your focus as much as possible—without letting any of your responsibilities fall by the wayside. Table 4.1 lists several of those responsibilities.

Once you review the table, you can see that we clearly outlined your responsibilities here in Chapter 4 so that there are no surprises down the road. After seeing such a transparent display of the balls you have to juggle, we hope that you find it easier to wrap your mind around the real responsibilities ahead. Don't despair. You can do this. Students do it every semester, every year—and not only do they survive, they succeed. In the sections that follow, we provide you with an overview of the stress brought on by this juggling act, and guidelines for keeping each of the individual balls in the air so that you can decrease your stress and increase the likelihood of your survival and success.

Table 4.1   Your Responsibilities During the Internship

Classroom Responsibilities	University Responsibilities	Home Responsibilities
✓ Writing lesson plans and preparing materials	✓ Keeping up with two calendars—one for the university and one for your school placement	✓ Maintaining part-time jobs
✓ Providing quality instruction		✓ Coping with limited funds
✓ Learning and using technology	✓ Reflecting on your teaching through journals, blogs, and/or discussion boards	✓ Dealing with personal health/medical issues
✓ Managing the classroom		✓ Getting enough rest
✓ Assessing and evaluating student progress	✓ Preparing for and attending scheduled seminars, workshops, and/or other meetings	✓ Organizing child care or care for your parents or other family members
✓ Providing prompt feedback for students	✓ Completing required readings and submitting assignments on time	✓ Managing transportation issues
✓ Participating in parent–teacher conferences and individualized education program (IEP) meetings	✓ Meeting with your supervisor to discuss your performance or ask questions	✓ Maintaining relationships with friends and significant others
✓ Writing weekly newsletters or updating your class webpage	✓ Studying for and taking specialty area exams (if required)	✓ Dealing with unexpected events
✓ Attending team and faculty meetings and workshops	✓ Submitting paperwork required for graduation and/or licensure	✓ Desiring to have a life
✓ Completing paperwork required by your school or district	✓ Completing a portfolio or other culminating documentation	
✓ Participating in school events after school and on weekends		

STRESS: IT'S HERE, EMBRACE IT

What is stress? **Stress** is your body's way of responding to different kinds of demands or influences. Stress affects both the body and the mind, and at extreme levels, it causes people to become tired, sick, and unable to focus. Sound familiar? Student teaching is such a new, big, and important task that a level of stress naturally comes with the job.

> Most of the stress associated with student teaching is *environmental stress*—including frustrations from everyday life, such as pressure from work or family, and/or *stress from overwork and/or fatigue*—including struggles with managing your time or balancing work and relaxation.

Everyone gets stressed, and everyone experiences stress differently. In fact, it is our ability to channel stress that determines whether, and to what extent, we are affected by it (Joseph, 2000). During periods of stress, chemicals are released into your bloodstream that can give you more energy and strength. A little stress is good, in that the extra boost of energy allows you to perform at your best for short-term events. However, extreme stress drains you of energy and negatively affects your performance.

As stated previously, student teaching in particular is by no means exempt from stress. In fact, teachers have been stressed for decades. In the 1970s, the notion of teacher stress was just beginning to emerge; however, by 1980, a growing body of researchers were exploring the issue, and in the 1990s, teacher stress was recognized on an international level, prompting the rise of workshops and widespread public awareness regarding the issue (Kyriacou, 2011).

In the sections that follow, we examine three types of demands (your "juggling balls") that cause stress during the student teaching experience. We also provide you with several useful strategies for dealing with those demands and the stress that they cause.

BALL #1: CLASSROOM DEMANDS

The list of classroom demands in the previous section probably looks a bit daunting, but we believe you can handle it, if you plan ahead. To help meet your classroom demands, we recommend the following three basic strategies: getting and staying organized, managing time wisely, and dealing with deadlines.

Classroom Strategy 1: Get Organized and Stay Organized

Organization may or may not be your strength. Regardless, it is a critical strategy for managing the huge responsibility of teaching, which becomes exponentially more difficult when the tools you need are scattered and in disarray. Below are ideas for keeping track of materials, kids, and time—both for those of you who know nothing about organizing for effective teaching and for those of you who need a refresher.

1. *Give your stuff a home.* You probably recognize this old adage used by moms: "A place for everything, and everything in its place." Well, they knew what they were talking about. Not only does this strategy keep a house neat and orderly, but it can also make your teaching job easier because you always know where to find what you need. And for many teachers, finding their stuff is half the battle. One way to keep up with the many items you're responsible for is to make use of your personal workspace in the classroom. Some CTs may not realize the importance of providing a personal space for you. It is okay to ask for one. You may have to be creative due to the room arrangement or availability of supplies. There may even be surplus items that can be used temporarily, so ask around. This space may be a small teacher's desk or table, or a corner of the room set up just for you. Regardless of how this area is set up, you should work hard to begin organizing your area—while at the same time keeping your CT's items organized in the way that has already been established. However, if your CT isn't a role model for good organizational skills, do not follow suit. You still have to keep things in order. Maybe you can serve as the role model for the CT in this instance.

2. *Clean your desk.* As the saying goes, "a clean desk is a sign of genius"—or perhaps a sign of a respectful guest. When you were a teenager (after your mom finally gave up on the "everything in its place" rule), you could close the door to your messy room and no one would be the wiser. This is not the case with student teaching. Your chaos is often in the middle of the room for all to see—your CT, the students, their parents, and the principal. So, keep it neat. This is, of course, easier said than done. It can be so tempting to just drop everything on your workspace with the honest intention of

putting it away later. Resist the urge, and put it away now. If you wait until later, you have so many loose and unrelated items that the job becomes more intimidating—and you are even less likely to clean it until critical mass is reached. We know that many of you really believe you have a "system," but if your system looks like a tornado swept through your area, there's a problem. Our suggestion is to straighten your workspace every afternoon. This gets much easier over time, especially if you're putting most items where they belong throughout the day. This also helps you feel calmer when you return the next morning, because instead of cleaning and finding items, you can get started with tasks that are better uses of your precious time.

3. *Be your own secretary.* Getting organized isn't easy, but it can be less difficult if you have the right tools. For starters, you're going to need a three-ring binder to keep up with critical documents, such as meeting agendas, memos from the principal, and handouts from workshops you attend. You may also wish to include information specific to your class or the internship, such as the class roster, the school handbook or conduct code, and contact information for your CT and supervisor. Use dividers and label them so you can further organize your paperwork and easily find what you need. (Note: Lesson plans should be kept in a separate notebook that is accessible to your CT and supervisor at all times.) And if you've gone digital with your documents, you need to collect and combine them in meaningful ways, and create meaningful folders on your computer as well. Dropbox (https://www.dropbox.com/) is a wonderful way to keep up with your documents no matter where you are. You can also download free and inexpensive apps for scanning documents using smartphones and tablets (try Genius Scan and CamScanner for starters). If you keep your documents on your own device, you'll definitely eliminate a lot of clutter! And you'll always know where they are.

4. *Save time with class rosters.* One of the best organizational strategies for keeping up with what's going on in your classroom is the basic class roster. We use rosters to keep up with everyday information as well as student academic progress. This is a basic grid with all students' names in order on the far left column, and additional columns for keeping up with critical information, such as attendance, who paid for the field trip, who completed the Unit 12 History Test, and so on. Print several copies of the roster (with names only) and keep them on hand (or filed away) for easy access. Or better yet—save them electronically and become even more successful at keeping up with the information!

5. *Track your time.* Part of staying organized is learning to have an awareness of time. This includes making realistic estimates of how much time different tasks take, as well as the recognition of time as it is actually passing. While a school day might have seemed torturously long when you were a student, you may notice that as a teacher, time passes in the blink of an eye. This makes it easy to get behind, both during teaching and planning periods. The obvious recommendation is to watch the clock—but this doesn't always work. Another suggestion is to use a timer, which may help you focus and stay on task—and prevent you from arriving late for lunch and dismissal every day.

✓ Keep a timer nearby, and set it for the amount of time you think you'll need to complete a task. When it rings, stop and reflect briefly on the following questions:

✓ Did I use my time the way I intended?

✓ Did I allot enough time (or too much time) to get this job done?

✓ How can I make better use of my minutes in the future?

Remember, there are no rollover minutes in teaching. You can't use today's leftover minutes (what leftover minutes?) tomorrow, so use your minutes wisely while you have them.

Classroom Strategy 2: Manage Your Time

In the previous section, we touched briefly on the necessary tool of time management, but it bears mentioning again. You must manage your time well, or it will be wasted. Having said that, we have four words for you: Plan during planning time. You really don't want to spend all of your nights and weekends creating materials, grading papers, and writing lesson plans, so try to protect this sacred few minutes dedicated to planning. Of course, there are team meetings on some days and other days when unexpected events arise, but for the most part, you should plan during your planning time. Resist the urge to hang out in the teachers' lounge—at least for more than 5 minutes or so—and get back to your classroom to deal with all the projects that need grading.

Most student teachers only get one block of planning time per day, and this is usually somewhere between 40 minutes and 1 hour. So, let's assume you have 50 minutes of allocated time. How easily will that time slip through your fingers? Very easily, if you're not focused. Figure 4.1 illustrates how quickly 50 minutes of planning time is wasted without time management.

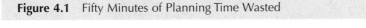

Figure 4.1 Fifty Minutes of Planning Time Wasted

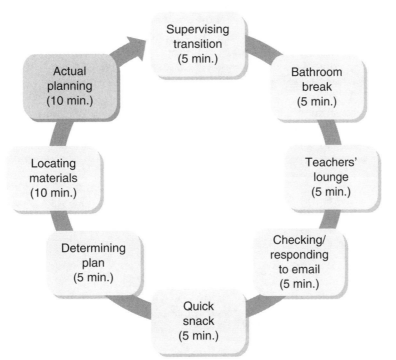

And now, here are a few tips to *maximize* your planning time:

1. *Multitask.* Pack a non-messy snack and drink that you can enjoy while checking your email or working.

2. *Plan to Plan.* So much of planning time is lost on trying to determine what to do and locating the right materials. To save time, create a planning folder that you keep on your desk at all times. Use an actual folder on an actual desk, or you can do it electronically on your computer desktop. Use sticky notes (also available electronically!) to remind yourself what you need to do, and toss them into your planning folder throughout the day and week.

3. *Prioritize.* As far as planning for instruction is concerned, you can prioritize by urgency or complexity—whichever makes the most sense for you on any particular day. However, for email, respond only to messages that are critical during planning time. Return the others after school or when you are at home.

4. *Chunk.* When jobs seem too large, break them up into manageable pieces and tackle them one task at a time. You'll feel a sense of accomplishment as you tick items off your to-do list, even if they're small items.

5. *Collaborate.* Find someone else—either another student teacher or someone on your grade level or team—who is teaching the same unit. Work together and share ideas. If a lesson or activity emerges that both of you like, then one of you should prepare all (or most) of the materials for both of your classes. Be sure to share the load. If you didn't take on the first unit, volunteer to round up the materials for the next one. Bring your own good ideas to the table so it doesn't appear that you are always taking, never giving.

6. *Delegate.* Set up and rotate student jobs so that all of the daily work doesn't fall on you. Let students pass out work and materials, file nonconfidential items, and help with maintaining some of your classroom areas. Have a kid who's a tech whiz? Let her update your class webpage (with your direction and approval, of course). Designate the responsibility for some of your jobs to your instructional assistant (IA)—if you have one. We know this may sound strange or wrong, but this is how IAs work in the real world—the IA assists you. Your instructional assistant can transport students, supervise transitions, make copies, distribute work, prepare instructional materials, and help with bulletin boards and displays. Also, a growing number of IAs are able to carry out valid instructional duties, especially when training is provided. However, be certain that you are not using your IA as your own personal assistant. Your IA needs to see that you are pulling your own weight and not dumping all of the "grunt work" on him or her.

Following the six strategies above can really save time and make your important planning period feel less hectic. So, what does that new and improved planning period look? Figure 4.2 is an example of an improved time management scenario. Additional tips for maximizing your planning period are also provided.

Figure 4.2   Fifty Minutes of Planning Time Well Spent

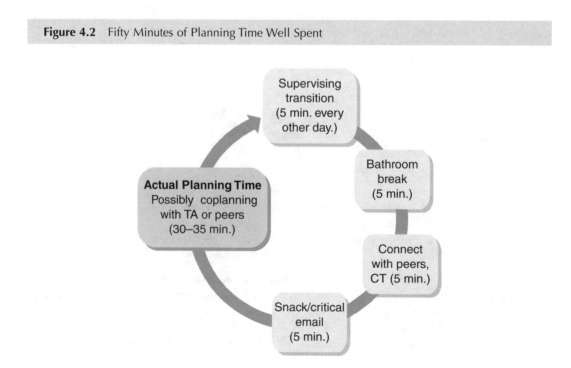

MORE TIPS FOR STAYING ON TOP OF PLANNING

✓ *Find an organizational mode that works for you.* Observe other teachers who seem to have it together, then develop your own style. Note: Chaos is a state, not a style.

✓ *Find good templates and stick with them.* Templates save time and help ensure consistency and completion in your documents. Thousands of templates (e.g., for lesson plans) can be found online and downloaded for free.

✓ *Prepare your lessons a week ahead of time for feedback.* Your CT might be able to give you a little insight about what will or won't work—and you'll have enough time to make changes if necessary.

✓ *Prepare your classroom in the afternoon before you leave.* Never trust that there will be time in the morning, because it is likely that something will come up—an emergency faculty meeting, a flat tire—and you'll end up prepping your room while simultaneously fielding questions from students who arrived early for school.

✓ *Think about long-term plans.* Keep a folder to collect materials for upcoming units and activities. When the time comes to write the plans, you'll already have an idea of what you're doing. For those of you who are tech savvy—Don't forget about Pinterest (www.pinterest.com)! It's a great way to keep track of all of the awesome teaching ideas you've found online.

Classroom Strategy 3: Deal With Deadlines

As we said before, student teachers comment every semester about the amount of paperwork they are responsible for during the internship. Here are a few ideas for taming the paperwork beast:

© iStockphoto.com/michaklootwijk

1. *Carry a calendar to all meetings, and keep it by your side as you check your email.* When you hear, read, or are told about a new responsibility, add it to your calendar immediately. Don't assume that you will remember to jot it down later. Chances are, later your mind will be on something completely unrelated, and you won't remember it again until later becomes too late.

2. With any type of assignment, make certain that you are clear on what is expected, when it is due, and how and to whom it should be submitted. Often, school administrators (and even teachers) forget that student teachers are still learning about how schools truly function (even though you have the advantage of having read our advice on school culture). Consequently, instructions aren't always provided clearly. It's quite likely that you transitioned so well into your teacher role that others in the school assume you know what they're talking about, but if there's something you don't know, ask. However, don't expect everything to be explained to you. It's not uncommon for others in the school to expect you to find some things out on your own. Just think how much more powerful and lasting the learning is when you discover it for yourself.

3. *Use your technology to set reminders.* Take advantage of what you can do with your cell phone, email alerts, and electronic calendars. You can program even the most basic cell phone to remember family members' birthdays and significant anniversaries. So, it is just as easy to set a cell phone reminder, such as "March 30, Benchmark data due— Mr. Sanders—5 p.m." Cell phones and other gadgets with even more sophisticated capabilities are widely available and very affordable, so there's no reason to miss a deadline.

4. *Use your filing system to keep your critical paperwork organized.* Did you forget already? If so, go back and reread the section above on organization.

BALL #2: UNIVERSITY DEMANDS

This is the part of the juggling act that student teachers dislike the most. In fact, for many, it's the first ball to get dropped. The problem is that once the internship begins and student teachers are in their classroom environment, they feel they have "arrived" and are finally doing what they were put on this earth to do. "Now," they think, "If I could only get rid of those pesky university requirements, everything would be great." Not true. Your university or licensure program is still responsible for you and your learning during this training period. They have to ensure that they have told you everything, prepared you for everything, and given you the very best instruction they could possibly provide; in most cases, that involvement lasts right until the very end with program completion and/or graduation. And you do receive a grade for this period in your teaching program, so you want to make sure that you keep up with your requirements. Our recommended strategies for your university responsibilities fall under three different categories: researching the internship, communicating with university faculty, and collaborating to get jobs done.

University Strategy 1: Research the Internship

What exactly does your university or licensure program require of you? Are there on-campus sessions to attend? Is there a portfolio or other culminating project? Do you have official forms to complete? Below are tips for staying at the top of your game during the internship.

1. *Talk to recent graduates of your program.* Based on our past experiences within student teaching programs and our communication with faculty at other universities, we know that assignments and requirements usually don't change drastically from semester to semester. Thus, it's a good idea to communicate with someone who has recently completed the program regarding what you can expect. This person can give you hints about how to get the work done in the most efficient way and advise you on certain pitfalls to avoid.

2. *Go to class.* Talking to a recent program completer can be helpful, but it can also provide a wealth of misinformation, so beware. In order to get the full picture, you should also attend all scheduled meetings and seminars so you can be crystal clear on what your requirements are for the semester. Most instructors have a website or Blackboard page where information is housed and announcements are posted. Take advantage of this resource.

3. *Be an early bird.* In the beginning of the semester when your load is light, you should spend time reading over your requirements and starting to chip away at all of your obligations. Student teachers who don't do their research or don't get the ball rolling early often find themselves overwhelmed—when it is so much easier to get started when the load is lighter. Completing as much work as possible in advance allows you to experience a more balanced internship—with fewer periods of panic and fewer all-nighters.

THINGS YOU CAN TACKLE IN ADVANCE
✓   Studying for and/or taking Praxis II or other specialty exams (if they are required for your program area)
✓   Writing papers and completing projects, especially those not directly related to your classroom instruction
✓   Collecting and organizing items to use in your final portfolio or other culminating projects
✓   Filing paperwork for graduation
✓   Updating your résumé
✓   Organizing paperwork needed to apply for licensure

Simply getting one or two of these items out of the way can generate a more comfortable and manageable pace for completing the other tasks involved with student teaching.

University Strategy 2: Communicate With University Faculty

You are still connected to the university or licensure program, so please don't abandon your supervisor for 15 weeks (or however long your internship lasts), and then return for graduation. Here are a couple of tips to avoid seeing your face on the back of a milk carton:

1. *No disappearing acts.* You should be in regular communication with someone from the university, whether it is your supervisor, a student teaching seminar leader, or your academic advisor. Someone needs to know where you are and how you're doing, so be sure to share any information, such as sickness or family emergencies, that cause you to be absent or otherwise difficult to reach. In some instances, the university supervisor may be in the school quite frequently, and may pop in just to say hi between observations. However, with larger programs and limited faculty resources, supervisors are often stretched thin and unable to visit you outside of the required observations. Don't panic. Just confirm that your supervisor provides you with a reliable and preferred method of contact—whether it's phone, email, or text—and use it wisely, tactfully, and professionally.

2. *Check in periodically.* Of course, if you have concerns contact your supervisor right away. But it's also okay to simply check in to share brief information about how you're doing and what you're teaching, and to offer suggestions of good times to visit to see you in action. If nothing else, the supervisor knows you are alive and well and still teaching in his absence. Since many parts of an internship are interconnected, a good rule of thumb is to copy your seminar leader (or whomever you report to in addition to your supervisor) on all emails so that this person is always aware of your status. If you are experiencing challenges or need help, communicate your concerns early on, before they mushroom into problems that are larger than life or too difficult to fix within the remaining weeks of your internship.

University Strategy 3: Collaborate to Get Jobs Done

You are not alone in the internship, and we don't expect that you try to complete every task independently. Instead, we strongly recommend you seek out advice, resources, and assistance from others around you; of course, this includes university faculty, but we also suggest that you band together with your peers in the program to get jobs done.

For example, if you're studying for Praxis II, work with a few of your peers to set up a study group. Quiz each other, share ideas, even talk about how you are dealing with the stresses related to the test. For assignments, talk with your peers about the criteria to make sure that you are clear on the instructor's expectations. Once you have a first draft of a required paper, trade papers with your study group so your work is edited with a fresh pair of eyes. You can even collaborate on larger projects. For example, we know students who set up gatherings that were part work related, part social—such as a portfolio party (complete with laptops, a scanner, pizza, and *American Idol* on the television) so that no one felt alone in the process. We love this idea in particular because it allows the students to do double duty: work on a very important and potentially overwhelming task while collaborating in a relaxing environment with colleagues.

BALL #3: HOME DEMANDS

Another phrase in the arsenal of every mom is, "You can't take care of anybody else, if you don't first take care of yourself." While moms usually take care of everybody's needs before their own, they really are onto something with this advice. This is true of most of the moms we know (and plenty of responsible dads), although everyone reveals this truth in different ways. When you finish reading this chapter, call your parents—and/or others who looked out for your needs—and thank them. As a teacher, if you haven't met your own needs (i.e., "taking care of home"), you inevitably will do a disservice to your students.

Managing your responsibilities at home involves

✓ making healthy choices;

✓ staying connected with family and friends;

✓ doing things that make you happy; and

✓ saying no to jobs that you can't handle at that moment.

Home Strategy 1: Make Healthy Choices

First among your home demands is *personal health*. Be sure you're getting enough sleep (about 7-1/2 hours per night), eating properly (not too much junk food), taking any prescribed medications, and exercising (about 30 minutes per day). We know that you probably don't have a lot of time, and that gym membership you bought may go completely unused during your internship, so consider walking before school, during your lunch break, or immediately after school. Even if you can fit in only two 15-minute periods or three 10-minute periods of exercise, it all adds up to a healthier you. Some teachers even participate in walking clubs and Zumba class at their schools. Consider joining them. The conversation and collegiality that emerge help you de-stress and remind you that there is a life outside of your classroom.

Home Strategy 2: Stay Connected

The next home demand to address is *your need to be connected with family and friends.* Trust us—the internship isn't easy, and you can't do it alone. To survive, enlist the help of your personal support team. Whether it's through actual visits, phone calls, emails, Skype, or status updates on Facebook, you need to talk to people who are old enough to vote or rent a car (i.e., someone other than your students). And you need your support team now more than ever, just in different ways. First, make sure they understand the demands of student teaching. They need to know that you won't be as available for social calls as you were in the past, and that even though you (probably) aren't getting paid, this is a real job with real student outcomes at stake—not the fantasy gig with nights, weekends, and summers free that many uninformed people imagine when they think of teaching. So, tell them a little bit about what you're doing—but don't overdo it or they may stop listening or interject with a brand new conversation topic. Don't worry—you don't need your support team to listen to you go on and on about teaching—reserve that for your teacher friends. What you can do, however, is get their help with other tasks, such as walking your dog on Wednesdays because you'll be home late after grade-level meetings, or picking your child up from dance class because you'll be at Open House. Chances are, they'll be happy to help.

Home Strategy 3: Get a Life

The third home demand you must focus on is *your need to have a life.* We say it over and over throughout this book: Student teaching is a huge undertaking. It requires a lot of your time and energy. After you've spent the day teaching, the afternoon planning, and the early evening taking care of some basic personal needs (e.g., exercise, dinner), then what? More planning? Well, yes, if you are behind. But if you follow our advice and plan ahead, you will have a few minutes to focus on you and the things you used to spend lots of time on in a previous life. So pull out your scrapbooking, grab your Guitar Hero, or watch some totally guilt-free TV. You've earned it. Just spend this time doing something you enjoy. Remember: All work and no play may make you a very grouchy teacher.

Home Strategy 4: Just Say No

What about those projects you promised to work on? Remodeling the bathroom? Starting a neighborhood babysitting co-op? This might not be the time for those jobs. You should seriously reconsider most big projects for now, but you do have a couple of options.

You can postpone some projects by prioritizing your list and defining the critical items, then...

- ✓ If the task absolutely must be done, figure out a way to break it into manageable chunks, or enlist the help of your support team to complete it.

- ✓ If the task can wait, write down a realistic time to revisit it, and try your best to stick to it.

- ✓ If the task can be completely passed on to someone else—hooray. Cross it off your list.

It is quite possible that after you've prioritized your list and come to terms with what you can and can't take on right now, someone may come along and try to add another item to your list. What should you do? Most people's gut feeling is to say no, but they say yes anyway, in order to not disappoint someone. Sometimes it's okay to accept the new job—if you can honestly give it the time and attention it needs. But what if you really do need to opt out? When you just can't take on one more task, you need a respectful way to say "No" or "Not right now." In Appendix A there is a list of 20 ideas for learning to "just say no," plus a rationale for each response that makes the exchange guilt free.

WHEN THE DEMANDS ARE MORE THAN YOU CAN HANDLE

Sometimes, the internship just doesn't work out. This typically happens when financial challenges, personal or family health issues, or perhaps even the loss of a family member or dear friend is too much to handle during the internship. If this happens to you, you need to take a moment to honestly consider how you are doing and what you can feasibly undertake for the next several weeks. Whether or not you choose to remain in the internship is a personal and respected decision, but you must be honest with yourself; remember that regardless of who tackles the job, there are real students in this equation who deserve 100% from their teacher. Sometimes it is best for all involved for a student teacher to step away and return to the internship when he or she is emotionally capable of handling the demands of teaching.

Occasionally, a student teacher who is struggling with the demands of teaching may be put on an action plan by his or her university supervisor, or even asked to take some time off and revisit the internship after reviewing aspects of teaching in which he or she needs to grow. This does not happen often, but in extreme cases you should know that it is a possibility.

SPECIAL FEATURE SECTION FOR NONTRADITIONAL STUDENTS

"You Think You Know, But You Have No Idea"

We asked student teachers to share their thoughts on the myriad responsibilities that come with student teaching. Here's what they had to say. Notice that the majority of their comments had little to do with actual teaching, but instead with the ability to juggle all of the many tasks that are part of the student teaching experience as a whole.

Got Stress?

"Stress does not even begin to describe how I feel. Life . . . what's that? Didn't even know that existed. My stressors are: (1) student teaching, (2) money and work, and (3) family. I feel as if there isn't much I could balance, because I don't have the time to. My life revolves around this student teaching experience. I feel as if I could've prepared better, but I had no idea it was going to be like this."

"My areas of stress are finding the time to pull my materials together to get my taxes done, spend time with my husband and family, and to get enough rest. When I get enough rest, I relate better to the children in the class and really enjoy them. When I'm dragging, I just want to get through the day and I really feel like I'm cheating the students."

Keeping Up With Family and Friends

"I have a 2-year-old daughter, and it is so hard sometimes when I don't get to do as much with her as I want to because I am sitting at a computer (this is what drives me crazy). However, I am dealing with it, and I am loving my experience."

"There has been a huge change in the amount of time that we are used to spending together. So, what I've come up with is focusing on my daughter from the time I get home until she goes to bed. After I put her to bed, it's back to hitting the books. The only problem with that is that I have to retrain my brain to think during that time of night. I'm already pretty exhausted when I get home."

"It hit me a few weeks ago that I'm not really even a college student anymore. Even my weekends are taken up with writing lesson plans and pacing back and forth thinking about how I can get my struggling students to achieve these objectives."

"I try to keep Friday night as a fun night and do not do any student teaching stuff. Of course my house always looks a wreck nowadays. My kitchen table is covered with piles of teaching manuals, textbooks, lesson plans, etc."

Maintaining Personal Health

"I think that my two best friends are my daily vitamin and my extra dose of vitamin C. I swear if I miss a day, I can feel the germs creeping in."

"This experience has made me change the way that I eat (sorry, Steak n' Shake). I need more fruits and veggies just to make it through my day."

"Last week I slept. I went to bed every night by—if not before—9:30, and it felt good. . . . I found the kids a lot easier to deal with, and I was able to let almost everything roll off of my back."

Dealing With Disorganization

"I am very organized, but I have one area lately that I need to focus on. During teaching, I've been laying down stuff and then forgetting where I put it. Or, I do put things away and then can't remember where I put it. Help."

"My kitchen table is no longer used for eating, but for storage. I also find myself laying papers down in my classroom and forgetting where I put them. One time a student accidently took them and luckily returned them the next day. My organizational skills have gone into overdrive with all I have to keep up with."

Words of Encouragement

"Stress is a word that has become entirely too frequent in my vocabulary. However, I have been able to deal with it because I know that this experience will not last forever."

"One real important thing that helped me through the late nights and weekends on the computer was Starbucks. Starbucks is a great place to go relax and work. A hot peppermint latte calms you and gets those lesson plans flowing."

"My advice to all is to stay focused on the bigger goal—remember that this, too, shall pass and that we all have a lot to be grateful for and proud of. All of us know what it took to get to where we are now, and we have come too far to let this exhaustive student teaching process get us down. Keep your heads up, continue to take care of you—you are the priority here because you cannot be an effective teacher, mother, counselor, caregiver, etc., etc., etc., unless you are taking care of you."

FINAL THOUGHTS

This chapter is full of strategies for managing the numerous demands student teachers often encounter during their internship. We want to reiterate the importance of organization and time management and their crucial role in keeping up with the day-to-day items and tasks involved in the internship. Moreover, we want to remind you that you are not expected to progress through the internship without the help of others. In addition to calling on your "village" to help with certain activities, it is equally important to remain in close contact with your supervisor so that there are no "surprises." Clear organization of outside factors can help you focus more closely on those factors directly related to teaching and learning. The next chapter addresses the final necessary area of management—dealing with student behavior— which, when handled effectively, can lead to increased benefits for the entire class, including improved time-on-task during instruction.

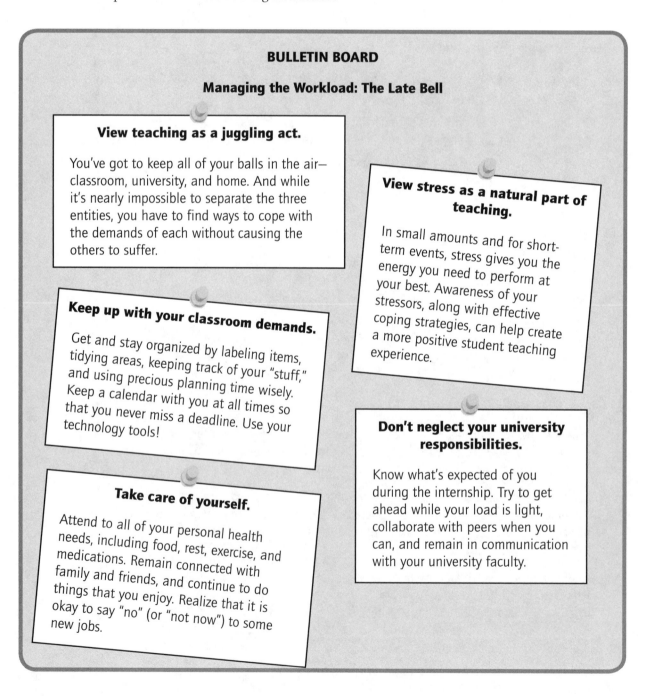

BULLETIN BOARD

Managing the Workload: The Late Bell

View teaching as a juggling act.

You've got to keep all of your balls in the air— classroom, university, and home. And while it's nearly impossible to separate the three entities, you have to find ways to cope with the demands of each without causing the others to suffer.

View stress as a natural part of teaching.

In small amounts and for short-term events, stress gives you the energy you need to perform at your best. Awareness of your stressors, along with effective coping strategies, can help create a more positive student teaching experience.

Keep up with your classroom demands.

Get and stay organized by labeling items, tidying areas, keeping track of your "stuff," and using precious planning time wisely. Keep a calendar with you at all times so that you never miss a deadline. Use your technology tools!

Don't neglect your university responsibilities.

Know what's expected of you during the internship. Try to get ahead while your load is light, collaborate with peers when you can, and remain in communication with your university faculty.

Take care of yourself.

Attend to all of your personal health needs, including food, rest, exercise, and medications. Remain connected with family and friends, and continue to do things that you enjoy. Realize that it is okay to say "no" (or "not now") to some new jobs.

EXTRA CREDIT

Read About It

Stress

Creel, R. (2013). *Twenty ways to say no.* Retrieved from RamonaCreel.com. at http://ramonacreel.com/beyond-organizing/organizing-checklists-and-tip-sheets/20-ways-to-say-no

Davies, L. (n.d.). *Coping with stress: Tips for educators.* Retrieved from http://www.kellybear.com/TeacherArticles/TeacherTip16.html

How to manage your stress. (n.d.). (student health pamphlet). Chapel Hill, NC: The University of North Carolina at Chapel Hill Campus Health Services. Retrieved from http://campushealth.unc.edu/healthtopics/stress/stress-management.html

Parks, B. (2013). ABCs for a low-stress school year. *Instructor Magazine.* Retrieved from http://www.scholastic.com/teachers/article/abcx2019s-low-stress-school-year

Ranskin, D. G. (1989). *The doctor told me that my stress caused my . . . (headaches, insomnia, burning stomach, or whatever your symptoms are).* (student health pamphlet). Manhattan, Kansas: Kansas State University Counseling Services. (Revised for online version by D. Lambert in 2000.) Retrieved from http://www.k-state.edu/counseling/topics/stress/drstress.html

Wilkins, B. (2008, August 1). *101 ways to cope with teaching stress.* Retrieved from SmartTeaching.org at http://www.smartteaching.org/blog/2008/08/101-ways-to-cope-with-teaching-stress

Organization

Katz, M. (n.d.). *Managing paperwork: Top priorities for organization.* LearnNC at University of North Carolina at Chapel Hill. Retrieved from http://www.learnnc.org/lp/pages/741?ref=search

Smith, K. J. (2005, August 19). *Templates to help you with paperwork.* Retrieved from LearnNC at University of North Carolina at Chapel Hill. Retrieved from http://www.learnnc.org/lp/editions/firstyear/254

Springer, S. (2005). *The organized teacher: A hands-on guide to setting up and running a terrific classroom.* New York: McGraw-Hill.

Thompson, J. G. (2009). *The first-year teacher's checklist: A quick reference for classroom success.* San Francisco, CA: Jossey-Bass.

Think About It

1. Think about the internship so far. Overall, what do you think is the most challenging aspect of teaching? For each aspect you listed, name two steps you can take to make this element of teaching easier or less of a challenge for you.

2. What kinds of outside demands (university, home) compete with your ability to do well in the classroom? Think of a plan for dealing with those demands. Use the chart below to jot down your ideas.

University Demands		Home Demands	
Demand/need	Who can help me, and how?	Demand/need	Who can help me, and how?
University Demands		Home Demands	

3. List at least five leisure activities that you want to engage in during your free time—these cannot be related to teaching. For each activity, determine what you need to do (or not do) in order to make it happen.

Try It

1. *Revisit Figures 4.1 and 4.2 on planning time.* For one week, track how you spend your planning time. Then, after the first 3 days, look and your chart and reevaluate how you spend your time. Are you wasting a lot of time, or is your time well managed? Make changes as needed, and make an effort to stick with those changes. At the end of the week, check how you spend your time again. Are you making progress? Are your minutes used wisely? Are you getting a lot done? Write about your growth in your reflection journal or log.

2. *Develop your organizational system.* Get started with a three-ring binder, several dividers, and a few three-hole pocket folders. Add whichever materials you need to create a system that works for you—one that allows you to keep up with all of the parent notes, faculty memos, paperwork, deadlines, and general stuff that teachers collect. (Resist the temptation to file your lesson plans here; they actually work best in a separate notebook.) At the end of each school day, when you are clearing your desk, be sure to file away any of these miscellaneous pieces in their appropriate sections. If you find that you are still struggling to locate items, either the particular system you chose isn't working, or you haven't given it a good try. Reevaluate and try again.

3. *Develop your organizational system electronically.* Sign up for an account with Dropbox or a different online storage site. Download a scanning app. Find an app that keeps up with group work and grading. Explore all of the technological possibilities that keep classroom organization literally in the palm of your hand!

4. *Revisit the chart you created above for tackling home and university demands.* Get the ball rolling by contacting those who can help you with tasks. Be sure to provide them with the necessary information and materials to help you by getting the job done the way you want it done—or be prepared to have it done their way. Either way, it will be done. In your reflection journal or log, write about how it feels to ask and allow others to handle some of your responsibilities. Is this something you're comfortable doing? Why or why not? Determine the level of support that feels right for you, and move forward.

5. *Each day after the students leave, try to focus on tackling an important job related to the internship, other than writing lesson plans and pulling resources together.* For example, you might tweak your résumé, review for your specialty exams, or create an interactive bulletin board for your students. Also, each day when you leave the school, make a point of engaging in at least one activity that is about you and not your students—even if it's only for 15 minutes. For example, you might work in your garden, shoot hoops with a friend, or catch a quick nap—whatever makes you feel temporarily indulgent. Keep a running tally of these activities in your journal or reflection log so that you can remind yourself of all you have accomplished and all you've done to maintain balance and keep your sanity.

5

Classroom Management During Student Teaching

The Principal's Office

Dear Student Teacher:

Welcome to one of the most challenging parts of student teaching—classroom management. There is simply no way to sugarcoat this—classroom management can be hard, really hard. Although you've taken on a great deal of responsibility in the classroom (lesson planning, teaching, grading papers, creating bulletin boards, completing running records, and so on) and you really are doing much of the work of a "real" teacher, the truth is you are not the "real" teacher. The students know this, your CT knows this, and you know this. Moreover, nothing is more fun for students (no matter the grade or age) than to test a new teacher.

So, what's a student teacher to do? How do you manage a classroom that's not totally yours to manage? How do you discipline students when you really want them to like you? How do you enforce your CT's rules, especially those with which you disagree? In this chapter, we provide you with strategies to help you and your students stay out of the principal's office. We help you to optimize the student teaching experience even though management is to some extent beyond your control.

Although classroom management is challenging (as it is for many of the most experienced teachers), you can implement strategies that eventually allow you to focus less on managing and more on teaching.

Sincerely,

Your Management Mentors

CLASSROOM MANAGEMENT

Classroom management is a colossal concern for new teachers. Other than content knowledge and effective pedagogical skills, we believe nothing is more integral to academic achievement than successful classroom management. We know your teacher education program provides instruction and training regarding classroom management. Still, now that you are actually in the student teaching internship, we thought a review of classroom management basics might be invaluable to your overall success.

What Exactly Is Classroom Management?

There are many definitions for classroom management, and often it's confused with discipline. However, it's important to understand that discipline and classroom management are not synonymous. According to Dictionary.com, **discipline**, or the act of training or punishment to obtain a certain behavior or outcome, is merely one of the many components that make up classroom management. Harry and Rosemary Wong (2009) defined classroom management as "all of the things that a teacher does to organize students, space, time, and materials so that instruction in content and student learning can take place" (p. 81). Now ask yourself—don't you need more than discipline to be able to teach and for your students to learn? Of course you do. So, it's nonsensical to define classroom management and discipline as the same issue. In truth, **classroom management** is a complex, yet organized, matrix of variables that teachers arrange to manage behavior and classroom processes, such as instruction and social interactions. Although only you can determine the exact variables necessary for your effective classroom management plan, let's review briefly what most educational researchers agree every good plan should have: procedures, rules, rewards, and consequences. (See Table 5.1.)

POPULAR MANAGEMENT PLANS

A Quick Review of Popular Tried-and-True Plans

You need more than just the basics to have a successful classroom, and there are a number of classroom management plans and philosophies that are very effective in helping teachers manage their classrooms. In fact, during your preservice training, you were probably introduced

Table 5.1 Classroom Management Basics

Rule (rool), noun. A principle or regulation governing conduct, action, procedure, or arrangement.	Every effective classroom management plan must have rules. In other words, you need a way to regulate actions and behavior in your classroom. Students should know what is expected of them; thus, classroom rules should be clear, concise, and consistently implemented and enforced.
Reward (rîwôrd′), noun. The return for performance of a desired behavior; positive reinforcement.	Rewards are often used as incentives for positive student behavior and/or excellent academic performance. Rewards should be developmentally appropriate and distributed fairly. Some examples of rewards are homework passes, extended recess time, free time, and assignment choices.
Consequence (kon-si-kwens, -kwuhns), noun. Something that logically or naturally follows from an action or condition.	Consequences in classroom management plans are most often enacted as a result of inappropriate behavior or breaking the rules. Consequences should be clearly communicated to students, appropriate for the infraction, and consistently enforced.
Procedure (prə-sē′jər), noun. A series of steps taken to accomplish an end.	This is the "how to" portion of the classroom management plan. You should clearly explain how to turn in papers, ask a question, label papers, sharpen pencils, get and return supplies, work in groups, complete seatwork, behave during interruptions, etc. Your class procedures could be extensive. The key is to make certain you explicitly teach and practice them with the students. Also, be sure to review class procedures when necessary.

to several key players in the classroom management field. Just in case your memory is a bit fuzzy on the strategies, Table 5.2 provides a quick review of a few plans.

All of these theories offer many great ideas for classroom management. Just remember: You can't really know what elements work best for you until you have your own classroom and can create your own plan. Regardless of the plan, the goal is always to optimize academic achievement and positive social interactions. This means that you must have a sense of order in your classroom. Order doesn't mean you blow a whistle or put names on the board every time a student fails to follow a procedure or breaks a rule. According to Doyle (1986), "Order in a classroom simply means that within acceptable limits the students are following the program of action necessary for a particular classroom event to be realized in the situation" (p. 396).

Table 5.2 Popular Classroom Management Plans Transformed for Student Teaching

Wonderful Wong		
Title and Author	*Strategies*	*Transform for Student Teaching*
The First Days of School by Harry and Rosemary Wong	• The first day will make or break your entire school year. • Have a plan with procedures and routines in place. Explain, rehearse, and reinforce procedures and routines at the beginning and throughout the school year.	• Make a good first impression on your CT and students. • Learn the class management plan and the flow of the class. Ask your CT questions about class routines.

• Consistency is crucial. • Greet students at the door, have a seating chart, and get them to work quickly. • Post the schedule and assignments in a visible location. • Manage the classroom rather than disciplining the classroom. • Structure is needed in well-managed classrooms. • Create a supportive community of learners.	• Always have a warm-up activity. • List due dates and assignments on the board. • Create an organized environment. • Encourage all students to value everyone's opinions.

Magnificent Marzano		
Title and Author	*Strategies*	*Transform for Student Teaching*
Classroom Management That Works: Research-Based Strategies for Every Teacher by Robert J. Marzano, Jane S. Marzano, and Debra J. Pickering	• Educational research is used to create Action Steps. • Establish effective rules and procedures. • Implement appropriate disciplinary interventions. • Foster productive student–teacher relationships. • Develop a positive mental set. • Help students contribute to a positive learning environment. • Activate schoolwide measures for effective classroom management.	• Read educational journals to stay current with the latest education research. • Reflect on class rules and procedures. Revise those that are least effective. • Create a positive environment through your actions and attitude. • Read the school's faculty handbook, and align class rules with schoolwide policies.

Can't Miss Canter		
Title and Author	*Strategies*	*Transform for Student Teaching*
Assertive Discipline by Lee Canter and Marlene Canter	• Catch students doing "good." • Use no more than five clear rules written in positive form (e.g., Do your own work instead of don't cheat). • Consequences should be on a spectrum directly related to the punishment. • Develop an appropriate rewards system. • Never embarrass students in front of their peers.	• Praise student accomplishments (e.g., behavior, academic achievement, peer interactions). • Discuss sensitive issues with students privately. • Review your CT's consequence system. Identify which consequence goes with which inappropriate action. • Discuss your CT's reward system. Help to expand or update the system.

Amazing Albert		
Title and Author	*Strategies*	*Transform for Student Teaching*
Cooperative Discipline by Linda Albert	• Identify why the student is misbehaving: attention, power, revenge, or avoidance of failure. • Handle misbehavior immediately. • Use encouragement strategies that build self-esteem and motivation to cooperate. • Build strong partnerships with students and parents.	• Students misbehave for a reason. Discuss behavior issues with your CT to learn more about the student's history. • Address misbehavior the first time (even if you are nervous). • Use cooperative learning and team-building activities to promote students' self-efficacy. • Write a letter or email to parents introducing yourself and your role in the classroom. Invite them to participate in your lessons (e.g., discussion of travels, reading tutor).

(Continued)

Table 5.2 (Continued)

Count on Kounin		
Title and Author	*Strategies*	*Transform for Student Teaching*
Discipline and Group Management in Classrooms by Jacob Kounin	• The teacher has "withitness" and knows what the students are doing and what is going on in the classroom. • Overlapping or attending to different events without being totally diverted by disruptions is a critical skill. • Lessons should be brisk and cues should be given to keep students focused. • Group alerting should be practiced to keep all students "alerted" to the task at hand. • Provide students seatwork activities that have variety and offer challenge.	• Don't stand at the board or sit for long periods. Circulate. • Visualize lessons to prevent unexpected events from distracting you. • Create signals to make students aware of transitions. • Differentiate assignments and allow student choice.
Judicious Jones		
Title and Author	*Strategies*	*Transform for Student Teaching*
Positive Classroom Discipline by Fred Jones *Tools for Teaching* by Fred Jones	• Use body language and physical proximity to prevent and correct misbehavior. • Help students to support their own self-control. • Focus on instruction to lessen management issues.	• Stand near students who are misbehaving or move the student near you. • Create student contracts to encourage self-monitoring of behavior and achievement. • Review the developmental stages of your students. Design lessons appropriate and relevant for them.
Controversial Kohn		
Title and Author	*Strategies*	*Transform for Student Teaching*
Punished by Rewards by Alfie Kohn	• Manipulating students with incentives only works in the short run. • Rewards produce only temporary obedience. • Build a classroom community to lessen management issues. • Curiosity and cooperation are encouraged—not competition. • Engage in discussions about actions rather than focusing on positive reinforcement.	• Don't rely solely on incentives or rewards. Help students make connections between the content and their personal goals. • Encourage students to work together and to resolve their own conflicts. • Create class goals and celebrate class progress. • Speak privately with students and discuss how their actions impact the class community.
Talented Tate		
Title and Author	*Strategies*	*Transform for Student Teaching*
Shouting Won't Grow Dendrites by Marcia Tate	• Create a classroom environment conducive to learning. • Develop a proactive plan. • Deliver brain-friendly lessons. • Deal with chronic misbehavior.	• Create a bulletin board, student display, or student work zone. • Anticipate challenges and create strategies to deal with them. • Review your lesson plans and use strategies to increase student engagement and minimize misbehavior.

Who's in Control Here, Anyway?

Now that we've reviewed the basics of classroom management, let's discuss a common fantasy that you might have regarding student teaching. During your teacher education program, you may have studied Wong and Wong's "give me five" technique to quiet down a classroom or Marzano and colleagues' "action steps" (Marzano, Marzano, & Pickering, 2003; Wong & Wong, 2009). Perhaps you envision yourself (in your best teacher outfit) in your quiet yet busy classroom at the head of a class of students sitting in perfect rows with raised hands. Or, rather than fantasizing about a perfectly managed classroom, perhaps you're on the opposite end of the spectrum and imagine names written in red on the board, students in time-out, or directing students to the hallway for a private conference about expectations? Whether you're fantasizing about the perfect class or agonizing about possible behavior problems, there is a common theme. You're attempting to alter students' behavior. You're either trying to get them to do something or to stop doing something so that instruction can take place. You want control.

However, in order to have control, you must have power. As a student teacher, you must come to grips with the fact that your power is limited. Everyone at the school knows you're not the "real" teacher. Consequently, you don't have the same power as your cooperating teacher or other teachers in the building. Still, even knowing you have limited power, you are required to demonstrate your understanding of basic classroom management concepts. So, even with very little power, you are held accountable for how students behave and how the classroom functions. You are asked to implement a set of rules and steps to get the students to do what you want, how you want it, where you want it, and when you want it. You can imagine how inherently difficult this can be. How easy is it to get your significant other, child, parent, or sibling (or cousin, fraternity brother, congressman, eccentric neighbor, etc.) to do what you want, how you want it, where you want it, and when you want it? It's not very easy, is it? Now, how easy is it to get 25 school-age children to do what you want them to do, how you want them to do it, where you want them to do it, and when you want them to do it—every single day of the school year? Is this even possible? Is this even a reasonable expectation? How, you might ask, can you be responsible for student behavior and what happens in your classroom at all times when you have no true power or control?

Here is a hard truth—control during student teaching is an illusion. However, even though you may not be able to control your students' behavior and what happens in your classroom at all times, you are nonetheless held accountable for it. That's right. You read that sentence correctly. Even though you cannot control it all, you are still held responsible for it all. You are ultimately responsible for everything that happens in the classroom because it affects academic outcomes. The goal of education in the United States is to prepare children to be productive citizens in our society. As a practice, schools push mastering curriculum concepts and social relationships as a means to achieving that goal. Thus, classroom management truly plays an integral part in the infrastructure of the entire United States. If you can't manage your classroom, then students might not be able to master fractions or become friends with other students. These failures might prevent them from becoming productive citizens in our now global economy. Without productive citizens to contribute to this global economy, our entire world order could collapse. Consequently, it could be argued that the success of the entire world depends on your ability to manage your classroom!

In truth, the success of the world doesn't depend on effective classroom management, but the success of your classroom does. According to Moskowitz and Hayman (1976), once a teacher loses control of his or her classroom, it becomes increasingly more difficult for that teacher to regain control. Also, research from Berliner (1988) and Brophy and Good (1986) reveals that the time teachers take to correct misbehavior because of poor classroom management skills results in lower rates of academic engagement in the classroom. It is extremely important that you understand the role classroom management plays in the learning process and, consequently, your internship. A great deal is at stake: your reputation, your CT's reputation, instructional time, academic achievement, a potential job, your stress levels, and your sanity. So, with all of this at stake—and still factoring in the fact that you cannot consistently control student behavior—how can you succeed at classroom management?

Michael Apple (1995) explains that teachers have a great deal of power when it comes to influencing student behavior. So, even though you don't have the power of a "real" teacher, you do have the power to *influence* behavior and implement basic classroom management skills. The key is to remember that your job is to manage your classroom, not control it. Managing implies you can prevent and handle issues as they arise because you have a plan in place. It doesn't mean problems won't ever arise—quite the contrary. It just means that when (not if) they arise, you are ready.

HOW DO I PRACTICE CLASSROOM MANAGEMENT DURING STUDENT TEACHING?

Right now, you are a guest in your CT's classroom. He or she already established a set of classroom rules that most likely you are expected to implement. Still, the student teaching internship gives you the opportunity to discover what works for you, so when you get your own classroom, you'll have the confidence to implement your own system. However, as your Management Mentors, let us repeat that now is not the time to do a lot of experimenting with classroom management strategies. Stay focused on your ultimate goal—demonstrating that you possess the knowledge, skills, and disposition necessary to join the teaching profession. Ultimately during student teaching, your only goal regarding classroom management is to show you can handle the very basics of managing your classroom. Now is absolutely not the time to test every strategy you've ever read about or witnessed during classroom observations. This doesn't mean you shouldn't try some of the strategies you've learned. The point is that this is not the time to try *everything*. You'll get the chance to integrate any management strategy you wish when you have your own classroom (and even then you'll probably find it wise to focus on just a few strategies at a time). We know you're full of enthusiasm and energy, and we know you've been anxiously waiting to test out all the ideas you've collected during your teacher education program. We promise you that you will get the chance—just not now. For this very brief and finite period of time, keep in mind the strategies reviewed earlier, but stay focused and ultimately follow the next important steps.

Know Thyself

It seems simple enough to say to begin with yourself; still, it can be difficult during student teaching to reflect on yourself when you are so incredibly busy. However, personal reflection requires you to take a long, honest look in the mirror (literally and figuratively) and assess your confidence level. You must believe in yourself and your abilities to successfully manage a classroom. This is not an option. If you don't believe in you, your students won't believe in you either. It is completely normal to be nervous about classroom management. All student teachers are worried about managing the classroom. However, not all student teachers show it. Instead of projecting insecurity and worry, they appear self-assured and confident (even if they are not).

It's certainly natural to have some anxiety about being an authority figure in the classroom. Still, there is a difference between feeling nervous and lacking confidence. So, if you are feeling a little weak in the knees about managing the classroom, we want to suggest a strategy called "practice and pretend." This strategy involves practicing confidence. How do you practice confidence? In classroom management terms, you follow a procedure and a rule. The procedure involves pretending to have a conversation with your students while practicing your tone of voice (projecting your voice and speaking clearly), perfecting your posture (standing up straight, shoulders back), and maintaining eye contact (talking to yourself in the mirror and looking yourself in the eye). The rule is that you must practice this routine every morning when you wake up and every night before you go to bed. Practice and pretend introducing yourself to the class, reviewing classroom expectations, giving the directions for an assignment, or redirecting a student. The topic of the practice and pretend exercise can vary; just pretend to have a conversation and practice your tone, posture, and eye contact. Regardless of where you are on the confidence spectrum, remember that you would not have made it to student teaching if you were not qualified. Confidence in your abilities is a key step in executing effective classroom management. Believe in yourself and your students will believe in you too.

Know Your Cooperating Teacher

If you haven't already read the chapters about the importance of a positive relationship with your CT, we encourage you to stop now and go back to read them. Remember, in general, cooperating teachers are chosen because they are highly qualified to guide you through the entire teaching process, which includes all aspects of classroom management. As soon as you can, familiarize yourself thoroughly with your cooperating teacher's classroom management plan. Recognize that your CT may not have an actual classroom management plan written down in a document like popular management plans or the one you created for an assignment in your teacher education program. Consequently, you may need to ask some very specific questions to make certain you understand your CT's system. Refer to questions in the Crucial Management Questions Guide (Figure 5.1) to help you discuss this with your CT.

Honestly, one of the most valuable strategies you have at your disposal for success with classroom management is simply to have a serious in-depth discussion with your CT about his or her management system. You need to know more than just what to do if a student is defiant. Also, you need to discuss in an open way any rules you think you might have a hard time enforcing. Sometimes just having a deeper understanding of why your CT has the rule in place can give you the fortitude to enforce it.

For most CTs, classroom management has become second nature. They're not always conscious of their system (what they do, and why, and when they do it) to keep the classroom running smoothly. Consequently, you need to put on your detective hat and do some investigating. Keep asking questions so that you can learn as much as you can.

What If My Cooperating Teacher Is Bad at Classroom Management?

As your Management Mentors, it's time for us to give you another bit of hard truth. Not all CTs are experts at classroom management. Because the spectrum of expertise can vary and this is an issue many teachers find challenging, it is possible (but not probable) that you are working

---

Figure 5.1 Crucial Management Questions Guide

Directions: During the student teaching internship, you need to know as much as you possibly can about your cooperating teacher's classroom management plan. Schedule some time with your CT to find out the answers to the following questions:

✓ Can you tell me a little bit about why you set up the room this way? Are you flexible with this arrangement, or do you want it to remain the same?

✓ What are your rules? How did you come up with them? Do the students follow them most of the time? Which rule is the most difficult for them to follow and/or for you to enforce? Are there any rules you're thinking about changing or adding?

✓ Are you open to creating a new system? Can you give me some parameters?

✓ What happens when a student breaks a rule?

✓ Are you using any kind of rewards system? Can you explain it to me? How do you track it? What happens to students who don't get frequent rewards?

✓ What is the parent reaction to your system? What do you do if a parent disagrees with the way an issue is handled?

✓ What organizing techniques are you using to keep the classroom flowing smoothly? How do the students know what to do and when to do it?

✓ How do you handle students who refuse to comply with your requests but who haven't broken a rule?

✓ What do you do if there is an emergency, such as a fight breaking out or a student getting sick in the classroom?

✓ How did you find out what motivates your students? What strategies did you use to get to know them?

---

with a CT who is not equipped to assist you in fully mastering the basics in classroom management. Still, even if your CT is struggling to implement an effective management system, you can learn from him or her. Take the time to reflect on what is not working. Perhaps there is no clear management plan in place, perhaps the rules are not clear or not consistently enforced, or perhaps your CT is more concerned about being the students' friend than teacher. Use this information to think about how you might handle these issues when you have your own classroom. Finally, carefully ask your CT if there is anyone else in the building whom you can observe to learn even more about classroom management. If you think this might offend your cooperating teacher, be certain to explain that you need to observe several teachers in key areas like classroom management in order to fulfill your university's requirement. Once you know the experts in your school, spend some time in their classrooms. Ask them questions about their systems and share your findings with your CT. The information you gain will be beneficial to both you and your CT. Your CT might even be willing to try or let you try to incorporate some of those ideas into the classroom.

Know Your Students

Great performers know their audience. As a teacher, you already know the students are your audience, and it's imperative you learn as much as you can about them. First and foremost, learn their names. It does not matter if you teach five students or 500, or if they have easy names or very difficult names. You show your students that you value who they are when you learn their names and pronounce them correctly. Create a seating chart with the students' names on them, use mnemonic devices, or make associations that help you to remember. For example, you have a student with red hair. The red hair makes you think of Lucille Ball, which makes you think of your Uncle Robert who watched the *I Love Lucy* show when you visited him in Georgia as a child during the summer. You remember that a city in Georgia is Athens, which sparks you to remember that your student's name is Athena. It might read like a long process, but this all happens in your amazing brain in mere seconds. Whatever strategy you choose, just learn their names correctly and quickly.

Second, make an extra effort to get to know what your students value. The only way to find out what your students are passionate about is to talk to them. Rather than writing lesson objectives on the board as your students are arriving in the morning, take the time to chat with them. Ask them basic questions: How was your weekend? Do you have any pets? What have you been doing since I saw you last? How are the rest of your classes going? Is there any good food in the cafeteria today? As your Management Mentors, we'd be remiss if we didn't remind you to be strictly professional in your approach to get to know your students. Be careful *where* (not alone in the bathroom) and *how* (not like a peer) you approach a student, as the location and manner of approach can impact how the student perceives your attempts to get to know him or her. It should be crystal clear that your intention is to build a teacher–student relationship and absolutely nothing more.

We are not suggesting that you waste instructional time by chatting with your students the entire period. However, taking some time to get to know your students is imperative. Do your best to make a connection with every student, even those students with whom you find it difficult to connect. Building positive relationships with your students helps to minimize management issues, thereby maximizing instructional time.

Know Your Space

In the world of architectural design, form follows function. We don't have a total grasp of the complexity of that concept (because we're Management Mentors, not designers), but we're pretty sure it means your space should work for you. In other words, you need to make certain the classroom is organized to facilitate teaching and learning. Your CT already organized the classroom, so pay careful attention to how it is arranged. Make note of where information is posted, where students store their items, teacher and student work areas, resources and supplies, and lighting options. Depending on your CT's flexibility, you may or may not be able to change much of your environment; however, having a greater awareness of it helps you to manage your classroom more effectively.

Know Your Lesson

You'll read all about instruction in Chapter 6. Still, it is worth stating now how important it is for you to have engaging lessons for your students. Marcia Tate (2006) explains that effective managers plan lessons that minimize classroom disruptions; they don't have any special magical talents. In our years of supervising student teachers in the field, we've sat in classes filled with perfectly obedient students until the lesson began. However, once the student teacher began to teach a poorly planned lesson, the students became bored and decided to entertain themselves. Once students disengage, more likely than not, the teacher has management issues.

You must do your best to create lessons that engage your audience. We don't mean you have to turn flips to explain gravity, or light your hair on fire to explain the principles of heat.

What we do mean is that you need to make certain you are employing brain-friendly strategies that will engage your students. Also, pay close attention to your students while you are teaching. If you see them begin to disconnect (you'll know this because their eyes are glazing over, they're passing notes, or they're sleeping), change your teaching strategy. Don't keep teaching a bad lesson just because it took you all night to create it and it's written in ink in your lesson plan book. It's a plan, not a binding legal contract. As the teacher, you get to make adjustments to your lesson as necessary.

Know the System

What we're calling "the system" includes the systems of both your CT and the school. Effective classroom management requires a plan, preferably a clear and concise plan that works for you and your students. Whether you are using your CT's plan, a popular plan, or a plan that you are creating and implementing, you must be clear about its components. It is imperative to really know it in order to show it and enforce it. However, if you see that you need to make changes to your plan, by all means, make those changes. Just beware: Don't make changes all day, every day. You'll confuse yourself and your students. You are the expert in your classroom, and you know yourself and your students. Take advantage of professional development opportunities, talk to seasoned teachers, and consult other student teachers. Do whatever you need to do; just be confident enough to consistently implement your plan and to make small changes when your system is not working.

AVOID THE MOST COMMON MISTAKES MADE BY STUDENT TEACHERS

Now that you have some ideas about what to do with classroom management, we want to give you some advice on what *not* to do during student teaching.

Teaching Is Not a Popularity Contest

As your management mentors, we want to warn you about the number one classroom management misstep that student teachers make—they want to be friends with their students. Many student teachers have a powerful desire for their students to like them. It can

be hard not to fantasize about being the engaging, challenging teacher who is also beloved by all the students. This doesn't mean we think it's bad for your students to like you; however, teaching is not a popularity contest. If your students like you, that's great. If they don't, continue to do your best to make personal connections with them while staying focused on your goal to deliver meaningful lessons and to create an environment conducive to learning. Think back to your motivations for becoming a teacher. Some common reasons people join the teaching profession are a love of their teaching content and a love for working with children. Your motivation to become a teacher was not to become friends with 25 kindergartners. If you are in need of increasing your social network, there are many avenues you can explore for expanding your friendship base. However, becoming BFFs (best friends forever) with all of your students is not one of them.

So, even though the plot line in many popular movies about teachers involves phenomenal breakthroughs once the teacher cultivates authentic friendships with the students, remember that is not reality. You can be friendly to a student without focusing on being their friend. You are the teacher. Friendship is not your primary objective. The job description of a teacher does not include "befriend the students." In addition,

I dare you to find one teacher evaluation instrument that lists befriending students as a requisite. So, be friendly. Rapport matters, but being a friend does not. Get to know your students. Ask about their lives and care about them—just don't depend on them to be your social network. If you focus on friendship, you do them and yourself a disservice; plus, your ability to effectively manage the classroom becomes severely compromised.

Yelling Is Telling

As a student teacher, we know you are often unsure of yourself. However, you would never tell the students, "Class, I'm not sure of myself today, and I'm feeling really nervous inside. I don't know if I have what it takes to be a teacher. I'm really terrified you'll figure out that I'm not sure what I'm doing. Sometimes it just feels like I'm winging it." Most of you would never say this aloud to your students because it would simply confirm your inexperience. However, when you resort to raising your voice (also known as yelling) in the classroom in an attempt to gain control—that is exactly what you're doing. Your yelling is telling. It is a clear (and very loud) signal to the students that you don't know what you're doing.

If you find yourself yelling to get your students' attention, stop and take a deep breath. Recognize the need to review and enforce the management system. Do not talk over the students; just wait (with your best "I mean business" face) for them to listen to you. Do not talk until the room is silent. The students will eventually stop talking (this might take 2 minutes or 10). Now, calmly and quietly review your rules, consequences, and classroom policies. Ask the students to repeat them back to you, resume your lesson, and consistently enforce your system.

Use, Don't Abuse, Your CT

We strongly suggest that you work cooperatively with your CT regarding classroom management. However, make certain you do not rely on your CT to handle all of your discipline issues. This may be really hard for you and extremely hard for your CT. It could be hard for you because you're probably a little nervous and afraid about implementing the consequences of the management plan. If your CT is willing to handle behavior disruptions, it might be easier for you to let him or her take over than to face your fears of disciplining students. On the other hand, it might also be extremely challenging for your CT to let go of the reins he or she is so used to holding. Sometimes, it's just hard for your CT to hand over all aspects of classroom management, especially those involving discipline, to an inexperienced student teacher. Your CT understands that instructional time is extremely valuable, so it could be difficult for him or her to completely turn over the reins to you while you figure out the realities and complexities of management. Also, because your CT is ultimately held responsible for the management of the classroom, he or she might jump in to rescue you rather than risk losing valuable instructional time.

Nonetheless, whether you are using your CT's system or not, you simply must not rely solely on your CT to enforce the consequences for misbehavior or enforce classroom procedures. If you constantly look to your CT when misbehavior or procedural issues occur, you lose all credibility with your students. Effective teachers position themselves as confident leaders in the classroom. It is important that you demonstrate your ability to confidently and consistently guide procedures in your classroom and implement consequences if problems arise.

SPECIAL FEATURE SECTION

If You Are . . .

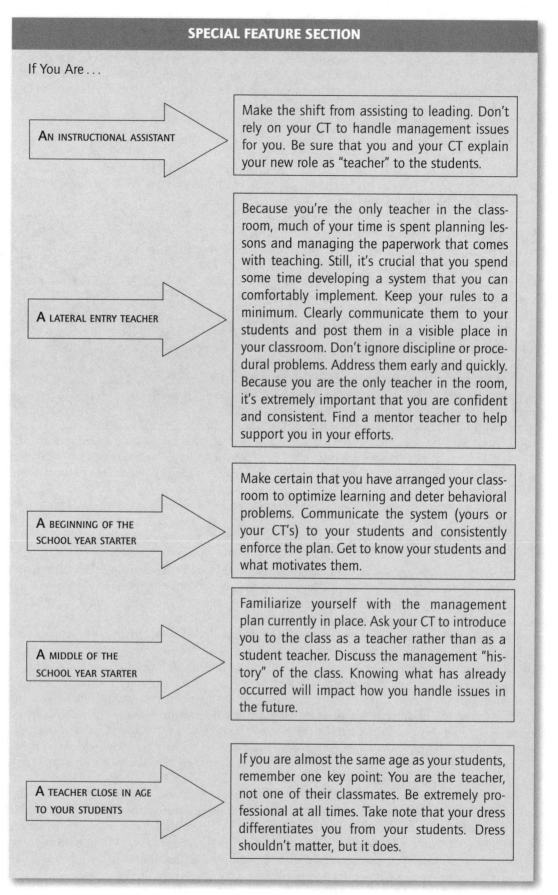

AN INSTRUCTIONAL ASSISTANT → Make the shift from assisting to leading. Don't rely on your CT to handle management issues for you. Be sure that you and your CT explain your new role as "teacher" to the students.

A LATERAL ENTRY TEACHER → Because you're the only teacher in the classroom, much of your time is spent planning lessons and managing the paperwork that comes with teaching. Still, it's crucial that you spend some time developing a system that you can comfortably implement. Keep your rules to a minimum. Clearly communicate them to your students and post them in a visible place in your classroom. Don't ignore discipline or procedural problems. Address them early and quickly. Because you are the only teacher in the room, it's extremely important that you are confident and consistent. Find a mentor teacher to help support you in your efforts.

A BEGINNING OF THE SCHOOL YEAR STARTER → Make certain that you have arranged your classroom to optimize learning and deter behavioral problems. Communicate the system (yours or your CT's) to your students and consistently enforce the plan. Get to know your students and what motivates them.

A MIDDLE OF THE SCHOOL YEAR STARTER → Familiarize yourself with the management plan currently in place. Ask your CT to introduce you to the class as a teacher rather than as a student teacher. Discuss the management "history" of the class. Knowing what has already occurred will impact how you handle issues in the future.

A TEACHER CLOSE IN AGE TO YOUR STUDENTS → If you are almost the same age as your students, remember one key point: You are the teacher, not one of their classmates. Be extremely professional at all times. Take note that your dress differentiates you from your students. Dress shouldn't matter, but it does.

FINAL THOUGHTS

As your Management Mentors, we've done our best to advise you on the components and challenges of classroom management. Work closely with your CT, be confident, and know your plan. Our hope is that you now have a better understanding of what to do and what not to do. Still, we've supervised long enough to know there are a few common classroom disruptions most student teachers encounter. So, we provide you with Figure 5.2.

Figure 5.2   Solutions for Common Classroom Disruptions

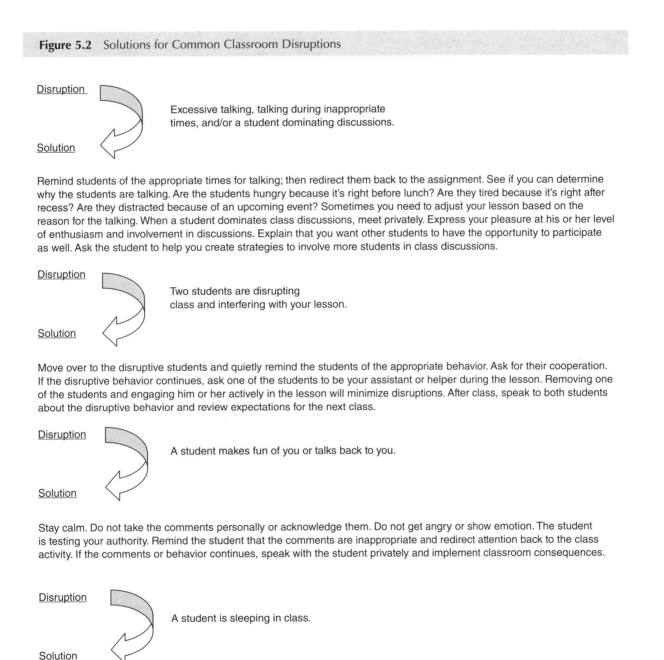

Disruption

Excessive talking, talking during inappropriate times, and/or a student dominating discussions.

Solution

Remind students of the appropriate times for talking; then redirect them back to the assignment. See if you can determine why the students are talking. Are the students hungry because it's right before lunch? Are they tired because it's right after recess? Are they distracted because of an upcoming event? Sometimes you need to adjust your lesson based on the reason for the talking. When a student dominates class discussions, meet privately. Express your pleasure at his or her level of enthusiasm and involvement in discussions. Explain that you want other students to have the opportunity to participate as well. Ask the student to help you create strategies to involve more students in class discussions.

Disruption

Two students are disrupting class and interfering with your lesson.

Solution

Move over to the disruptive students and quietly remind the students of the appropriate behavior. Ask for their cooperation. If the disruptive behavior continues, ask one of the students to be your assistant or helper during the lesson. Removing one of the students and engaging him or her actively in the lesson will minimize disruptions. After class, speak to both students about the disruptive behavior and review expectations for the next class.

Disruption

A student makes fun of you or talks back to you.

Solution

Stay calm. Do not take the comments personally or acknowledge them. Do not get angry or show emotion. The student is testing your authority. Remind the student that the comments are inappropriate and redirect attention back to the class activity. If the comments or behavior continues, speak with the student privately and implement classroom consequences.

Disruption

A student is sleeping in class.

Solution

Walk near the student's desk and speak loudly. If the student continues to sleep, once the other students are working, kneel down by the student's desk. Ask the student if he or she is feeling well or if something else is wrong. The student may be sleeping for a legitimate reason. If the student is merely disengaged, review lesson concepts quickly and focus the student back to the task. Remind the student how the task relates to upcoming or past lessons.

BULLETIN BOARD

Classroom Management During Student Teaching: The Principal's Office

Know your system.

Whether you're following your CT's system, a popular management plan, or using your very own creation, be very clear about its components. The key to classroom management is a reasonable plan you consistently enforce. However, if necessary, don't be afraid to fine-tune or make adjustments if your CT allows.

Familiarize yourself with popular classroom management plans.

There are many already developed effective management plans. Spend some time researching and/or reviewing current popular plans so that you have a basic understanding of management theory.

Control is an illusion.

Expect for issues to arise, and have a plan in place to handle them. It's an impossible task to expect students to behave the way you want at all times, so be as proactive as possible.

Avoid common management speed bumps.

Don't yell at your students or let your CT implement all of the discipline. It's okay to be friendly, but don't rely on your students to be your friends.

Teach engaging lessons.

One of the best deterrents for misbehavior is your ability to engage your students. Engage them before they begin to entertain themselves. Don't be afraid to adjust your lesson when necessary.

Get to know your students.

Learn their names and pronounce them correctly. Make a personal connection with every student. Knowing who they are, what motivates them, and what they value helps to minimize discipline issues and helps you to adapt your management plan to suit their needs.

Know the classroom environment.

Make certain you understand the function of all areas in your room. Students should also understand the flow of the classroom and any systems used for the smooth operation of the class.

Work with your cooperating teacher.

Your CT is a valuable resource, so use him or her. Your goal is to demonstrate competence. Wait to implement ambitious management strategies until you have your own classroom. If your CT has weak management skills, be sure to observe the experts in your building.

Be confident.

Confidence is an absolute necessity. Believe in yourself. If you're feeling insecure or inadequate, take immediate actions to boost your confidence.

EXTRA CREDIT

Read About It

Behavior Management

http://www.behavioradvisor.com/11583.html—*Dr. Mac's Behavior Management Site*

Classroom Management

http://www.education-world.com/a_curr/archives/classmanagement.shtml

http://www.nea.org/tools/ClassroomManagement.html

http://www.classroommanagement.com

Classroom Management Video Tips for Teachers

http://www.edutopia.org/classroom-management-video

Confidence

http://www.mindtools.com/selfconf.html

Education Information for New and Future Teachers

http://www.adprima.com/managing.htm

Student Teachers

http://www.inspiringteachers.com/beginning_teachers.html

Classroom Management

Brophy, J. E. (1983). Classroom organization and management. *The Elementary School Journal, 83*(4), 265–285.

Burden, P. R. (2000). *Powerful classroom management strategies: Motivating students to learn.* Thousand Oaks, CA: Corwin.

Canter, L., & Canter, M. (1993). *Succeeding with difficult students.* Santa Monica, CA: Canter & Associates.

Crawford, G. B. (2004). *Managing the adolescent classroom: Lessons from outstanding teachers.* Thousand Oaks, CA: Corwin.

Davis, B. M. (2006). *How to teach students who don't look like you: Culturally relevant teaching strategies.* Thousand Oaks, CA: Corwin.

Divinyi, J. (2003). *Discipline that works: 5 simple steps.* Peachtree City, GA: The Wellness Connection.

Edwards, C. J. & Watts, V. J. (2010). *Classroom discipline & management* (2nd ed.). Milton, Australia: Wiley.

Emmer, E., & Evertson, C. (2012). *Classroom management for middle and high school teachers* (9th ed.). Boston, MA: Pearson.

Evertson, C., & Emmer, E. (2012). *Classroom management for elementary teachers* (9th ed.). Boston, MA: Pearson.

Glasser, W. (1999). *Choice theory.* New York: HarperCollins.

Good, T., & Brophy, J. (2007). *Looking in classrooms* (10th ed.). Boston, MA: Pearson.

McEwan, E. K., & Danner, M. (2000). *Managing unmanageable students.* Thousand Oaks, CA: Corwin.

Smith, R. (2004). *Conscious classroom management: Unlocking the secrets of great teaching.* San Rafael, CA: Conscious Teaching.

Taylor, S. (2011). Behavior basics: Quick behavior analysis and implementation of interventions for classroom teachers. *The Clearing House: A Journal of Educational Strategies, Issues and Ideas, 84*(5), 197–203.

Tileston, D. W. (2004). *What every teacher should know about classroom management and discipline.* Thousand Oaks, CA: Corwin.

Think About It

Directions: Read the following real "stories from the field" while imagining you are the student teacher. What could you have done to prevent the issue from arising? What is the best course of action now? Are there any behaviors that make the situation worse?

1. Your CT announces to the class she is leaving the room for a few moments. She reminds the students of the classroom rules and informs them all that you are in charge. She explains that any student who breaks a rule will not be able to participate in the class pizza party on Friday. Still, as soon as she leaves the room, all of the students start talking to each other and stop working. You remind them of the rules, but they ignore you and continue to talk. You walk to the front of the class and wait for the class to quiet; yet, they continue to talk. So, you clear your throat and remind them again that their teacher will return momentarily and they all need to be working. A few students begin to work, but most of them continue to talk. Your CT returns to the room, and all students immediately quiet and begin working. She asks you how the class behaved while she was out, and all of the students turn to look at you.

2. Two students are talking loudly across the room to each other. You already reminded them of the class rule of no talking during seatwork, and you asked them nicely to work quietly. They apologize for talking and begin to work quietly. However, they start passing notes to each other instead.

3. It's your first day teaching full-time, and you're very excited. You start your lesson, and everything is going very well. The students are working cooperatively in groups, and you are circulating to offer feedback and remediation when necessary. One student asks to go to the bathroom. You remind everyone that bathroom breaks are not allowed during class time and he will have to wait for the period to end. You continue circulating, but when you return to his group, he asks more frantically, "Please, I really have to go. I just can't wait until the break." Since you began the internship, this student has been very helpful to you and has never been a discipline problem. With this in mind, you respond, "Okay, I'll let you go this one time during class, but you need to hurry. Come right back." The student agrees. Five minutes pass, and the student has not returned. You step into the hall, but

there is no sign of the student. Fifteen minutes pass, and the student still has not returned. Suddenly, another teacher on your hall appears at your classroom door with the student in tow, and asks, "Does this student belong to you?" The entire class laughs as you thank the teacher and usher the student to his desk.

4. You are reading a story to the class during circle time. All but two students are paying attention and participating in the lesson. Rather than interrupt the flow of the entire lesson, you decide to continue reading. However, although you planned to address their talking after class, their talking is becoming difficult to ignore. You pause during the reading and say, "I need your eyes on me and your lips closed. This is a great story, and I don't want you to miss a thing. If you can't keep quiet, you know what will happen." One student replies, "All right, I'll be quiet." The other student, however, replies, "Why'd you choose such a boring story? Our teacher always chooses good stories. You're not a real teacher anyway. I don't have to listen to you or do what you say."

5. Before class begins, you spy one of your students talking on a cell phone in the hall. She sees you watching her as she talks on the phone. You motion to her to put the phone away and come to class. Still talking on the phone, she turns her back to you and continues talking. As the bell rings, she starts to walk to your class. As you hold the door open for her, you say, "Thank you for joining us today. You know it's against school policy for you to talk on your phone during school hours. I'm going to pretend I didn't see you, okay? Just go ahead and take your seat." The student takes her seat, and you begin reviewing the previous day's lesson. While you are talking, a phone begins ringing. Everyone looks around, and the student who was talking on her phone in the hallway takes out her phone and answers it. She says quietly, "Hello? Yeah, I'm in class right now, so I'll call you back after class." She hangs up the phone and puts it back into her bag.

Try It

Activities to Cultivate Confidence

Directions: Review the following list carefully. Choose three activities to complete within the next 2 weeks.

1. *Make a list of every success you've had with classroom management during the student teaching internship.* Now, post the list on your desk, in your lesson plan book, or some other place where you will see it often. Continue to add your successes to the list and watch it grow.

2. *Review your CT's classroom management plan and other management plans of teachers in your school.* Also, review the summaries of popular classroom management plans listed in Table 5.2. Now, using all of this information and reflecting on your experiences in the classroom, create your own classroom management plan.

3. *Make a list of your strengths.* List all of your positive attributes. Ask your significant other, family members, and/or close friends to help you add to your list. Keep your list in a visible space and read it daily.

4. *Make an "I Did It" or vision board* (Byrne, 2006). Cut out pictures from magazines and make a collage celebrating all of your accomplishments and/or goals. Place your board where you'll see it often.

5. *Create a playlist of songs that make you feel strong and powerful.* Listen to the songs on your way to work, during your planning period, and at any other free time.

6. *Watch teacher movies, such as* The Ron Clark Story, Freedom Writers, Stand and Deliver, The Great Debaters, *and* To Sir With Love. Take the time to identify qualities in yourself that are similar to the teacher heroes in the movies.

7. *Spruce up your look.* Go through your wardrobe and identify five professional outfits that make you look and feel great. Work out, get a new haircut, or do something else that will make you feel good.

Take the necessary steps to look your best on the outside so that your confidence radiates from the inside.

8. *Get in touch with your fans.* Pretend you're a rock star, and figure out your fan base. Is it the Cub Scout group you led, or is it your 6-year-old son? Find all of the people who think you rock and as often as possible spend time with them.

Part III

Planning

6

Strategies for Effective Teaching

The Planning Period

Dear Student Teacher:

At this point, you've had a chance to figure out how you fit into your school's big picture, how to manage your multitude of new responsibilities, how to work effectively with your cooperating teacher, and how to keep the students in control (most of the time). That just about covers it, right? Wrong. You still have to teach.

Undoubtedly, the methods classes you took in your teacher education program provided you with a wealth of ideas for teaching in your subject area or grade level. Having experienced this from both sides of the teacher–student coin, we are well aware that much of this information often doesn't transition to long-term memory because (a) it hasn't become "real" yet, and (b) your brain has been overloaded with information from so many courses that you haven't had a chance to fully process it yet.

In this chapter, we provide a review of strategies that are currently considered best practice in the field of education. While our assumption is that these strategies are not new to you, our hope is that revisiting them during the internship not only helps you remember them but also ignites a very real responsibility for student learning and a desire to try them out with real students. With our combined years of experience teaching and observing learners from pre-K through adult, we feel confident that you'll finish this chapter with a repertoire of tried-and-true ideas (and perhaps some new and innovative ones) for keeping your students engaged, challenged, and constantly learning.

Signed,

Your Strategy Support Team

CHAPTER OBJECTIVES

After reading this chapter, you will be able to

- explain why lecture is a good instructional strategy in small doses;
- define brain-friendly learning and share several strategies that fit this philosophy;
- discuss the relevance of infusing technology into instruction for 21st-century learners; and
- develop engaging ideas and activities that fit your personal style and (we hope) try some of them out in your internship classroom.

Few of us can focus for extended periods of time, except on activities we choose and enjoy. Sadly, school does not top (or even appear on) most people's lists of "Favorite Ways to Spend a Little Free Time," so consider a traditional learning environment as the context for the following section.

LIMIT YOUR LECTURES

A common saying in the field of education is that "the average attention span, in minutes, is a person's age divided by one." So, according to this revolutionary mathematical concept, 5-year-olds in a kindergarten class can focus their attention for . . . 5 minutes. The typical teenager in a civics class has drifted off to la-la land in less than 15 minutes. And what about adults? Do you remember that last meeting, lecture, or conference you had to sit through? Your mind probably started to wander long before the first 20 minutes had passed. Of course, we all come up with strategies for keeping focused, such as voluntarily taking notes or secretly checking text messages, but it's easy to succumb to the millions of thoughts racing through our heads at any given point in time—no matter what our age.

With so many types of media available, instant access to information, and constantly changing images on TV and computer screens, children and adolescents essentially expect to be entertained—and if they aren't, they quickly lose interest (Elias, 2005). Moreover, young people are also more adept at multitasking, prompting some to suggest that children's and adolescents' brains are changing—allowing them to multitask more efficiently than those in previous generations (Elias, 2005).

Don't get us wrong—we're not suggesting that screen time is the root of all "short-attention-span" evil. However, when you think about it, the average television show has commercials approximately every 8 minutes, which allows us to regroup, get a glass of water, or run to the bathroom. Even if you have a digital video recorder (DVR) or personal video recorder (PVR), you still have the option to bypass the advertisements or to channel-surf to see if anything better is on. You can even rewind and fast-forward if you want to see or hear the program again, or if you want to skip a segment. When surfing the Internet, you have the ability to immediately switch pages with the click of a mouse. We can't think of a single person who has ever uttered the words, "Gosh, I was so bored surfing the Internet today. There was nothing new or interesting." More often, we hear, "I have no idea how I lost 3 hours surfing the Internet today."

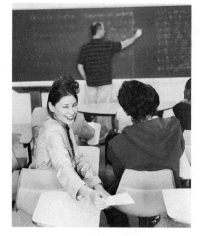

Students in a classroom environment aren't so fortunate as to be able to change channels or click a mouse to regain interest and attention. In fact, they're pretty much held hostage for the learning period and punished if they try to escape in any way. So, our advice is this: Give your students a commercial break. In other words, about every 7 to 10 minutes (perhaps less for younger learners), stop talking and let them do something—even if it's simply a 30-second task (Bowman, 2008). This "doing" could be partner-to-partner sharing of what was learned so far, tossing a small beach ball around so several students can provide an example of a concept, or answering a reflective question in small groups. When your students learn to expect this "commercial break" (and the understanding that it is content related rather than random chitchat), they are more likely to pay attention during your presentation.

With this knowledge in mind, we can start on the path to effective teaching by no longer implementing "death by lecture" (Bowman, 2008) and beginning to think realistically about how much information our students can digest before their eyes begin to gloss over or they fade completely. Consider this additional common quote from the field: "The one doing the most talking is doing the most learning." We believe that this is true—so who wins in a lecture format? The teacher wins. The students, however, are tying their shoelaces in a knot, decorating their notebooks with graffiti, planning an escape to the bathroom, and secretly listening to their iPods under their hoodies. They are not learning the difference between *homonym* and *homophone* or the cell structure of a plant. When too much time is spent with the teacher at the forefront, that time is, unfortunately, wasted. (Cue the commercial. Quick!)

So, if prolonged lecture is taboo, what are your options? We compiled a review of strategies to move your teaching from dull to dynamic and to move your students from fast asleep to fascinated. In the following sections, we cover two of the hottest topics in schools today— brain-based learning and technology infusion.

BRAIN-FRIENDLY TEACHING AND LEARNING

On July 17, 1990, President George H. W. Bush proclaimed the years from 1990 to 2000 as "The Decade of the Brain." In the years that followed, millions of dollars were spent on activities and programs that enhanced "public awareness of the benefits to be derived from brain research" (Presidential Proclamation No. 6158). Over time, practical application of research on the structure and function of the brain is now quite common in educational settings as teachers and administrators use this information to positively impact their learning communities (Jensen, 1995, 2000; Sousa, 2001; Sylvester, 1995).

Brain-friendly (or brain-compatible) teaching and learning helps increase student engagement and retention through instructional methods that are grounded in research and an understanding of how the brain functions. As a quick review, here are the main components of this approach, along with some of the underlying principles.

Nuts and Bolts of Brain Research

- *The primary function of the brain is to learn.* That's precisely what it does—what it was made to do. As a parallel processor, the brain is capable of completing multiple tasks at once—so many that we don't even realize when our brain is doing its job. So, not only can everyone learn, but everyone does learn. The problem arises when the brain's natural needs are stifled. So, what does the brain need to best function?

- *The brain craves novelty.* To satisfy the brain, we must learn and do things in new and different ways. When activities become monotonous or routine, our brain tunes them out. In a sense, it says, "Been there, done that. Engage auto-pilot." However, when a new element or mode is introduced, it serves as a wake-up call for the brain: "Hey. This is new. Pay attention."
- *The brain must make connections.* It is constantly searching for patterns and ways to map new information onto what is already known. This is how the brain produces meaning. When you have an idea of how information is organized and its relationship with your prior knowledge (e.g., similarities, differences, and hierarchies), it is easier to both store and retrieve information when it's needed.
- *The brain must actively process new information to assure retention.* In other words, we must do something relevant with the information to make it stick. When teachers provide opportunities for choice, collaboration, and reflection, information is able to move from short- to long-term memory. But how do we make the information stick? Table 6.1 provides some examples.

Table 6.1 Make It Stick

	What Happens	*Why It Matters*	*How It Looks*
Choice	The teacher provides activities that allow students choice in how they process and store knowledge.	Choice leads to motivation (Guthrie, 2001). Learners are more invested in their work when it is meaningful.	Students choose what to learn (within parameters). Students choose activities. Students choose how to work (alone, with peers). Students' activities include "must dos" and "may dos." The teacher gradually introduces more choices for students.
Collaboration	The teacher orchestrates a variety of opportunities for students to work together to solve a problem or complete a task.	The brain is social. Collaboration increases students' interest in the content (Hootstein, 1995; Zahorik, 1996). Collaboration leads to sustained active participation in learning (Nolen & Nicholls, 1994).	Students work together as partners, triads, or in small groups. Student groups are self-selected or preestablished. Groups are heterogeneous or homogenous. The teacher uses peer helpers (experts) to capitalize on student strengths. The teacher periodically makes changes in groups depending on the activity's purpose.
Reflection	The teacher intentionally and frequently includes opportunities for students to reflect on both the process and the product of their learning.	Reflection is a powerful tool for self-assessment. Students' awareness of their performance on a task can lead them to continued success or to make changes that might bring about success in the future.	Students write in journals. Students practice visualization. Students and teachers engage in class discussions. Students create reproductions of objects and simulations of events. Students use interactive notebooks. The teacher uses graphic organizers. Students perform guided note taking.

What does "making it stick" mean for educators?

- It can make teaching and learning fun. (It may increase student engagement.)
- It can reduce behavior problems. (Engaged students are less likely to be off-task.)
- It can increase achievement for all. (Isn't this the ultimate goal, anyway?)

A FEW IDEAS TO GET YOU STARTED

Some of you may already be in a school setting in which the instruction is quite brain-friendly. This environment creates a sense of safety and well-being that influences cognition (thought processing), which in turn affects interest, motivation, and recall. That's great. However, for some of you, brain-friendly teaching is a foreign concept because you have no real-world models to emulate. The next section provides specific ideas you can use to develop a positive classroom climate where students feel comfortable and take risks.

Setting the Stage: Creating a Brain-Friendly Atmosphere

Use music in your classroom. It alters brain chemistry—and can be used to energize students or help them relax, depending on the BPM (beats per minute).

Use sound. Vary your tone, volume, and rate of speaking to fit your activity or purpose. You can use books on tape or CD, sound effects, and even think-alouds to model a process.

Use color. You can use it on transparencies, on the whiteboard, and around the room. Print important documents on colored paper. Teach students to use different colors of highlighters or sticky notes to indicate important information on a page.

Use humor. It reduces stress and increases alertness and memory. Funny stories, jokes, and cartoons—very brief ones—can do the trick.

Use movement. It increases the flow of oxygen to the brain. Have students stretch, move into groups, or provide physical responses to your questions (e.g., with thumbs up or thumbs down, "Every Pupil Response" cards, or standing to share their answers).

Hydrate. The brain functions more efficiently when it's properly hydrated. Allow students to bring bottled water or provide water breaks to decrease lethargy and inattention.

When possible, give students a choice. This lowers stress and triggers the release of good brain chemicals. And, as stated before, it leads to increased interest and motivation for learning.

The Big Interactive Performance: Teaching in a Brain-Friendly Way

Remember—brain-friendly teaching involves choice, collaboration, and reflection. As a result, students are more interested in their learning, more accountable for their learning, and more likely to recall and retain their learning. Need a few ideas?

Start class with a ritual. The ritual can be as simple as a greeting or an overview. Dr. Shepherd on *Grey's Anatomy* begins each surgery with the line, "It's a beautiful day to save lives." Some teachers begin with "Good morning. Today is a Magnificent Monday (or Terrific Tuesday, etc.). I'm so glad you're here." Be creative. Think of ways to make the greeting interactive, and have your students join in.

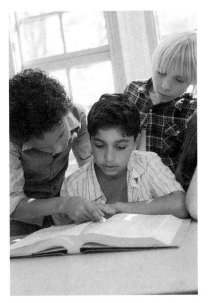

Begin with meaningful information. Save the "housekeeping" items (e.g., taking attendance, collecting homework) for later, once the class has gotten started on a purposeful and relevant task.

Set a purpose for learning. Knowing the big picture can help students follow along appropriately because they have an idea of where they're going. Furthermore, purposes should be revisited throughout and at the end of a lesson or activity, in order to rethink and revise expectations.

Start with the known so that new learning can be linked to students' existing knowledge. Additionally, it is helpful to begin with familiar contexts and gradually move on to new and/or unfamiliar contexts. Try using analogies to link known and new information.

Use graphic organizers. **Graphic organizers** (such as Venn diagrams, bubble maps, and flow charts) are powerful visual tools for helping students recognize what's important and understand how all the bits and pieces fit together. Consider using advance organizers for content-heavy courses, because these frameworks allow students to see ahead of time (and focus on) the important information as it is being provided. This is a far easier method than the way that most students take notes: writing down everything the instructor says or writing nothing at all. When used appropriately, the organizer can later serve as a study guide.

Pose a problem for students to attack in small groups. This strategy is effective because the brain grows by trying to solve problems. With brain-friendly learning, the goal is the attempt rather than finding a correct answer, so seek out problems that have more than one right answer, or more than one way of getting there.

Use affirmations to keep students thinking positively. Employ a few stock phrases (e.g., "Great thinking," "Way to go," and "You rock") to let your students know their participation is appreciated and that their responses are valid. Make them responsible for the positive climate by having them give a neighbor a high five or a fist bump, give themselves a pat on the back, or say a group cheer.

Add some spice to your presentation. Remember, the brain craves novelty. In addition to the ideas mentioned in the section above, you can also use games, props, role-play, simulations, group work, challenges, video clips, and so on. However, be sure to change your activities often (even in small ways) so that they don't become old and boring.

Incorporate nonlinguistic representation. Information is stored in the brain both linguistically and visually. The linguistic (spoken) forms usually come naturally for teachers. However, according to brain research, the nonlinguistic forms are the ones that have been shown to increase brain activity. To keep the brain alert (and to make learning stick), use images, models, and movement—by you and your students—to represent the information and relationships you're teaching.

Provide lots of opportunities for practice. After modeling has taken place, it's the students' turn to give it a try. We suggest many tries, because practice leads to increased speed and accuracy with a given concept. Students can try out activities in small groups or complete work independently.

Use collaborative and cooperative learning. **Cooperative learning** incorporates small-group work that requires input from each member to complete a task or solve a problem. When set up effectively, it can help students feel comfortable and supported. Each student must be accountable for some part of the team's work, and students must depend on each other to complete the task successfully.

Review often. Weave repetition and practice with lots and lots of review to see if your students are "getting it." Review can be done in pairs, on paper, or even chorally. Rather than you providing the recap, make your students accountable for sharing key information. If they make mistakes or leave out critical points, that's a good time to chime in with clarification.

Provide regular feedback. Let students know how they're doing and if they're on the right track. Use checklists, rubrics, and even verbal comments to give students an idea of how their understanding and application of the content measures up to your expectations.

Encourage self-evaluation. Find out what students think about their own learning and processing. Have them discuss their strengths, areas for improvement, and insights gained.

THIS SOUNDS A LOT LIKE LEARNING STYLES

At this point, you might be thinking that quite a bit of brain-friendly teaching is similar to strategies focusing on learning styles (Dunn & Dunn, 1978). **Learning styles** refer to learners' strengths and preferences for taking in information. Like brain-friendly teaching, an awareness of students' individual learning styles can help teachers modify the learning environment to increase the likelihood that learning transfers to long-term memory. In a nutshell, the Dunn and Dunn model (1978) outlines five categories (environmental, emotional, sociological, physical, and psychological) that help teachers think about 18 or so modifications (e.g., sound, lighting, seating arrangement, groupings, level of structure, ability to get snacks/drinks) that can impact how well students are able to receive and remember information. Some reports even suggest that using the learning styles approach can lead to higher scores on achievement tests for average students, struggling students, and students with special needs (Dunn & DeBello, 1999).

If you think that it sounds difficult to try to meet each of those 18+ individual needs for every child, every lesson, every day, you are not alone. You probably won't want to spend your first days of school mapping out learning styles for your entire class. Rather, we think it's more useful to

- know that different learning styles exist;
- be aware of and provide the types of modifications that appear to be critical for some of your students; and
- think about learning styles from a broader perspective (e.g., visual, auditory, and kinesthetic preferences) so that you can meet your students' needs without becoming overwhelmed.

There are numerous assessments and inventories available online that can help you quickly determine your own and your students' learning styles. One link is provided in the "Read About It" section at the end of this chapter. Additionally, there is an opportunity for you to think about the relationship between your style, your preferred mode of instruction, and modifications you might need to put in place to make sure you are reaching all of your students.

We hope you have a better picture of what brain-friendly, learner-centered instruction looks like in the classroom. Now is a good time to talk about technology, which is actually a very brain-friendly tool. The next section of this chapter deals with ways to use technology to keep your students engaged and to maximize time spent on teaching and learning.

TECHNOLOGY-BASED INSTRUCTION

Being "in the know" requires a lot of work. And as our global community grows, we have access to increasingly more information—information that changes from day to day, hour to hour. (We still find it hard to believe that we are more than 10 years into the 21st century. It seems that just yesterday we were stockpiling bottled water, canned goods, and cash in preparation for Y2K.) We are reminded of how quickly times are changing as we observe the students who enter our classrooms each day. These students, born between the mid-1990s and the late 2000s, are often referred to as Generation Z, "**digital natives**" (Prensky, 2001) and "new millennium learners" (OECD, 2008) because they have spent a majority of their lives surrounded by and using technology. They have a voracious appetite for technology and expect instant gratification. They appear to be constantly connected to devices—laptops, smartphones, iPods, iPads, tablets, and handheld gaming systems, just to name a few. Additionally, these students are constantly connected to each other through email, texting, status updates, and social networking. And between the time the current edition of this book is written and the time it reaches the bookstore shelf, even more exciting technological advances will undoubtedly have been made and in the hands of your students.

With all of the glitz and glamour of technology, how can teachers compete? Our answer is this: Jump on the bandwagon. Technology is not the enemy. In fact, it can bridge the gap between you (the dinosaur) and your students (the ones who have always had instant access to everything). There are many ways to use technology in your instruction—as well as for student practice and sharing of knowledge—that can keep you in tune with the interests and learning needs of your students. And, as a nonlinguistic representational tool (remember—images, models, and movement), technology can be a wonderful way to boost your students' brain activity.

The first thing you need to do is find out what is available at your school. Most schools have the basics (computers, DVD, and CD players) in either the classroom or a lab. Perhaps there are also digital cameras, document cameras, and laptop or iPad carts that you can reserve or check out. Many schools have interactive whiteboards available as well. Make an appointment with the school's technology specialist to learn about the available options. And if some new type of technology is mentioned, make an appointment to learn how to use it. In many schools, the equipment is in a room collecting dust because no one knows it's available or has the time to figure out how it works. Be a pioneer. You might even be able to teach your CT a thing or two.

The Tried and True—and Possibly Overused

When it comes to activities, there are the traditional technology forms, such as educational software and websites. These are great, especially if you find programs and activities that allow you to tailor the content to meet individual students' needs and to keep track of their progress.

Then, there's the other all-time favorite—PowerPoint. Remember when we told you that the brain craves novelty? Well, after a while, listeners often begin to tune out these presentations, particularly if the slides are bland, too busy, or being read verbatim. To spruce up your PowerPoint presentation, try adding color and sound—but don't overdo it. Also, try some other ideas, such as embedding related audio and video, linking to a related webpage, making the presentation interactive, and/or breaking it up with small-group activities. Or, try your hand at Prezi (a cloud-based presentation software), or SlideRocket (an integrated presentation tool) to solicit more engagement from your presentations. For other alternatives to PowerPoint, view the Technology section in this chapter's "Read About It."

Dig in to the Digital Age

If you're pretty good at scheduling individualized computer time, you can efficiently search for and bookmark appropriate links for your students, and your students don't refer to your PowerPoint presentations as "coma inducing," then you can also try the following "techy" suggestions.

Virtual Field Trips

Can't afford to take the class to China to learn about the Great Wall? Need to go back in time, but your time machine is on the fritz? A virtual field trip may be right up your alley and in your budget. A **virtual field trip (VFT)** is a guided exploration of prescreened and thematically based webpages (including any combination of text, images, video, and audio content) that, when woven together appropriately, can create an effective online experience. Some VFTs are arranged in a logical thread with prompts and questions to guide the learner through the process; others merely provide links and leave the rest up to the teacher. Either type can be effective. However, we do believe that the best VFTs are created and reviewed by educators who understand child and adolescent development.

Internet Scavenger Hunts

This is a new take on an old concept. The interactive **Internet scavenger hunt** allows individuals or small groups to learn about and review concepts. Essentially, they include a set of questions followed by links to teacher-approved Internet sites where the answers can be found. The hunt can be as simple or as complex as you wish. Many hunts are readily available on the web. In addition to being engaged in a fun activity, the students are able to learn content and practice technological skills simultaneously.

WebQuests

Similar to an Internet scavenger hunt, a **WebQuest** allows students to participate in a scaffolded learning experience using teacher-approved web resources to investigate a topic. However, unlike most scavenger hunts, a WebQuest includes (a) an authentic, meaningful task, such as a problem or a challenge, and (b) a structured group environment where each member takes on a specific role and is responsible for searching for, discovering, and sharing specific information with the group. There are many WebQuests available on the Internet, as well as sites for helping teachers develop their own.

Multimedia Projects

Technology is great for use during instruction. How about using it for students to share their knowledge with others? We all remember the dreaded book report, the poster, and the brochure. And don't forget the dioramas—you know, the scene in the cardboard box. Is there anything else out there? Sure, there is. A **multimedia project** is a method for sharing knowledge, which may include any combination of text, graphics, animation, video, and sound. In the earlier grade levels, these projects may require more adult assistance and may even be completed as a whole-class or small-group collaboration. However, many older students (intermediate grades and beyond) are technologically advanced and require only the parameters of the project. Your job as teacher is to set up the guidelines, create the rubric, and watch as your students' creativity blooms.

Student Response Systems

In addition to using technology to share student learning at the end of a unit of study, you can also employ digital checks of learning along the way. Some teachers are now using devices like clickers to tap into student responses using a wireless connection. If you're unfamiliar with clickers, they are the same type of device used by contestants on the game show "Who Wants to Be a Millionaire" when contestants ask the audience for help with a particularly tough question. Since school systems have limited budgets for purchases like classroom sets of clickers (which can be very expensive), many teachers use online sites, such as Poll Everywhere and Socrative to meet their audience response needs. These sites are often free on a limited basis and allow students to use the devices they already own (smartphones, tablets, laptops, etc.) to submit responses by text, web, or Twitter. When used appropriately, student response systems can be a fun, quick, and effective way of seeing—in real time—the concepts your students understand and those they still find a challenge.

Cool Teaching? There's an App for That

When we were student teachers many moons ago, it was not uncommon to spend our precious time and our own limited funds purchasing and developing the tools of our trade. (Back then, this usually involved index cards, construction paper, markers, and our schools' laminating machines.) Fortunately, for today's teachers, a multitude of educational apps are available for download on smartphones and tablets, and many of them are absolutely free. So, whether you are looking for a way to let your first graders practice reading high frequency words or a method of keeping track of the higher-level thinking you require of your 8th grade social studies class, there is probably an app that does what you want. All you have to do is search, install it on your device, and go! Be sure to check the "Read About It" section at the end of this chapter to see some of our favorite apps for productivity and learning.

Podcasts, Wikis, and Blogs—Oh, My!

Our final section on technology in the classroom deals with strategies that may require a little more technological prowess. Here, we address three additional ways to elevate your use of educational technology—through podcasts, wikis, and blogs.

Podcasts

Have you ever wondered how to help students catch up after they are absent or missed out on important information? Or wondered how to make your lectures available to a group of students? What if some of your students require audio or visual support as they participate in your class? A **podcast** may solve this problem. It is a digital recording that is presented electronically for future viewing or listening. You record your critical lessons and activities (audio or video) and make the podcasts available for your students to download online. In addition to using podcasts to catch up with any missed work, students can create podcasts (e.g., radio style shows) to share their learning each week with parents and others in the community. Additionally, podcasts are great for use in a flipped classroom. The flipped classroom inverts traditional teaching methods, delivering instruction online outside of class and moving "homework" and practice opportunities into the classroom.

Wikis

A **wiki** is an online database (or a collection of webpages) that allows users to freely add and edit content. Yes, it can be edited by anyone, at any time, from anywhere with an Internet connection. Consequently, the pages you pull up may not be accurate or complete, so you should regularly use other sources to check your facts.

Some claim that wiki stands for "what I know is . . . " while others state that wiki is the Hawaiian word for "quick." Either definition applies because a wiki allows users to add their own content to a community page, and it's pretty instant. Many of you are familiar with Wikipedia, the free online encyclopedia that uses wiki software. This site can be a great resource for teachers because it provides instant, up-to-date answers to thousands of questions that you or your students may have. So—how can you use a wiki in your class? Basically, it could be a class webpage where everyone is allowed to add content—such as photos, video, lecture notes, handouts, articles, discussion, links to related websites, and so on. The wiki becomes a repository of information that your students can access and add to as needed.

Blogs

Some of you may remember the good old days of journaling in a spiral notebook or a composition book with a black-and-white marbleized paper cover. Well, technology has allowed us to move forward past this archaic (though, for many of us—nostalgic) practice. Today, many teachers are setting up a **blog** (or online journal or discussion board) for students to write about what they are reading and learning. The advantage of a blog is its interactivity: Students are able to respond to other students' posts, as opposed to simply receiving feedback from the teacher. Dialogue causes the learner to feel more engaged in the process and more connected with others in the class—including the teacher. Blogs aren't only for literacy, however. Teachers can also set up theme-related blogs where students can post their connections to and reflections on their learning. Just remember that you have to set up guidelines about how to respond to each other and what types of comments and exchanges are allowed. Some older students may be familiar with open blogs on the Internet, in which respondents "slam" each other or post other negative remarks. Remind your students that they are part of a classroom community and that only positive comments and constructive feedback are permissible.

SPECIAL FEATURE SECTION

There May Be No "I" in TEAM, But It's Time for "U" to Step Up to the Plate

If you're an instructional assistant or lateral entry teacher, you're in a unique situation when it comes to being innovative, engaging, and effective. And just as in other chapters, we're here to guide you through any murky waters you might encounter during your internship. Table 6.2 illustrates how your expectations and reservations may differ from those of the traditional student teacher, and then provides suggestions on how to move forward to find your voice, and subsequently provide the best instruction for your students.

Table 6.2 Differing Expectations for the Instructional Assistant and Lateral Entry Teacher

	How Your Situation Differs From the Traditional One	*Strategies for Making the Most of Your Experience*
Instructional Assistant (IA)	You have a previously established role in the school, which typically was not a leadership role.	*Think like a teacher.* Drop the role of IA (as much as your administration allows) and become a (student) teacher. This means that you are learning, but you are increasingly capable of taking on more instructional responsibilities.
	You may be used to being told what to do, as opposed to making suggestions for what to do.	*Act like a teacher.* As you begin to view yourself as a teacher, start to take more initiative with instruction. You have years of methods classes (and your professors) to back you up.
	You may not have been involved in classroom instruction at all.	*Be a teacher.* Now is your time to show what you know. You are a professional, and you can do more than make copies and check homework. Share some ideas that you wanted to try. Speak up at grade-level meetings. Do not disappear into the background.
	You may be uncomfortable with the role reversal (i.e., delegating responsibilities to your CT while you engage in instruction).	*Be part of a team.* By all means, don't let your discomfort lead you to undertake everything on your own. Instead, talk sincerely with your CT about how this makes you feel. Your CT may feel weird about it, too. Be aware of your tone when making requests of your CT. Also, remember that the environment is more positive when the two of you work as a team. This is even more important for you than for traditional student teachers.
	Your CT has a distinct style, and up until now, you basically followed it.	*Be mindful of your tone when making suggestions.* This is tricky. Making suggestions can cause your CT to think that you believe something is wrong with how he or she handles instruction—and therefore to wonder why on earth it is wrong all of a sudden. To prevent this reaction, be careful how you express your ideas. Rather than saying, "Your style stinks" (because often it really doesn't), perhaps try saying that you'd like to try some other strategies to help discover your personal teaching style. "I'd like to try some new strategies to fulfill the requirements of my university. I hope you don't mind."
Lateral Entry Teacher	You are the teacher, and this can be overwhelming.	Give yourself some time to be in survival mode, but not too long. You will probably begin with some tried-and-true instructional strategies, but we encourage you to gradually introduce some of those new and innovative ones you've been meaning to try. And you've got it made—because there's no one to tell you that you can't.
	You haven't gotten a chance to see what others are doing.	Capitalize on your in-school planning period to visit other teachers in order to observe their instruction. If this isn't possible, simply ask them what they're doing.
	You've seen what others are doing, and it's nothing to write home about.	Don't fall into the rut by only following what others are doing. You have a wonderful opportunity to break the mold.
	You've seen what others are doing, and it's amazing.	You will be expected to follow suit. Give yourself some time to get in the flow, and make time to learn the strategies and technologies that are important to your school.
	You may be worried that the other teachers will label you a "radical," or reject you from the group if your instructional ideas are different.	Let's be honest. You really do want to fit in. Fitting in is part of the job. You wouldn't have picked this job if you didn't want to be part of the team. This doesn't mean that you leave your own personal style at the door, but it does mean

(Continued)

Table 6.2 (Continued)

	How Your Situation Differs From the Traditional One	Strategies for Making the Most of Your Experience
		that you have to be careful not to "flaunt your newfangled teaching styles" as if everyone else was out of touch. You have to find a balance where you can be yourself within the group. Start by tapping into the different areas of expertise in the group. It may sound a bit like brownnosing, but it can be effective if it is sincere. As always, be mindful of your tone.

FINAL THOUGHTS

We hope we held true to our word—that by the end of this chapter, you would have a wealth of ideas for creating an engaging, brain-friendly, and technology-infused classroom environment. Now that you have these great ideas, it's time to think about how to pull them all together in a clear and effective format called—you guessed it—the lesson plan.

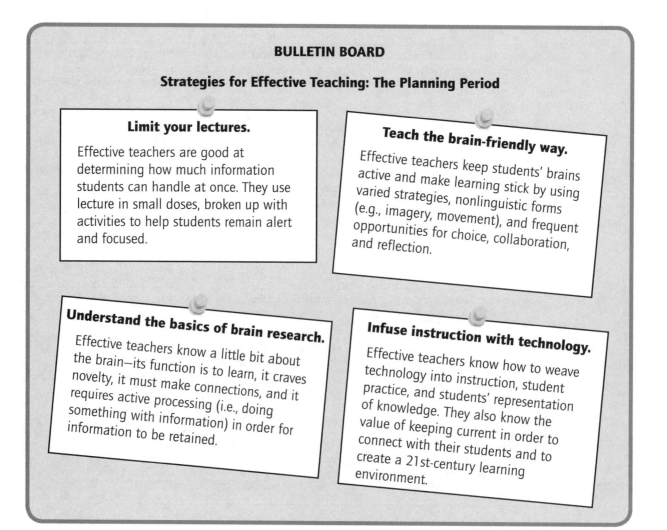

BULLETIN BOARD

Strategies for Effective Teaching: The Planning Period

Limit your lectures.

Effective teachers are good at determining how much information students can handle at once. They use lecture in small doses, broken up with activities to help students remain alert and focused.

Teach the brain-friendly way.

Effective teachers keep students' brains active and make learning stick by using varied strategies, nonlinguistic forms (e.g., imagery, movement), and frequent opportunities for choice, collaboration, and reflection.

Understand the basics of brain research.

Effective teachers know a little bit about the brain—its function is to learn, it craves novelty, it must make connections, and it requires active processing (i.e., doing something with information) in order for information to be retained.

Infuse instruction with technology.

Effective teachers know how to weave technology into instruction, student practice, and students' representation of knowledge. They also know the value of keeping current in order to connect with their students and to create a 21st-century learning environment.

EXTRA CREDIT

Read About It

Brain-Friendly Teaching Strategies

Dr. Spencer Kagan's Structures for Cooperative Learning:

http://www.kaganonline.com

Kathie Nunley's The Layered Curriculum:

http://www.help4teachers.com

Dr. Marcia Tate's Worksheets Don't Grow Dendrites:

http://www.developingmindsinc.com

More Teaching Strategies

Marzano, R. J., Pickering, D. J., & Pollock, J. E. (2001). *Classroom instruction that works: Research-based strategies for increasing student achievement.* Alexandria, VA: Association for Supervision and Curriculum Development.

Learning Styles

Learning Styles: The Dunn and Dunn Model—Learn about the different domains and their implications for classroom environment and instruction.

http://fc.lovett.org/~kkalnin/studybuddies/Learning%20Styles%20GISA.pdf

What's Your Learning Style?—Take the quiz and determine what your results signify.

http://people.usd.edu/~bwjames/tut/learning-style

Technology

American Tapestry: The Millennial Generation.

http://www.docstoc.com/docs/122953020/American-Tapestry-The-Millennial-Generation

Blogspot and Wordpress: Create your own blogs, free.

https://www.blogger.com

http://wordpress.org/

Edmodo: A free and safe way for students and teachers to connect and collaborate.

https://www.edmodo.com/

Glogster: Online interactive posters.

www.glogster.com

PowerPoint Alternatives:

http://www.ragan.com/Main/Articles/10_PowerPoint_alternatives_that_make_meetings_fun_46415.aspx

Online Audience Response Systems:

www.polleverywhere.com

http://www.socrative.com/

Wikis in Education: Create your own wikis, free.

http://wikisineducation.wetpaint.com

WebQuests: Learn about and search a database of WebQuests.

http://webquest.org/index.php

Educational Apps

48 Free Education Apps Sorted by Grade Level:

http://www.edudemic.com/free-education-apps-sorted-by-grade-level

60 Educational Apps in 60 Minutes:

http://prezi.com/swceiv2g3bbt/60-educational-apps-in-60-minutes/

Top Free Education Apps from Google Play:

https://play.google.com/store/apps/category/EDUCATION/collection/topselling_free?hl=en

50 Free Android Apps Used in Education, Right Now:

http://www.edudemic.com/2012/10/50-free-android-apps-being-used-in-education-right-now/

More on Web Tools

Richards, W. (2009). *Blogs, wikis, podcasts, and other powerful web tools for classrooms* (2nd ed.). Thousand Oaks, CA: Corwin.

Warlick, D. (2007). *Classroom blogging: A teacher's guide to blogs, wikis, & other tools that are shaping a new information landscape.* Raleigh, NC: The Landmark Project.

Think About It

1. What are some ways you see teachers in your school engaging in brain-friendly teaching and learning?
   - Novelty in learning
   - Making connections
   - Active processing
     o Choice
     o Collaboration
     o Reflection

2. Are there some barriers to using brain-friendly teaching and learning? How can teachers overcome those barriers?

3. Prior to student teaching, how did you use technology in the classroom?

4. Are there barriers to using technology in the classroom? If so, how can teachers overcome those barriers?

5. Develop a list of at least three new ways you will use technology in your classroom during student teaching, with the resources you have available.

Try It

1. *Review the brain-friendly strategies for classroom atmosphere and instruction.* Select three to try out within the next week. How did your students respond? Did you notice any differences? Write about your observations in your reflection journal. Consider whether you will stick with these strategies or add new ones. Be sure to reflect after attempting each new strategy.

2. *Take a learning style inventory.* (We recommend the "What's Your Learning Style?" test listed in the "Read About It" section above.) What kind of learner are you? How does this impact your teaching style? What strengths does your style bring to the classroom? What can you do to meet the needs of your students who have different learning styles?

3. *Become familiar with the technology in your building.* Who is the technology specialist at your school? Make an appointment with this person. Discover the technology available at your school:

   - in the classrooms
   - in the media center
   - in the computer lab

4. *Make an appointment with your school's technology specialist to be trained in at least one piece of equipment that is unfamiliar to you.* At the end of the training, be able to list at least three ways you could potentially use the equipment in your upcoming lessons. To take it a step further, plan to teach someone else (e.g., your CT, a fellow student teacher) how to use the equipment, and demonstrate how you will use it to deliver your lesson.

5. *Search the Internet for a WebQuest, Internet scavenger hunt, or VFT that is related to an upcoming lesson or unit.* Follow through the steps of the activity to determine if it is appropriate for your students. If so, share it with your CT, and if you get approval, incorporate it into a lesson. Be sure to reflect on your use of technology in your reflection journal.

6. *Help your CT develop a wiki, blog, or podcast related to a unit of study.* Set up the parameters of use, and model your expectations for students. It might be a good idea to begin with a small group rather than the entire class, but allow everyone in the class to view your product. As students become familiar with the concept and process, they can teach more students in the class how to participate. In your reflection journal, write about what worked well and what you might do differently next time.

7 Preparation and Performance

The Lesson Plan

We hope you finished Chapter 6 feeling satisfied with a variety of ideas for stimulating your students' brains with instruction that is interesting, innovative, and challenging. Now, it's time to take those ideas and organize them in a coherent and complete format—a lesson plan—that shows that you can carefully design a full activity from start to finish. This activity, by the way, should include a variety of effective instructional strategies to meet the needs of a diverse group of learners. That doesn't sound so bad, does it? Writing lesson plans involves thinking through an entire process, and great strategies, such as wikis and WebQuests, are only a piece of the process.

You probably heard horror stories about the dreaded lesson plans required for student teaching: They are long (we've seen faculty members with 17-step plans), you must write them for everything you teach (which is true), and you spend all of your waking moments composing them at the computer while your friends are in the next room playing a zombie survival game on the Xbox 360 (that is totally up to you—and depends on how much you follow the advice in this chapter).

Once you are armed with the information we provide, we feel very confident that you will wow your CT and your students with some fantastic lessons that showcase all you've learned. Good luck, and go get 'em.

Sincerely,

Your Power Planning Pros

CHAPTER OBJECTIVES

By the end of this chapter, you will be able to

- describe the relationship between assessment and instruction;
- discuss ways in which assessment-driven instruction can help teachers get the most out of their instructional time;
- explain the importance of differentiation and individualization for optimal student learning;
- list and define the essential components of lesson plans;
- compare and contrast different formats for writing lesson plans, and discuss the extent to which different formats address the essential components; and
- develop written lesson plans based on state and national standards.

THE LESSON PLAN: BEST BASIC PRACTICES

Effective instruction involves very thoughtful planning. During student teaching (and even once you've landed your dream teaching job), you should have a written plan for everything you teach. In the beginning, your plans need to include substantial detail, but over time, you will become more at ease with teaching, and your instruction will flow more naturally with less of a reliance on step-by-step, word-by-word plans. Even though the plans required by your CT may look different from the structure you were taught at your university, you should know that all good lessons have some very basic elements that focus on content and grade-level expectations prescribed by national associations, your state, and/or the needs of your particular students. In the sections that follow, we provide a brief overview of critical elements for developing sound instructional plans. Additionally, we provide an overview of differentiation and how it can also lead to effective instruction.

Know the Expectations: National Standards, State Standards, and School Pacing Guides

In order to be an effective teacher, you have to know the requirements for the different subjects you teach, from a national perspective all the way down to your school level. To begin, determine whether or not your state has adopted a set of national standards, such as Common Core State Standards for Math and English Language Arts, National Curriculum Standards for Social Studies, and Next Generation Science Standards. Otherwise, you begin with the adopted state or district standards. Regardless of where the standards originate, they define the specific content knowledge and skills your students need to master in order to progress to the next grade or course. Links for national standards can be found in the Read About It section at the end of this chapter; state standards are usually available online through your state's Department of Education website.

To be most effective, it is a good idea to familiarize yourself with at least one grade level above and below your grade. This is good practice for at least two reasons. First, by exploring outside your grade level, you get a better picture of the knowledge and skills your students should typically bring to the learning environment, where they need to be performing at different points during the school year, and what the expectation is for the next school year. Additionally, this deeper exploration of standards helps you build up your repertoire of skills and strategies for working with students who need more or less challenge in a particular area.

After exploring the standards (and you will undoubtedly come back to them again and again), ask your cooperating teacher if there is a **pacing guide**, which outlines the topics to be taught at different points in the school year for a particular grade or course. Sometimes, pacing guides are set up by grade-level teams within a school, using state or national standards as a guide. Other times, pacing guides may be set up system-wide and available online for teachers to access and use. However, if no official pacing guide is available, you should ask your cooperating teacher to give you an overview of the topics that will be covered during your time in the internship, and ask approximately how much time is devoted to each topic. (Sample pacing guides are included in Appendix B.)

Use Assessment to Guide Your Instruction

Once you have a clear idea of *what* you are supposed to teach and *when* you are to teach it, you can begin thinking about *how* to teach it. To determine more precisely the level and scope of instruction necessary, you need to implement one or more carefully chosen assessment measures. **Assessment** involves the formal and informal collection of information used to ascertain what students know, what they have learned, and what they need to learn next. In Figure 7.1, note how assessment and instruction are related in a recursive process.

Figure 7.1   The Assessment–Instruction Cycle

- *Assess:* Use formal pretests, discussion, KWL charts, and other quick methods for determining your students' current level of understanding. (Recall that a KWL chart is a student-driven visual representation of what they already **know** [K], what they **want** to learn [W], and eventually what they have **learned** [L] about a given topic.)
- *Instruct:* Locate or develop lessons and activities to teach and reinforce the concepts and skills your students are lacking or focus on which areas require more assistance.
- *Assess:* Use discussion, posttests, projects, and other activities to determine if your students "got it" or not.
- *Instruct:* If the students "got it," move ahead to the next concept. If they didn't "get it," reteach the challenging concepts in new and different ways.
- *Continue with the assessment–instruction cycle until you are able to move on to the next major concept or unit of study:* Keep in mind that all of your students are entitled to learn, even if they already mastered the concepts you planned to teach. If you are unable to move on because some students are not yet ready, consider using a combination of remediation for some and extension and enrichment for others until the class is ready to move forward with the next major concept.

Think of this cycle as a time-management tactic: If you know what your students know, you can focus your sacred planning time and valuable teaching time on areas that actually require additional instruction. Furthermore, you can tailor your lesson specifically for those students who need it and provide other instruction for those who don't.

Another key point to consider regarding assessment is that you are actually expected to demonstrate a positive impact on student learning during the internship. When you analyze your pre- and post-assessment data from the subjects you taught, you should be able to clearly show how well your students learned the content you presented. Table 7.1 provides several key questions to ask yourself as you examine your impact on student learning.

By investigating what your students learned in light of what you presented and how you presented it, you can determine whether or not you are really meeting the needs of all of the young people who fill the seats in your classroom each day. And, as the assessment–instruction cycle describes, your instructional plan has to be different to accommodate the different levels of understanding you discover.

Table 7.1   Examining Impact on Student Learning

Measuring Students' Prior Knowledge	• What did the students know before I began this unit? • How was this measured?
Assessing Students at or Near Mastery Level	• Did some students already have a full and clear understanding of the content? • Did I make sure that these students continued to learn? How?
Assessing Students Requiring Additional Instruction	• Were misconceptions noted? If so, were these pockets of errors or widespread confusion? • What was the most problematic area for the students? • Did I choose lessons and activities to address these students' needs? What were they?
Assessing Students' Gains	• What gains did my students show by the end of the unit? • Did all students have an opportunity to be challenged and increase their learning?

Examining Lessons I Learned	• What have I learned about:
	   ○ my efficacy as a teacher?
	   ○ my students' learning styles?
	   ○ how my students and I work together in our learning environment?

DARE TO DIFFERENTIATE

Have you ever been in a classroom where the teacher spent a considerable amount of time teaching the entire class using the same type of instruction? What was the behavior of the students? Our guess is there were three distinct categories:

1. One group of students was paying attention. They were able to learn from both the type of instruction and level of challenge provided.

2. Another group of students initially paid attention, but perhaps became confused with the content or bored with the presentation, and they began to engage in off-task behaviors.

3. A final group of students stopped paying attention long before the instruction even began. Perhaps they already understood the content, or the lesson didn't present a challenge for them—so, like their confused and bored peers, they also tuned out and began to engage in off-task behaviors.

Likewise, when the entire class is offered the same exact type of practice activities, projects, and products for assessment, only a fraction of the class is motivated or able to complete the tasks set before them. This is a serious problem, but one that can certainly be overcome through the use of **differentiated instruction.** When teachers differentiate, they adapt instruction so that all their students can reach their potential. This instructional strategy is very useful, for example, for learners with a wide variety of learning styles, students with learning disabilities or exceptionalities, academically gifted students, and English-language learners.

According to Elksmin (2001) and Whitaker (2001), teacher education programs often fail to demonstrate the use of differentiation strategies in their own teaching. Consequently, we're willing to bet that many of you have never seen an actual model for differentiation in your own schooling or your teacher preparation. We admit it—allowing differentiation in your classroom is an invitation for "organized chaos" (Sands & Barker, 2004); however, effective teachers recognize that they cannot have a "one size fits all" philosophy of instruction because their students have different interests, learning styles, and learning needs.

In classrooms with **differentiated instruction**, the teachers modify the materials, content, projects, products, and assessments to meet those varying and student-specific needs. They use **flexible grouping procedures**, which means that the groups are monitored and adjusted as needed, based on student interests, learning styles, and readiness. Sometimes groups and assignments are selected by the teacher to make sure that students get what they need; at other times, students are allowed to choose assignments that appeal to their own particular strengths and interests.

STRATEGIES FOR DIFFERENTIATION

✓ Breaking coursework into more manageable chunks

✓ Accelerating coursework for those who need it

✓ Focusing on curriculum basics

✓ Extending the curriculum for students who need more challenge

✓ Guiding small groups through tasks

✓ Encouraging independence

✓ Promoting higher-level thinking for all students

Remember: Your students will not all fit a predetermined mold, so refrain from "teaching to the middle." Provide activities that engage all of your students, and encourage them to work to their potential. Admittedly, it takes work to figure out what your students need, then to tailor your instruction to the groups that emerge. The more you do it, though, the easier it becomes. Trust us on this one.

LESSON PLAN BASICS

A **lesson plan** is a framework for presenting instruction in a clear and cohesive manner. However, if you ask five different people what elements should be included in a lesson plan, you are likely to get five different answers. Actually, the answers may seem different on the surface, but they are probably very similar at the core—with different names or a different order for each of the components, and some extra stuff added to fit personal styles. We believe that there are some "must-haves" (or nonnegotiables), when it comes to lesson plans:

- *Objective/Purpose.* There must always be a purpose for the lesson or activity—even if you want students to discover it during the lesson rather than having it stated up front.

- *Teacher Input.* You must have a role, whether you are providing instruction, modeling, or facilitating. Your level of guidance and direction varies depending on the type and purpose of the lesson. During input, you can try some of the instructional strategies mentioned in the previous chapter.
- *Opportunities for Practice.* This is where the students get to do things—to move around, to discuss, to write, to explore, to experiment, to share, and to play (yes, we said play) in ways that help teach and reinforce the target skills and content. This practice can be guided, where you literally walk students through a task, or independent, where students demonstrate skill mastery on their own.
- *Checks for Understanding.* You have to include these checks periodically throughout your lesson to make sure students are on track, understand the content, and know what they are expected to do. If students seem to have missed the boat, you must go back and reteach the content in new and different ways; then check again to confirm that the group is back on track.
- *Closure.* This is a must, and even though it's a simple concept, it is often misunderstood or completely omitted. Every lesson needs a wrap-up to remind, summarize, and reinforce the objective to the students. We recommend having students take the lead on closure by taking turns sharing the lesson's main points or concepts.
- *Assessment.* You must have a way to determine whether or not the class "got it" overall. This could be based on students' verbal or written responses, observations of their performance on a task, or even (at times) a test or quiz. Many teachers now use "exit slips," which is a procedure where students must answer a question or respond to a prompt related to the day's learning before they can be dismissed or move on to the next subject. For more formal assessment, consider using rubrics and checklists (which are typically made available to students ahead of time) to clearly indicate areas of mastery and areas of need.

TIME-SAVING TACTICS

Need a Wheel? It's Already Been Invented

Like most of you, we are fairly busy people with plenty to do and never enough time to do it. Consequently, we are firm believers in finding someone else's wheel rather than reinventing one. By this, we mean finding someone else who already created a template or model of the item you need. Of course, you may need to tweak the preexisting material to make it useful for you and your particular style, and in certain cases (i.e., to avoid plagiarism) you'll definitely need to give credit to the original authors, but that's so much easier and less time consuming than starting from scratch. We recommend that you use templates to save time and minimize accidental omissions (such as forgetting to include the "check for understanding" and "closure" procedures in your lesson plans—which seems to happen a lot). Sample templates for lesson plans are provided for you in Appendix C.

Make Your Plans "Sub-Proof"

In addition to using templates to streamline your lesson plans, we also recommend that you make your lesson plans "sub-proof." No, this doesn't mean that you guard your sacred lessons from substitute teachers with Fort Knox–level security. On the contrary, it means that with short notice and very little effort, a substitute teacher (or parent volunteer, or even your principal) could pick up your plan book and teach your lessons almost exactly as you designed. When you make your plans sub-proof, you don't have to develop a set of extra "sub plans"—which usually involve a lot of worksheets and pointless activities meant to keep the sub's head from exploding, or to make sure the sub agrees to come back in the future. When your plans include engaging lessons that the sub can actually follow, the sub may even see the job as that of a teacher rather than as a babysitter for your class while you are away. There's an added bonus: When you do return to the class, you won't have to double up or skip lessons, or extend your unit to make up for lost time.

TIPS FOR TEAMWORK—OR HOW NOT TO STEP ON YOUR CT'S TOES

By now, your bag of tricks is bulging at the seams, you've got multiple strategies on a variety of levels, you know what's nonnegotiable in a lesson plan, and you're ready to hit the classroom. You walk through the door, bright-eyed and ready to take on the world (or at least a group of fourth graders), and you're hit with one of the following realities:

1. It's everything your professors said it would be. *Woo-hoo! Bring it on.*

2. It's nothing like your professors said it would be. It's all lecture, worksheets, skill, and drill. *Beam me up, Scotty.*

3. It's sort of like what your professors said, but these teachers are in overdrive. You're going to have to spend some evenings and weekends catching up on the new programs and technology that your all-knowing professors somehow failed to mention—yet you need to have these strategies incorporated in your lesson plans by the end of the week. *Can you say "energy drink"?*

If you walk into the first situation, we're happy for you. That's the best-case scenario. And if you walk into the third situation, that's not bad, either. It just proves that different schools have different materials and programs and structures, far too many for us to teach, and that we were at least on track with the foundation we provided for you. But, if you walk into the second situation, we feel your pain.

Every year, at least a handful of students inform us that "the teachers aren't doing this stuff" (and by "stuff" they mean brain-friendly teaching, infusing technology, differentiating instruction, etc.). Even though we try to expose our students to cutting-edge strategies for teaching and learning, sometimes a disconnect exists between what is learned at the university level and what is experienced in the actual classroom. Now, we hope that this is more the exception than the rule, but it does happen, and we would like to offer a few suggestions for how to move beyond the feeling that somehow you have been hoodwinked.

Take Initiative—but Get Permission

Sometimes teachers (and entire schools) get in a rut. They've been doing things the same way for years. It is quite possible that their methods have been successful, too. You know, "If it ain't broke, don't fix it." But, really, there's nothing wrong with adding a little variety to teaching—as long as the results remain positive. Perhaps you are just the right person at the right time to come in with some fresh ideas. We have even heard from cooperating teachers who list this as one of their reasons for agreeing to host student teachers. If you see an opportunity to try some of the strategies and activities that you've heard and read about, find a way to tactfully suggest this to your CT. Try infusing some of the teacher's current practices with some of your new ones. For example,

"Ms. Smith, I am thinking about adding about 10 minutes of role-play to Thursday's social studies lesson. After the class reads the first three pages of the chapter, I want to let them work in groups of three to act out what they've learned. Then, they can answer questions 1 and 2 individually in their journals, as usual. Does that sound okay to you?"

or

"Mr. Price, I am so excited. I found an amazing website on the Amazon rain forest that includes a virtual field trip with pictures, sounds, and unbelievable video. I've also practiced using the interactive whiteboard so I can display the screen for everyone to see. Would it be all right if I showed this website to the class next week? I have the link in case you want to look at it ahead of time."

(Notice that in these scenarios, the CT is given the final say as to whether or not you should move forward with your idea. Also, the idea is introduced with enough time to create Plan B, if your CT's answer is no.)

We hope the answer will be yes. If you plan the activity just right and give students reasonable expectations for behavior in the modified learning environment, it might actually go really well. You might be asked to share your success with others on your grade level. On the other hand, you might get no response. But no response is far better than "Don't ever do that again"—so don't worry.

Make Reasonable Modifications

Always keep in mind that you are a guest in your CT's classroom for a limited period of time. With that in mind, you should never attempt a complete overhaul of your CT's current program. When your time ends, your CT has to continue instructing the students, and no one wants to have to reteach an entire class. Reasonable modifications might include slight changes to the teaching and learning environment, such as adding a "think-pair-share" component that partners students to share responses, or some other slightly different approach to the way the work has traditionally been done:

"Ms. Brown, I bought several small dry-erase boards and markers on clearance at the drug store. For tomorrow's math lesson, I want to try letting the children use the individual boards to work out the problems that will be written on the board. That way, more than one student gets to do board work—and they'll probably enjoy using the boards, too. Do you mind if I try that?"

Work *With* Your CT

A positive student teaching environment—for you, for your CT, for your students, and for their parents—comes about when you and your CT work as a team. During your initial period, as you are phasing into full responsibility, find ways to work alongside your CT to get the job done. While the two of you are team teaching, this is a great time to bounce ideas off each other about new or different strategies. Your CT will appreciate that you acknowledge her expertise—your acknowledgment should be genuine, of course—but you are also developing a relationship of mutual trust and respect. As a result, your CT may be more likely to let you try some of the strategies you've highlighted, bookmarked, and pinned on Pinterest for the past two years. Furthermore, if you and your CT are team teaching, you can try new strategies with a small group first to see how well they work or to determine how you might need to modify them for next time.

Ask for Feedback

In every situation, but especially when you are trying a new strategy, always ask for feedback on how it went. It might help if you start by reflecting on it first, then asking your CT what she thought:

"Mr. Smith, I'm so glad you agreed to let me try out role-play in today's lesson. The kids really got into it. I did realize about halfway through the activity, though, that I probably need to set up the groups ahead of time rather than let the class pick their groups. But I do think they paid more attention overall and got more out of the chapter because their performances were pretty accurate, and their written answers were clearer than they were last week. What did you think of the lesson?"

If you reflect on the lesson first, it lets your CT know you have processed the lesson and you are not merely looking to her to tell you everything. In other words, you can think for yourself, but you also *value her input*. (Note: This little golden nugget will take you very far in student teaching.)

SPECIAL FEATURE SECTION

Determining Your Level of Detail for Lesson Planning

If you are an instructional assistant or a lateral entry teacher, you already have an established role (and numerous additional responsibilities) within your school before the internship even begins. This role affects a good portion of your experience—even down to the type of lesson plans you're expected to prepare. Figure 7.2 provides a handy flow chart to help you determine how to proceed in this often tricky area.

FINAL THOUGHTS

We trust that this review of lesson planning basics served as a helpful tool as you begin to develop your instructional program. You have a clear idea of what to teach, the bare minimum components of a lesson plan, the importance of differentiation for the most effective teaching and learning, and how to function as part of a team. Now that you have the essentials of planning under your belt, you can think about performance. The next chapter focuses on the process of student teaching, how you grow and change as you reflect on the process, and the role that formal observations play in this transformation.

Figure 7.2 Determining Your Level of Detail for Lesson Planning

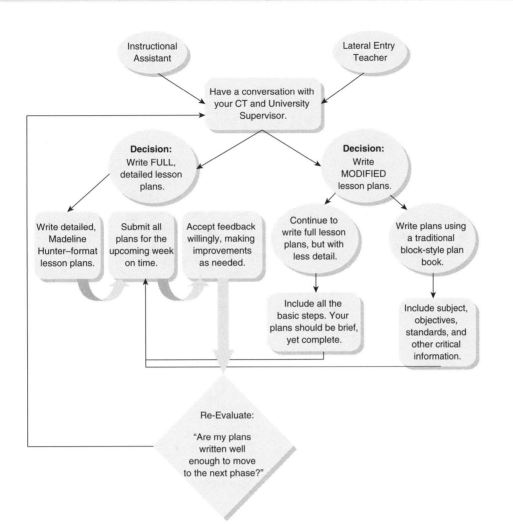

Notes:

1. EVERYONE must write lesson plans. However, the level of detail required varies from school to school.

2. Your role does NOT matter! The process of determining your level of detail <u>always</u> begins with a conversation.

3. Before moving on to the next level of detail, you must <u>always</u> return to the conversation step.

4. Be aware that your CT and University Supervisor reserve the right to require MORE detail if your lesson plans are not satisfactory!

5. For more information on what to include in your "Madeline Hunter–format lesson plans," revisit the section called *Lesson Plan Basics* at the beginning of this chapter.

BULLETIN BOARD

Preparation and Performance: The Lesson Plan

Utilize the assessment–instruction cycle.

Before teaching, effective teachers use assessment to fine-tune their instruction. After teaching, they use assessment to determine what has been mastered by which students and what needs to be retaught and to which students. They then repeat as necessary—saving time and energy by focusing on what the data say the students need to learn next.

Include lesson plan basics.

Effective teachers include the "must-haves" in their lesson plans: (1) objective/purpose, (2) input, (3) practice, (4) check for understanding, (5) closure, and (6) assessment. They use templates to save time, and they make their plans sub-proof so that learning continues even if they have to be absent.

Differentiate to meet the needs of diverse students.

When planning, effective teachers keep their students' learning styles, preferences, and abilities in mind. They provide opportunities for learners to play to their strengths, but also encourage them to branch out and work in those areas that don't come as naturally for them.

Be a team player.

Remember that you are a guest in your CT's classroom, and you can't institute a complete overhaul of any of the procedures that are already in place. Get permission, start small, and show some respect, please.

EXTRA CREDIT

Read About It

National Standards

Common Core State Standards—General Information

    http://www.corestandards.org

Common Core Math Standards

    http://www.corestandards.org/Math

Common Core English Language Arts Standards

    http://www.corestandards.org/ELA-Literacy

National Curriculum Standards for Social Studies

    http://www.socialstudies.org/standards

Next Generation Science Standards

    http://www.nextgenscience.org/next-generation-science-standards

Readymade Lesson Plans

The Educator's Reference Desk

    http://www.eduref.org/Virtual/Lessons

Scholastic—Timely Lessons and Units for All Your Teaching Needs

    http://www2.scholastic.com/browse/lessonplans.jsp

Teachers.Net Lesson Plans

    http://teachers.net/lessons

Common Core Lesson Plans

    http://commoncore.org/maps/unit/lesson_plan_submit

Planning Guides and Templates

10 Steps to Developing a Quality Lesson Plan

    http://www.lessonplanspage.com/WriteLessonPlan.htm

Scholastic: How to Develop a Unit of Study

    http://www2.scholastic.com/browse/article.jsp?id=3749710

Common Core Lesson Plan Template

http://commoncore.org/maps/unit/lesson_plan_submit

Differentiation

Differentiated Instruction—Theory, Planning, Links, etc.

http://www.Internet4classrooms.com/di.htm

How to Differentiate Instruction

http://www.teach-nology.com/tutorials/teaching/differentiate/planning

IRIS Center Star Legacy Module on Differentiating Instruction

http://iris.peabody.vanderbilt.edu/di/chalcycle.htm

Think About It

1. View the pacing guides provided in Appendix B.

   - In what ways do these pacing guides build on prior knowledge and extend concepts? Why is this so important for learners?
   - Why is it helpful for educators to develop and use pacing guides? What are some barriers to effective instruction in the absence of such guides?
   - Find out if your school or district developed pacing guides for the content you teach. If so, find out how to get a copy. If not, ask your CT to help you create a "big picture" for the content you'll be teaching during the internship.

2. Take some time to explore the concept of lesson planning.

   a. What are the principal's expectations for lesson plans?
      - How often are they submitted?
      - How much detail is required?

   b. How does your CT prepare for instruction?
      - Does she write full plans or use a block-style planning book?
      - Has she been teaching so long that she can teach without the written plan, notes, or teacher's manual on hand? What evidence do you have to support this assumption?

   c. Examine the lesson plans used by teachers on your hall or in other classes in your school.
      - What level of detail is used?
      - Is differentiation addressed? If so, in what ways?

   d. How will **you** prepare for actually teaching **your** lessons?
      - Will you read and reread your plans until they become familiar?
      - Will you practice in front of a mirror?
      - Will you use an agenda on your board or note cards to help you recall key points from your lesson?

3. Observe your CT's approach to determine what to teach.

   - Does your CT use assessment to guide instruction? How do you know?
   - What forms of assessment does he or she use

      o *before* instruction?
      o *after* instruction?

- Are instructional strategies chosen to meet students' specific learning needs? If so, provide some examples.
- If you are **not** observing a CT who uses assessment to guide instruction, what opportunities do you see that easily lend themselves to informal assessment? How comfortable are you with suggesting these tactics during your teaching time?

Try It

1. *Examine lesson plans for inclusion of "the basics."* Visit one of the readymade lesson plan sites listed in the "Read About It" section above. Select at least three lesson plans written by different authors. As you read through the lessons, see if you can identify the basic components that should be included in every lesson plan. Does the author label the lesson components using the same language you were taught in your teacher education program? In what other ways is the lesson similar to or different from your own plans? What structural designs do the authors use that you might consider incorporating into your own plans?

2. *Begin to plan for your students.* Have a conference with your CT to determine what you will be teaching. You may want to refer back to the pacing guide as an additional resource. Ask if there are any preferred strategies (e.g., assessment, instruction, practice) that are nonnegotiable for the upcoming lessons and which ones you can choose freely. Make a list of potential assessment measures you can use before and after instruction, as well as brain-friendly strategies for making the content engaging for your students.

3. *Write your own lesson plan(s) tailored for your students.* When you have the go-ahead from your CT, write a lesson plan (or a series of plans) that includes at a minimum: the basics, a mode of delivery that is reasonably engaging, and ideas for differentiation of instruction based on what you discover from your preassessment measures. Submit your lesson plan to your CT several days before it is to be taught, and ask your CT for feedback. Make suggested modifications in a timely manner.

4. *Teach your lesson, then reflect on it in a reflection journal.* Consider how well your students mastered the objectives you outlined in your plan. Did they "get it"? How do you know? Was there a part of the lesson that went particularly well? Or a part that didn't go well at all? Why do you think this happened?

5. *After teaching a unit, consider your impact on student learning.* How well did your students meet the objectives set forth in your unit? Did they master the broader content? How do you know? Revisit Table 7.1 to address the key questions.

6. *Add your plans and reflections to your lesson plan notebook.* This notebook was introduced in Chapter 4. Make sure that you separate your plans, using labels such as "Current," "Past," and "Upcoming"—or other labels that make sense and keep you organized. Additionally, use your lesson reflections to begin to determine what and how you will teach your next lesson.

Part IV

Performance

8

Developing Confidence in Your Teaching Ability

The Evaluation

Dear Student Teacher:

As Student Teaching Gurus, it is our job to help you have a successful and enjoyable experience by giving you the inside secrets. Well, hold onto your hats because this chapter is really an eye-opener. As a student teacher, you go through many phases within your internship. Although there are formal phases (which we define and explain later), we like to compare the student teaching experience to a carnival ride. You know, the one roller-coaster ride that only a few brave men and women want to attempt. It goes too high, too fast, has too many loops, and looks like a lot of fun. Your university supervisor and cooperating teacher are willing to help you manage the ride. It is through their guidance (and your willingness to accept it) that you build confidence in your ability to not only successfully complete student teaching but also to transition into a full-fledged solo teacher.

Additionally, we offer even more strategies to help you get organized, create balance, and reflect on your strengths and challenges. Expect to make mistakes, but more important, expect to grow. Remember, at the end of the day, the loop-de-loop is just part of the roller coaster. Student teaching should be fun and rewarding. Be certain that you're not so wrapped up in trying to be perfect that you don't take the time to truly enjoy and appreciate the experience.

Good luck,

Your Student Teaching Gurus

CHAPTER OBJECTIVES

By the end of this chapter, you will be able to

- describe the different roles and responsibilities of university supervisors and cooperating teachers;
- compare and contrast the multiple phases and stages of the student teaching experience;
- value the significance of each stage as it relates to building confidence in your ability;
- provide concrete examples of how the stages affect your teaching responsibilities;
- relate the experiential learning cycle to the acquisition of skill development; and
- identify how to utilize reflection as a tool for self-exploration and professional growth.

ROLES AND RESPONSIBILITIES

Ask teachers about their memories of the most challenging yet rewarding experience of their teacher education program, and we're sure (hands down) that most will share stories about their student teaching experience. Historically, student teaching was, and continues to be, the capstone experience. So much so that all 50 states require a student teaching practicum, further testifying to the significance of the experience. This experience has a significant impact on you as you juggle the responsibilities of being a student and teacher (and all that it entails), while establishing and developing relationships with cooperating teachers, principals, additional school staff, and a university supervisor. Thus, student teaching is a complicated emotional and interpersonal experience that is critically important to the making of a great teacher.

> *Student teaching is one of those things that will make you and break you. I have learned so much about myself—more specifically, I feel I am now a better judge of how far to push myself. I realized during student teaching that I do have limits and I should be aware of them, not afraid of them.*

> —Henry, Elementary Education major

As mentioned earlier, you are guided through this full-time teaching experience by a knowledgeable and resourceful university supervisor (US) and cooperating teacher (CT). Their roles are extremely important during the internship, as they are responsible for the almighty final observation report. Some of you have already broken out into a cold sweat just thinking about being observed. Well, we wish we had a magic pill to relieve your anxiety, but we are only your Student Teaching Gurus, not pharmacists. However, we can offer you this bit of advice: Take a deep breath, try to relax, and stay positive. We know this may be hard to do, but you'll have less anxiety if you are well organized (revisit Chapter 4).

Your CT and US are there to help you learn how to be a great teacher. They can't provide you with constructive feedback unless they actually watch you in a variety of teaching settings. It's really okay if your US drops in to observe you while you are lining the kids up to go to lunch (this informs him or her how you handle transitions). This is just as important as when your CT observes you teaching a geometry lesson. Both of these observations give them insight into your knowledge, skills, and dispositions. Just face it—evaluation is an ongoing part of this experience. People talk about what and how you are doing, so you may want to get used to living in the fishbowl for a while. Regular conferences between you and your CT or US (or with all three of you together) are an integral part of the student teaching experience. The university supervisor should be kept informed of any problems or challenges that are identified, and your cooperating teacher should discuss your performance with the university supervisor on a regular basis.

Ingrad Smith (2009) notes numerous reasons for evaluating student teachers during their experiences in K–12 settings. Among them: Certification programs need to prove to state or national program approval agencies that student teachers are doing what the institution says they require during their field experience (remember the National Council for Accreditation of Teacher Education (NCATE) conversation from Chapter 2). While this reason is important, more significant is that evaluation is used to inform you about skills that need to be strengthened. If all goes well, you receive both formal and informal feedback from both parties that provides you with positive reinforcement and constructive criticism along with communication of clear goals and expectations. Later in this chapter we discuss how to use their feedback to your benefit. Teacher education programs vary, but Figure 8.1 provides you with a handy checklist for understanding the roles and responsibilities of your support team.

Your successful completion of student teaching is determined by your meeting not only the expectations of your CT but also the performance expectations established by your teacher education program. Trust us—you should not hesitate to seek out the guidance of your US or CT. Think about it: If you do well, they get to claim some of the credit.

Figure 8.1   Roles and Responsibilities

Cooperating Teacher	*University Supervisor*
Regular supervision includes the following:	Regular supervision includes the following:
✓ communicating clear expectations regarding planning, classroom management, curriculum, student assessments, and performance;	✓ visits (often a minimum of 3) to the classroom to observe and discuss performance in accordance with state and teacher education program guidelines;
✓ weekly observations (at a minimum) of performance in the classroom along with communication/reflection of those observations;	✓ continuing availability to both the student teacher and the CT for consultation regarding any issues that may arise during the course of the internship;
✓ weekly discussions (at a minimum) to address expectations regarding planning, classroom management, curriculum, student assessments, and performance; and	✓ completion of formative assessments of the student teacher's performance, in accordance with state and teacher education program guidelines; and
✓ completion of a formative assessment provided by the teacher education program and participation in collaborative feedback conference(s) with the student teacher, CT, and US.	✓ a summative assessment of performance at the end of the student teaching internship in accordance with state and teacher education program guidelines.

We know that many educators think that the best way to support student teachers and provide them with experience use the "sink or swim" philosophy and just "throw them in." But in most cases, this can be a recipe for disaster, which is why teacher education programs usually proceed with a gradual immersion marked by **phases** or distinguishing events that are part of the internship. These plans vary widely, depending on the state department of education and/or accrediting institution, although the typical student teaching experience begins with a phase plan that transitions you into and out of full-time teaching. The overall plan should include a negotiation and clarification of the expectations, needs, and desires of both you and your CT—this facilitates the process of gradually increasing your responsibility until you're able to fly solo.

Phases of Responsibility

Phase In

Due to the many variables involved in student teaching placements, phase-in plans may vary, but they typically begin with you observing your CT, handling classroom routines, and assuming noninstructional duties, and then gradually the responsibilities increase, and you phase into teaching one or more subjects. A specific plan should be established during the initial meeting or during the first week of the placement.

Typical duties may include, but are not limited to

- managing transitions (e.g., taking students to specials, lunch, bathroom breaks);
- cooperative planning involving you and your CT (or other teachers);
- team teaching with your CT;
- preparing and administering assessments;
- teaching part of a class; and
- teaching one or two subjects or one or two class periods.

As you progress through this phase, your responsibilities should increase in preparation for full-time teaching.

Full Responsibility

Whether it is for a period of 1 week, 4 weeks, or longer, this phase is when you take control of the classroom and you are the full-time teacher. When this takes place and when you are ready to handle it, this responsibility is negotiated by you and your CT (and sometimes your university supervisor is a part of the process). At this phase, if you can name it, then most likely, you are in charge of it. Your CT may still prefer to handle some crucial tasks, such as parent conferences and report cards, but even these tasks offer you the opportunity to monitor and learn best practices.

Phase Out

During this time, you begin to gradually release the responsibility and "give back" the teaching reins to your CT. You may still teach some subjects, but this decreases as the semester comes to an end. Some student teaching programs may want you to include visits to other classrooms and/or schools during this time to gain additional exposure to other grade levels, teaching styles, and school cultures.

Stages of Development

While teacher education programs may vary as to courses, schedules, and student teaching phase plans, within these three broad components of your experience, research shows us that the student teaching experience is universally similar (Meijer, de Graaf, & Meirink, 2011). Moreover, it is guaranteed that every new teacher has to pass through five distinct developmental stages. We discuss the technical terms for those stages in a moment, but first, we want to help you visualize these stages using our previous roller-coaster analogy.

The Student Teaching Roller Coaster

If you've never been on a roller coaster, hang tight (you'll quickly understand the analogy). In this case, we like to refer to the five stages as

1. *Raring to Go.* You want the ride to begin, but first you have to observe the people who successfully got on and off the ride before you (preferably, studying the ones who managed to keep their lunch down).

2. *Climbing.* You finally get on, and you're slowly inching your way up to the top, enjoying the view, and taking it all in as you go along.

3. *The Loop-de-Loop.* It's here. You are at the top (and sometimes the bottom), twisting and turning. Sometimes you want to scream, laugh, shout, and cry. You want to get off, but there is still a long way to go.

4. *Coasting.* You see the end in sight. It's all slowing down, and you're not so sure that you are ready for it to be over.

5. *Relief.* Time to exit and reflect on the best parts of the ride. It doesn't hurt to remember the parts that didn't go so well either—as long as you learn from your mistakes (e.g., don't sit in the front car next time).

Source: Adapted from Moir, E. (1990). Teaching phases. This article was originally written for publication in the newsletter for the California New Teacher Project, published by the California Department of Education (CDE). Santa Cruz, CA: New Teacher Center.

Phases of Teaching

Meijer et al. (2011) offered the following developmental stages to characterize the first year teaching experience: *anticipation, survival, disillusionment, rejuvenation,* and *reflection.* The research refers to these stages as first-year teaching experiences, but we have adapted the ideas to reflect the entire student teaching experience. It should not be surprising that these stages also follow a similar "bumpy" (albeit exciting) ride. Figure 8.2 gives you an idea of how the phase plan is related to the developmental stages. Keep in mind that this is a general example, as your specific student teaching experience may differ in number of weeks. We discuss each of the stages and give you important tips and strategies to help build your confidence as you move through each stage. Confidence comes from being prepared. Recognizing and understanding these stages and knowing "how to deal" with them is essential to being prepared and having a positive experience.

Figure 8.2 The Student Teaching Experience

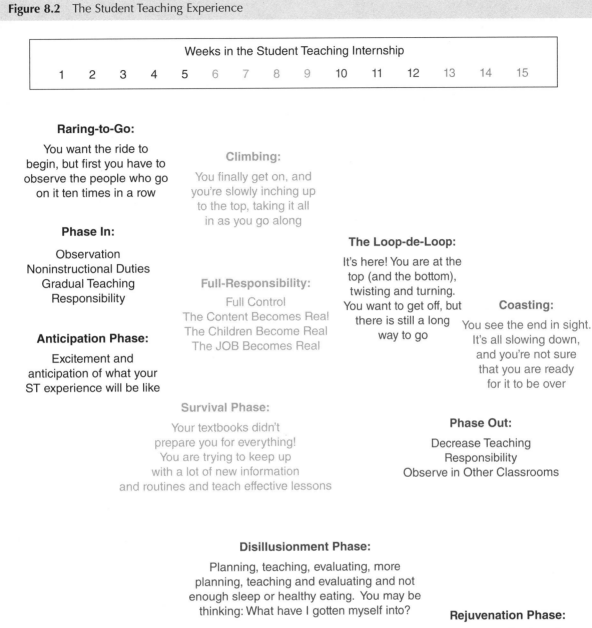

Weeks in the Student Teaching Internship

1 2 3 4 5 6 7 8 9 10 11 12 13 14 15

Raring-to-Go:

You want the ride to begin, but first you have to observe the people who go on it ten times in a row

Climbing:

You finally get on, and you're slowly inching up to the top, taking it all in as you go along

Phase In:

Observation
Noninstructional Duties
Gradual Teaching
Responsibility

The Loop-de-Loop:

It's here! You are at the top (and the bottom), twisting and turning. You want to get off, but there is still a long way to go

Full-Responsibility:

Full Control
The Content Becomes Real
The Children Become Real
The JOB Becomes Real

Coasting:

You see the end in sight. It's all slowing down, and you're not sure that you are ready for it to be over

Anticipation Phase:

Excitement and anticipation of what your ST experience will be like

Survival Phase:

Your textbooks didn't prepare you for everything! You are trying to keep up with a lot of new information and routines and teach effective lessons

Phase Out:

Decrease Teaching
Responsibility
Observe in Other Classrooms

Disillusionment Phase:

Planning, teaching, evaluating, more planning, teaching and evaluating and not enough sleep or healthy eating. You may be thinking: What have I gotten myself into?

Rejuvenation Phase:

Renewed Spirit and Confidence

Relief:

Time to exit and reflect on the best parts of the ride. It doesn't hurt to remember the parts that didn't go so well either (next time, don't sit in the front car)

Reflection:

Think about the various changes that you'd like to make during and after your ST experience

ANTICIPATION PHASE

The anticipation phase begins during the semester before you actually begin your student teaching. The closer you get to student teaching, the more excited and anxious you become about the student teaching placement. You may spend a lot of time thinking about who your CT might be, the wonderful class of kids that you will have, the supportive families you will work with, and your equally supportive school staff. Student teachers enter their new role with a tremendous commitment to making a difference and a somewhat idealistic view of how to accomplish their goals. This feeling of excitement carries new teachers through the first few weeks of school.

> *My student teaching experience was pretty great once I got comfortable with being in someone else's classroom. I was nervous when I first began because I didn't know what to expect from myself or the kids.*
>
> —Leslie, Secondary Science major

Potential Pitfalls (may include, but are not limited to)

- A tendency to idealize the responsibilities of the teaching position
- Forgetting to have a formal meeting with your CT to negotiate his or her expectations of your role in the classroom

How to Deal

Create a Plan. Be honest about your strengths and challenges.

Listen, Watch, and Learn. Basically, observe and ask a lot of questions to help you transition.

Be Flexible. Prepare for the realization that everything you think you know will probably change.

Reflect and Request. Think about how you can continue to grow and ask your CT, the instructional assistant, and your university supervisor for feedback.

Source: Adapted from Moir, E. (1990). Teaching phases. This article was originally written for publication in the newsletter for the California New Teacher Project, published by the California Department of Education (CDE). Santa Cruz, CA: New Teacher Center.

SURVIVAL PHASE

The first month or so of the student teaching experience is very overwhelming. You are observing, taking on new tasks, getting to know the kids and the school. Additionally, you are expected to learn a lot at a very quick pace. Most student teachers are instantly bombarded with a variety of unanticipated situations. Despite the A's and B's (and perhaps even an occasional C) that you received in your methods coursework and field experiences, you may still be caught off guard by the realities of teaching. You will find that you become very focused on the day-to-day routine of teaching and preparation (it is not uncommon for new teachers to spend up to 70 hours a week on schoolwork), and you may lose sight of other responsibilities, such as eating healthful meals. In spite of this, you will probably be surprised how your body continues to function on sheer excitement, adrenaline, and commitment.

My advice for future student teachers is to be open to new things. Yes, student teaching is the time to shine, but it is also time for experimenting and challenging yourself.

—Dean, Middle Grades major

Potential Pitfalls (may include, but are not limited to)

- Difficulty finding appropriate times to talk with your CT (you both are always teaching)
- Constant struggling to stop and reflect on your experiences
- Creating a balance between schoolwork, teaching, and your personal life

How to Deal

Be Flexible. Remember that each school day is different. Try to start every day with a fresh, renewed outlook.

Get Organized. Establish a plan to keep all of those little details in line (lessons, materials, extra responsibilities, etc.).

Think Again. Revisit subject content and pedagogy.

Ask for Help. Be honest about what you know and what you don't know.

Source: Adapted from Moir, E. (1990). Teaching phases. This article was originally written for publication in the newsletter for the California New Teacher Project, published by the California Department of Education (CDE). Santa Cruz, CA: New Teacher Center.

DISILLUSIONMENT PHASE

After 6 to 8 weeks of nonstop work, you may enter the disillusionment phase. The intensity and length of the phase varies, as it is typically defined by the ongoing reality of the particular job. The vicious cycle probably includes lots of planning and teaching; sustaining your days with Red Bull, 5-Hour Energy, coffee, or some other caffeinated product; no leisure time; exposure to lots of sick kids; getting sick yourself; getting behind on work, having to make up days; getting stressed; lack of sleep; not eating; and so on. See where we're going with this?

(Continued)

(Continued)

This is a very difficult and challenging phase. You will surely be missing your regular schedule (when exactly was the last time you actually exercised or watched a whole episode of your favorite TV show?), and your family and friends are definitely missing you. In fact, getting through this phase may be the toughest challenge you face along your journey toward becoming a teacher.

I was an instructional assistant at the school where I did my student teaching and at first I was afraid to ask questions because I thought that I should already know the answer. But, my CT encouraged me to ask questions since I will only have one chance to be a student teacher. I'm glad that I did. It really helped a lot.

—Bruce, licensure candidate

Potential Pitfalls (may include, but are not limited to)

- Realizing the extensive time commitment and that things aren't going as smoothly as you hoped
- Low morale, which may contribute to a period of disenchantment
- Questioning your commitment and competence
- Questioning your ability to manage the classroom

How to Deal

Keep Your Cool. There are going to be many opportunities to lose patience or get frustrated. But nothing helps you get through something more than holding your tongue and being patient. Remember the temporary nature of the internship and always be respectful to your cooperating teacher, to your students, to the staff, and to yourself.

Be Flexible. Clearly, we can't stress this enough. Don't get upset if things do not always go as you planned. Review your lesson plans for any missing instructional strategies and try to anticipate discipline problems before they arise so that you can have solutions already prepared.

Just Do It. At least twice a week, do something that you enjoy (but haven't thought about doing since you began your internship). It might be working out, getting eight hours of sleep, going to the movies, or just eating a meal that is not served through the window of your car. The unfinished plans will still be there when you return.

Source: Adapted from Moir, E. (1990). Teaching phases. This article was originally written for publication in the newsletter for the California New Teacher Project, published by the California Department of Education (CDE). Santa Cruz, CA: New Teacher Center.

REJUVENATION PHASE

The rejuvenation phase is characterized by a slow rise in your attitude toward teaching. Sometimes, all it takes is a long weekend, a teacher workday, or the realization that things do get easier with time. This breath of fresh air may give you a broader perspective that comes with renewed confidence. By now, you have completed your full-time teaching responsibility, have a better understanding of how the system works, have gained new coping strategies, have accepted the realities of the job, and most important, have a sense of accomplishment. Give yourself a pat on the back.

> *One thing to take advantage of, are the people on your grade level team who offer to help you because every teacher is different and can help you in their own unique way.*
>
> —Monica, licensure candidate

Potential Pitfalls (may include, but are not limited to)

- Having moments when you question your confidence (Did I teach the concepts correctly? Will they pass the test? Do my 1st graders know how to decode texts? Can they explain the life-cycle process?)
- Getting too comfortable (You are still in learning mode, and this time is important, as it gives you an opportunity to still be a part of the classroom and to show your CT that you are still respectful of the learning environment.)

How to Deal

Put on a Happy Face. Try to exude confidence. Even if you aren't feeling confident, act as if you are. Confidence typically comes from a teacher's enthusiasm, excitement about the content, and genuine pleasure in teaching.

Go on Vacation. If possible, use this phase-out time to visit other classrooms and/schools. This helps give you a better perspective. You may have always thought that you wanted to teach kindergarten, but spending time in a 5th-grade class might make you rethink your choices. Plus, at the end of the day, you are certified to teach a range of grade levels, not just one.

Source: Adapted from Moir, E. (1990). Teaching phases. This article was originally written for publication in the newsletter for the California New Teacher Project, published by the California Department of Education (CDE). Santa Cruz, CA: New Teacher Center.

REFLECTION PHASE

Reflection should be occurring throughout the entire student teaching internship, so although it is called a phase, it really is interwoven in everything that you do. It begins the first day of your experience, and in reality never ends. Reflection is the key to growth

(Continued)

(Continued)

and sustaining a successful career. You should never be intimidated by the reflection process, as it provides you with the most information for ways to improve your craft.

Teaching is a real "minds on" profession. You have to be prepared to analyze and think about everything that you do. This is the only way to become a better teacher.

—LaTanya, secondary candidate

Potential Pitfalls (may include, but are not limited to)

- Only reflecting on the negative and not the positive
- Only reflecting at the end of your student teaching experience
- "Throwing the baby out with the bathwater" (You don't have to start from scratch every time you want to revise a lesson, or idea, or try a new strategy.)

How to Deal

Have a Vision. Reflect on all of the positive and negative experiences and think about how you will make changes for your own classroom. Write them down in a journal so that you won't forget your ideas when you get your new job. Inevitably, when you start the new job, you are led right back to the anticipation phase, where you will begin the whole cycle all over again, but this time you are older and—more important—wiser.

Source: Adapted from Moir, E. (1990). Teaching phases. This article was originally written for publication in the newsletter for the California New Teacher Project, published by the California Department of Education (CDE). Santa Cruz, CA: New Teacher Center.

EXPERIENTIAL LEARNING

Realize that all of these phases and stages converge in an effort to help you to think about how to improve and build on the teaching skills you currently possess. This also translates into helping you build confidence in your abilities as a teacher. Those in the teaching profession understand that learning requires developmentally appropriate teaching and learning strategies along with a healthy dose of "trial and error." This idea can be equated to the theory of **experiential learning** (learning from direct experience) that was championed by Dewey (1933). He noted that it is possible for people to have different approaches to learning and/or ways of learning when they are presented with direct, well-designed, and facilitated hands-on experiences.

The Experiential Learning Cycle

As basic as it sounds, experiential learning helped to shape teacher education programs as we now know them. Over the years, many other theorists added to and updated Dewey's ideas in this area. Most notably, the educational philosophy of Lewin (1951) and the social psychology theory of Kolb (1984) have merged to give us the *experiential learning cycle* (ELC) model for understanding the process of learning. This model is distinct from other models of learning (i.e., behavioral models or social learning models), in that it views your experiences and how individuals reflect on them as integral to the learning process. According to this model,

- all experiences should be viewed as a continuous process;
- each experience influences each future experience;
- purposeful reflection, questioning, and planning bring about a transfer of learning; and
- the entire process may happen in minutes or over an extended period of time (days, weeks, or even months).

These ideas are displayed in Figure 8.3, which portrays the steps in the cycle. The technical, historical model suggests that you have a *concrete experience,* followed by a *reflective observation,* and then a formation of *abstract conceptualizations* occurs before you finally conduct *active experimentation* to test out the newly developed principles, which leads to a transfer of learning. However, we also offer a nontechnical explanation in Figure 8.4.

A Simpler Approach

Even though the ELC model is the most commonly cited model and its popularity is widely accepted, there is considerable debate as to whether it adequately represents all learning situations. However, we think that the model has considerable value and merit in education. Although we understand that using this model sounds like a lot of work (and it is), so is teaching. And if you want to get better at it, you should think about how you can apply this model to your everyday experiences. To help you facilitate this process, we ask you to abandon the technical terms in favor of our more streamlined approach to this learning process. Think of the model as the four easy steps in Figure 8.4.

STRATEGIC REFLECTION

The art of self-reflection is probably the most overlooked learning process, and we feel that it is the most important aspect of any teacher's day (or year for that matter). It receives less attention than collecting lunch money, parent conferences, administrative observations, and just plain sheer exhaustion. Let's be honest—we ask children to reflect on their behavior all day long: "Why did you solve the problem that way? Why did you skip Lisa in the lunch line? Why didn't you tell your dad to call me?" and so on. If we expect reflection from students, then perhaps we should at least take the time to understand better what it entails. *Reflection* is defined in many different ways. It usually includes or is prompted by some level of uncertainty that needs to be resolved (Dewey, 1933). The process of reflection involves a continuum, which is defined as a gradual transition from one condition to another without any abrupt changes. You'll have days where you are actively reflecting all of the time, consistently questioning the choices that you've made. You might be jotting notes on a piece of paper about new activities, attending a professional meeting where you are collaboratively working in groups to solve instructional challenges, or in a meeting with your CT after delivering a lesson. However, some days you won't actively reflect at all, thereby saving your mental energy to just make it through the day.

Figure 8.3   The Experiential Learning Cycle

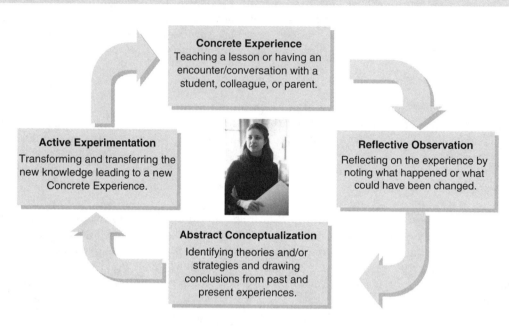

Source: Lewin, K. (1951). *Field theory in social science: Selected theoretical papers.* D. Cartwright (Ed.). New York: Harper & Row.

Figure 8.4   Four Easy Steps to Learning

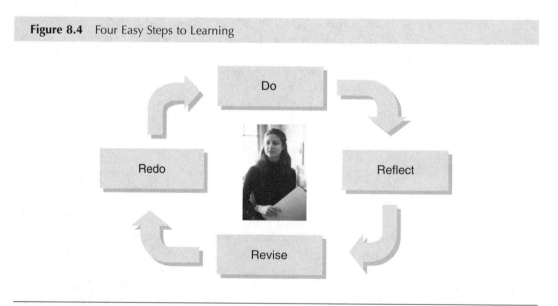

Source: Daniels, Patterson, & Dunston, 2010. Adapted from Lewin, K. (1951). *Field theory in social science: Selected theoretical papers.* D. Cartwright (Ed.). New York: Harper & Row.

Why Is Self-Reflection Important?

Why reflect at all? Simply put, reflection can improve your practice. Your CT and US began the process when they provided you with constructive criticism and feedback about your knowledge, skills, and/or dispositions. But you aren't doing anyone a favor if all you ever do is smile and nod your head as you are given priceless teaching advice. You must do something with any proposed recommendations. The initial step is easy—just do what is asked of you—but for long-term growth and development you need to take additional steps and continue the process through the use of purposeful self-reflection. The use of reflection can

- help you organize your thoughts and make sense of classroom events,
- lead to goal setting and professional growth,
- frame your teaching as an ongoing process of knowledge building, and
- lead to conversations and collaboration with your mentors (Cook, 2012).

Levels of Self-Reflection

Reflection is not so much about one day or a single event as about the process that occurs over time as you better understand your role and relationship to others (your students, their families, your colleagues, etc.). The ups and downs are to be expected; they typically go along with the job. The "aha" moment comes when you realize you must reflect in order to make changes.

Reflection, however, is more than "just thinking hard about what you do" (Bullough, 2011). The process should involve posing questions, searching for alternative answers, and seeking the deeper meaning of what you do. To be useful, reflection should include both individual and collaborative questioning about what you teach and how you teach it. Initially, reflection may focus just on what you are doing. This is referred to as the *technical level*, where you may be interested only in refining teaching strategies. Typically the questions that occur to you are prompted by challenges you have about the quality of your teaching or the effects of your teaching on your students (e.g., "I thought those changes I made for Alicia in the math materials for today's lesson were exactly what she needed. . . . I wonder why they didn't work very well"). You may also begin to ask yourself (and others) questions that focus on the relationship between your actions (and the actions of others) and specific situations that occur in your classroom, as well as in the context of a program, the school, and/or the community. This is the *contextual level*, which is marked by a realization of cause-and-effect relationships (e.g., "My response to Mary's behavior was great yesterday. I know what she did today is due to the same reason, but she didn't respond as well. I wonder what else was going on that could be getting in the way").

Reflection also occurs when you find yourself contemplating issues about your teaching and its impact on larger systemic issues. This is the *critical level*, which is the broadest form of reflection and may focus on ideas like social justice. Researchers note that these levels are developmental and that not everyone progresses through all levels to reach critical reflection. For example, "How is access to health care related to how my students learn?"

But in order to progress and reach the critical level, there has to be "method in the madness." Reflection should be strategic as well as systematic. Basically, this means that you have to be organized and have a system in place that specifies how you will reflect. Will you keep a daily journal, keep a small tape recorder handy, and use a flip camera to record yourself, or use some other recording method? These are all very simple ways to hold yourself accountable for the reflection process. Specifically, the goal is:

- to think about what you are doing,
- to challenge or validate your beliefs, and
- to develop and test cause-and-effect theories related to connecting your actions to student outcomes (for more information on this process, see the Bridges to Success website: www.tr.wou.edu/bridges/contact.htm).

At the end of the day (week, month, and year), if your goal is to become a better teacher, the process is simple. You may need to ask some hard questions, but the answers you get and the actions you take will help you be more confident and productive; ultimately, this benefits both you and your students.

SPECIAL FEATURE SECTION

So, now that you have a good idea of the scope and sequence of the student teaching experience, it is important to review what you've learned. In true teacher form, we felt it was important to leave you with something that you would find not only easy to read but also memorable. To that end, we provide you with Figure 8.5, titled The ABCs of Student Teaching. Figure 8.5 is an invaluable list, including everything from A to Z that you want to keep in mind as you get started and continue with in your student teaching placement. You will probably want to keep this list handy as a way to remind yourself of all the important points.

Figure 8.5   The ABCs of Student Teaching

- **A**dmit your mistakes—and learn from them
- **B**e flexible
- **C**ommunicate with your cooperating teacher, university supervisor, and classroom parents
- **D**ream a little dream (i.e., get a good night's sleep)
- **E**xplain, examine, expect, experience
- **F**ind time to attend some after-school events
- **G**et to know all the teachers in your school and make friends with the cafeteria staff, custodians, aides, and secretaries
- **H**ave the courage to try something else, if what you're doing isn't working
- **I**nvest time in yourself—outside of the school day
- **J**ust listen—both to what the kids are saying and to what they're not saying
- **K**eep a journal
- **L**earn your school's policies and procedures
- **M**odel the behavior that you'd like your students to display

- **N**obody's perfect
- **O**verplan—you might just need it
- **P**repare lessons that are exciting, innovative, creative, and engaging
- **Q**uit worrying and just do your best
- **R**eflect, reflect, and then reflect some more
- **S**tay alert
- **T**ake pictures (lots and lots of pictures)
- **U**nderstand that the learning process involves everyone—teachers, students, colleagues, and parents—and get everyone involved
- **V**olunteer to share projects and ideas, and don't be afraid to ask others to share their ideas with you
- **W**ork within your limits
- e**X**pect the unexpected—and plan for it!
- **Y**ell if you need support
- **Z**ero in on your strengths, not your weaknesses

Source: Adapted and updated from Lowman, 1984.

FINAL THOUGHTS

After reading this chapter, you should be feeling a bit more confident in yourself as a student teacher. You now know more about the roles and responsibilities of your cooperating teacher and university supervisor. Although their evaluations and feedback on your performance may seem intimidating at first, they are an important part of the process. Each phase and stage of the internship is as exciting as a roller-coaster ride, and your CT and US are right there beside you with every slow climb and fast fall. But in order to be adequately prepared, you must take responsibility to anticipate these ups and downs. This can be accomplished through active learning and strategic reflection. Remember: Do, reflect, revise, and redo—and then do it all over again. You are all set. You have the resources that you need to complete your internship with a smile. Now all you need is a job (well, most of you will need a job). Chapter 9 is designed to get you one step closer to that goal.

BULLETIN BOARD

Developing Confidence in Your Teaching Ability: The Evaluation

Roles and Responsibilities

Everyone has a job to do to ensure that you have a successful student teaching experience and that you are prepared to fly solo when you are ready. Your CT and US are your support team, and you shouldn't be shy about tapping into their knowledge. You frequently will be observed and evaluated during your internship. This is part of the process of moving you toward independence.

Experiential Learning Cycle

Make every experience a learning experience. The experiential learning cycle provides a process for you to analyze day-to-day situations. Remember:

Do

Reflect

Revise

Redo

Phases and Stages

It is imperative that you sit down and talk with your CT about how you will plan to gradually take over the teaching. Student teaching is like a roller coaster. You will have many bumps, dips, and fast turns. This is normal. Understanding these stages, and preparing for how to handle the accompanying issues associated with each phase, will take you far in developing your confidence.

Strategic Reflection

Reflection is incredibly important in all stages of the internship. You should set a plan for how you will reflect, and make it a regular part of your day and/or week. Whether you reflect formally or informally, it is the key to professional growth and development.

EXTRA CREDIT

Read About It

Student Teaching

http://www.education-world.com/a_curr/curr152.shtml

http://www.nmsa.org/AboutNMSA/PositionStatements/StudentTeaching/tabid/289/Default.aspx

http://www.middleweb.com/1stDResources.html

Observations and Evaluations

http://preservice-teacher-training.suite101.com/article.cfm/classroom_observations

Managing Multiple Responsibilities

http://voices.yahoo.com/surviving-student-teaching-guide-coming-33040.html

The Reflection Process

http://www.viu.ca/iel/teachlearn/guide/files/UofManHandbook5.9-5.12.pdf

http://learnweb.harvard.edu/alps/reflect

Alternative Licensure

http://www.ncei.com/Alt-Teacher-Cert.htm

Nontraditional Undergraduates

National Center for Education Statistics. (2008). *Special analysis: Nontraditional undergraduates.* Washington, DC: Institute of Educational Sciences, U.S. Department of Education. Retrieved from http://nces.ed.gov/pubs/web/97578e.asp

Research Article: Lee, E. D., & Mark, A. (2011). Non-traditional entrants to the profession of teaching: Motivations and experiences of second-career educators. *Christian Perspectives in Education*, 4(2), 3.

Think About It

Special Analysis: Nontraditonal Undergraduates

Access and read "Non-traditional Entrants to the Profession of Teaching: Motivations and Experiences of Second-Career Educators," a research article that compares and contrasts confidence levels of traditional and nontraditional student teachers. If you are unsure of your status, reading this article will be especially important for you. Answer the following questions based on the findings in the article, and see how well you can interpret the results. Spoiler alert: The results are probably exactly what you expect.

1. Nontraditional students with children or child-rearing experience display fewer concerns for self than do others.

   True or False

   Explain your reasoning.

2. Nontraditional students who are twenty-five years old or older display fewer concerns across all stages.

   True or False

   Explain your reasoning.

3. Discipline issues surface more often for nontraditional career switchers.

   True or False

   Explain your reasoning.

4. There is no difference between traditional and nontraditional groups when comparing higher levels of concern about student achievement and fewer concerns about interactions with adults (principal, other teachers, TAs, etc.).

   True or False

   Explain your reasoning.

5. Nontraditional student teacher groups are more self-confident than their traditional counterparts.

   True or False

   Explain your reasoning.

Source: Adapted from Lee, E. D., & Mark, A. (2011). Non-traditional entrants to the profession of teaching: Motivations and experiences of second-career educators. *Christian Perspectives in Education, 4*(2), 3.

Understanding the Phases of Student Teaching

The student teaching internship is marked by distinct phases. We've provided you with an outline of these phases in the hopes that you will be prepared for the events that occur during your experience. Use the following activity to develop tangible strategies to help you identify and anticipate what may come next.

The *anticipation phase* is marked by the following:

   1.

   2.

   3.

When I see these signs, I will do the following to avoid potential pitfalls:

   1.

   2.

   3.

The *survival phase* is marked by the following:

    1.

    2.

    3.

When I see these signs, I will do the following to avoid potential pitfalls:

    1.

    2.

    3.

The *disillusionment phase* is marked by the following:

    1.

    2.

    3.

When I see these signs, I will do the following to avoid potential pitfalls:

    1.

    2.

    3.

The *rejuvenation phase* is marked by the following:

    1.

    2.

    3.

When I see these signs, I will do the following to avoid potential pitfalls:

    1.

    2.

    3.

The *reflection phase* is marked by the following:

    1.

    2.

    3.

When I see these signs, I will do the following to avoid potential pitfalls:

    1.

    2.

    3.

EXPERIENTIAL LEARNING CYCLE

Use the case study to help answer the questions that follow.

The IA (Instructional Assistant) Who Wanted to Be a Teacher: A True Story

Pat always knew that he wanted to be a teacher. He loved learning as a child and always enjoyed school. In college, he wanted to major in education, but his parents talked him into majoring in business (they thought it was a more fitting occupation for a man). Even though he continued to take as many education courses as his schedule allowed, by his junior year he declared a major in business management. After graduation, he spent 10 years as a business consultant. Although he enjoyed the job, he derived the most satisfaction from organizing his company's community service events and volunteering at the local elementary school as part of the company's partnership efforts. Then, due to the failing economy, Pat lost his job. Although most of us would not welcome this situation, he saw it as a sign that he could finally enjoy a teaching career. He promptly started researching what he needed to do in order to become licensed as a teacher. While it didn't seem that it would be difficult, it did mean going back to school. After a bit of time, he was lucky enough to find a job as an instructional assistant. It was hard in the beginning, working during the day and going to school in the evenings, but he felt that finally he was on the right track. Even though there were some difficult days, he really enjoyed the classroom. He looked forward to going back each day. He spent a lot of time envisioning what it would be like when he had his own class: how he would do things differently (than the teacher he worked with), what he would say to the parents, and the creative, engaging lessons he would plan. The teacher he worked with was great, and it was partially because of her and the rest of the staff that he asked the principal to let him stay and complete his student teaching experience. It also helped that he wouldn't lose his income, which he needed. He wasn't really certain how it was going to work, but he knew he would be able to stay at the school where he had already built relationships, and he wouldn't have to quit his job to fulfill the student teaching internship, as was the case for many of his classmates. In any event, he looked forward to student teaching with more excitement than anxiety.

The first day of student teaching was a bit chaotic (and it didn't have anything to do with the kids). He was assigned to a class for student teaching, but the teacher was under the impression that he was there to be her new assistant. So he spent the better part of the morning talking to the university site supervisor in hopes of getting things resolved. Progress was made, and midway through the day he was moved to another class. Unfortunately, that was not the last time that problems occurred. On one occasion, the school building administration scheduled professional development training during class time, and they put Pat on the schedule to cover a kindergarten class. This took him away from his teaching duties. He had not yet assumed full responsibility, but he was teaching two subjects. He tried to be respectful and informed the administration that he should really stay with the CT's class, but they insisted that they needed him to serve his regular TA duties. Although Pat's CT supported him and echoed his concern about being pulled away from teaching duties, it didn't help alter the situation. He had to cover the class and figure out how to squeeze in teaching the two subjects that he missed. The situation was so stressful that he decided if he was ever put in that situation (or a similar situation) again, he would have to give up his position as a TA.

Answer the following questions:

1. How can you apply the experiential learning cycle model to Pat's unique situation?

2. This case study exemplifies many concurrent experiential learning cycles. Show the complete process by filling in the missing stages.

3. What are the strengths and weaknesses of this experiential learning cycle?

(Continued)

(Continued)

Pat's Assessment

"I really feel that in the end, the biggest issues seemed to stem from the administrators and teachers not realizing (or understanding) that I was now a 'teacher' (at least for 15 weeks). Also, I didn't always receive a welcoming response from other IAs. The response to my complaining was always the same, 'At least you still have a job.' In my school, teachers and IAs work together, but they definitely live in separate camps. Some of the IAs didn't feel respected, and that translates into resentment toward some teachers.

"I had to live in both camps. I got to hear the gripes of teachers about IAs and the gripes of IAs about teachers. I had to walk a fine line to appease both camps. This just added to my already full plate along with lesson plans, classroom management, and trying to keep my CT happy. Although there were a couple of false starts and some stalls, I walked away from the ST experience feeling as if I successfully completed a tightrope act. I learned a lot from my CT and the children, and I definitely feel that I am ready to be a teacher. But if anyone asks, I definitely have an opinion about things that could have been managed differently in order to make the process smoother. I could give you a long rant, or a laundry list of bewares, but it all really comes down to one thing—communication. My school doesn't usually have student teachers; therefore, I don't think the administration fully understood the commitment they were making when they agreed to let me student teach. That lack of understanding sometimes put me in uncomfortable situations where I had to remind the administration that I had to fulfill certain requirements as a student teacher. I think if my CT and I had communicated at the beginning with the administration and worked out some of the important details about the role of a student teacher, some of the 'surprise responsibilities' wouldn't have been such a surprise. It is worth the extra time to lay everything out initially. Perhaps having your university supervisor in on the meeting could also help. All in all, I still really like the school, and the experience really helped me to understand how schools run from both perspectives (teachers and IAs) as well as to understand some of the school politics. I'd even be happy teaching there. I look at it like this—every experience is different, and once you commit to being a great teacher, you take the good with the bad because in the end, you know that you are dedicated to the kids."

Try It

Strategic Reflection

Strategic reflection prepares you to monitor your own thinking and make connections between your experiences, thoughts, and text readings. You've purchased a lot of books during the course of your program. It's now time to dust them off and crack the spines again. This activity helps document a variety of experiences, which are designed to help you make concrete changes. Once you make the connections, you can document how to change or alter your behavior to produce an alternative result (or you may decide to continue to do things the same way). In order to get maximum value out of this activity, be as specific as possible when completing the "I read . . ." column. Start by using this text, and when you have more time, branch out and use your other education texts.

Experience	I thought . . .	I read. . . .	I will . . .
I planned a great lesson, but midway through it some kids kept asking a lot of questions, which took my attention away from Sara. When she didn't get my attention, she ripped up her paper and refused to participate.	What is wrong with these kids? This lesson was awesome. I even had them working in cooperative groups and they didn't get into it. And what is up with Sara? She's going to have to do it for homework.	"Identify why the student is misbehaving: attention, power, revenge. or avoidance of failure. Handle misbehavior immediately. Use encouragement strategies that build self-esteem and motivation to cooperate. Build strong partnerships with students and parents."	Think about planning better for all of the students next time. Maybe because the lesson wasn't differentiated, it made it too easy for some and too hard for others. Sara obviously maxed out on waiting for me to help her and got frustrated. I won't assign it for homework, since if she couldn't do it in class, she probably won't do it at home. I'll figure out a way to help her understand the lesson tomorrow.

9

The Last STEP

Student Teacher Exit Plan

Dear Student Teacher:

Congratulations. You survived student teaching. We know the last few months were very challenging. You had to figure out ways to navigate school politics, plan and present lessons, assess students, cooperate with your CT, collaborate with parents, manage the classroom, and build your confidence. Way to go. Now that you've turned the classroom back over to the cooperating teacher, the students have thrown you a party, and you've completed all of your teacher education or licensure program assignments, you are finally free. Even if you're a lateral entry teacher, you're now free to concentrate completely on teaching rather than meeting certification requirements. Regardless of your category as a student teacher (e.g., traditional student, licensure only, or lateral entry teacher), once you've completed the internship, you are free, free, free, right?

Actually, you're almost home free. The journey to becoming a teacher has really only just begun. Remember, the student teaching internship provides you with the opportunity to demonstrate that you've mastered the knowledge, skills, and dispositions necessary to acquire licensure. In order to actually get hired as a teacher (or keep your job if you are a lateral entry teacher), you must jump over a few more hurdles. Some are higher than others, but you'll have to jump all of them in order to officially join the profession. So, lace up your sneakers and get ready to jump. The information in this last chapter helps you complete these last few hurdles and actually be free—free to do it all over again, but this time you'll get paid for it. ☺

Sincerely,

Your Career Coaches

CHAPTER OBJECTIVES

After reading this chapter, you will be able to

- identify the components of a teaching portfolio;
- develop organizational techniques for the portfolio;
- differentiate audiences for the portfolio;
- analyze and explain the benefits of an electronic portfolio;
- explain the importance of a résumé and create a teacher résumé;
- utilize strategies for studying for the Praxis II examinations;
- outline the process of applying for licensure; and
- prepare for the job interview and hiring process.

THE PROFESSIONAL PORTFOLIO

Before You Go, You Need a Portfolio

If there's one thing you've learned by now, it's that educators believe in documentation. This concept is no more evident than in the universally required teaching **portfolio**, a collection of artifacts that summarize major teaching accomplishments and strengths (Shore, Foster, Knapper, Nadeau, Neill, & Sim, 1986). Practically every student teacher in the United States must complete a portfolio of some kind by the end of the student teaching internship. This requirement is due in part to the Council for the Accreditation of Educator Preparation, or CAEP, which is the professional accrediting organization for schools, colleges, and departments of education in the United States and requires teacher education programs to assess their programs (see www.caepnet.org). Thus, programs use student teaching portfolios not only to document that they are preparing candidates with the knowledge, skills, and dispositions necessary to enter the teaching profession, but also as assessment instruments to help them to revise and strengthen their programs. Consequently, practically every teacher education program requires candidates to compile a portfolio.

The portfolio serves as an assessment tool and documentation for teacher education programs. More important, it serves as documentation for you. Your portfolio allows you to paint a clear picture of who you are as a teacher, your beliefs about teaching and learning, and how you facilitate learning in the classroom. It allows you to demonstrate your understanding of pedagogy, content, and classroom management. Additionally, the portfolio offers you the opportunity to show the full range of your professional self. This includes your involvement in the school community, professional development activities, professional goals, personal reflections, leadership and teamwork skills, technological expertise, and any other unique strengths and talents you bring to the profession.

Thus, your student teaching portfolio is extremely important and serves not only as a mechanism for documenting that you've met program standards but also as tangible evidence of your abilities as a teacher. You need this evidence once you begin the interview process, as most school districts require candidates to show a sample of their work during a job interview (Darling-Hammond, 2006; Lee & Herner-Patnode, 2011; Wetzel, Strudler, Addis, & Luz, 2009). Consequently, the teacher portfolio is a multipurpose device essential to your success.

The Basic Portfolio

In all probability, your teacher education program provides you with a list of requirements for your teaching portfolio. However, at a minimum, all student teaching portfolios should include some basic elements:

✓ *Résumé.* This is the document where you list your education credentials, all relevant teaching experience (including student teaching, volunteering, and observing in the schools), other professional employment positions, and any other relevant skills, awards, and/or community service. A sample résumé is provided in Appendix D.

✓ *Educational Philosophy.* Explain your position regarding education and the kind of teacher you are. You can show your knowledge of educational theories, but your use of theory should be written so that it is clear and simple enough for anyone to understand. Remember, you are not writing for a class or a professor. Put a piece of yourself in your philosophy while grounding it in research and theory. Write it so that it's brief (preferably one page), clear, and memorable. Do this by using specific examples and anecdotes to support your thinking about education. Stay away from clichés, such as "I think all children can learn," "I love children," and "I've always wanted to be a teacher." These sentiments are true for most people who go into the teaching profession. In a nutshell, explain your beliefs about education while infusing them with memorable anecdotes.

✓ *Classroom Management Plan.* Stakeholders reviewing your portfolio want clear and convincing evidence of your ability to manage the classroom. Therefore, define your philosophy and plan for management in very simple terms. Explain your rules, consequences, incentives, and classroom procedures. If possible, show an example of your classroom layout through pictures or a simple diagram and provide a rationale for your setup. It is not enough to say you have a plan. You need to SHOW EVIDENCE of your plan.

✓ *Lesson/Unit Plans.* Be sure to include several examples of excellent lesson plans you use (or will use) as a teacher. Include all assessments and supplemental materials (readings, handouts, tests, project guidelines, etc.) so that your lesson comes to life. Make certain you include a variety of lesson plans that show how you incorporate technology, infuse diversity, differentiate instruction, and engage your students. If you used the plans before, it is also helpful to include samples of student work with your feedback to students.

✓ *Student Teaching Observations.* During the internship, you are observed by your university supervisor and often by your cooperating teacher and/or other teachers and school administrators at the school. Invite your supervisor or principal in to observe you when you are confident you have a superior lesson; include only your absolute best observations in your portfolio.

✓ *Reflections.* Adding reflections allows evaluators to see you as a reflective practitioner dedicated to improving your teaching. The reflections can be about your lessons, the internship, views on certain contemporary issues (diversity, technology, ESL—English as a second language learners, etc.), and/or your strengths and plans for improvement. Your reflections should do more than just describe and summarize; they should evaluate and analyze events and ultimately lead to insights into your teaching.

✓ *Accolades.* Show and explain your successes. Include letters of recommendation and/or appreciation. If you have received any educational awards or you presented at an educational conference, include those items as well as all relevant certifications. Most important, don't forget to include your teaching certificate once you receive it!

Portfolio Organization

As there are so many elements involved in creating the portfolio, a strategy for organization is essential. Although it's most likely you'll receive some guidance from your teacher education program, we offer these suggestions that we find most efficient for student teachers. You can also find additional pointers on creating your portfolio in Figure 9.1.

1. *Purchase your supplies.* You'll need quite a bit of stuff to organize your portfolio. Most portfolios are organized in a basic, two-inch, three-ring binder. You may also need some or all of the following: tabs to organize sections, paper for printing documents, ink for the printer, scissors or a paper cutter, a three-hole punch, plastic sleeves to protect important items, labels, and photo paper for printing pictures.

2. *Find a space to work.* You'll need a place to work on the portfolio where you can lay out items, take a break from the project (you will definitely need one), and be certain that everything remains untouched. Maybe it's the kitchen table, your bedroom floor, or your home office. You just need a spot where you can leave items and no one (not small kids, roommates, or pets) will disturb them. Choose this spot carefully and think about your needs while working. Do you like to watch television while you work? Is music a necessity? Do you need absolute silence? Take all of your personal preferences into consideration while remembering to choose the best possible spot that has a space that can remain undisturbed.

3. *Find your stuff.* Creating the portfolio can be a daunting task. Consequently, student teachers have a tendency to panic about locating and compiling the necessary documents. We want to reassure you that you do have the necessary items essential for your portfolio; you just need to find all of them. Presumably, you have access to your lesson plans, assessments, and all supplemental materials from student teaching. If you don't have copies of your observations, request copies from your supervisor and CT. If there is any item you can't locate that is critical for your portfolio, create or re-create it. Just do your best to locate existing materials so that you don't start from scratch for every item. If you have not written your educational philosophy, it's perfectly fine to cut and paste ideas from preexisting documents you wrote and then add and revise to create the appropriate document for your portfolio. Be sure to photocopy all of the documents you incorporate into the portfolio. Whatever you do, keep the originals (just in case something goes wrong).

This approach also applies to pictures. Get them out of your cell phone or computer! You probably already have several pictures of yourself teaching and interacting with students. If, however, you failed to take photographs (because you were too busy concentrating on teaching), it's quite easy to go back and re-create them. Have a classmate meet you after the school day and pretend you're teaching at the board or creating a bulletin board. Or, you can ask your CT to take pictures of you while you're teaching. You can also take pictures of projects you assigned or initiated. If you created the school's recycling club or spearheaded a book drive, take pictures of that activity. Before you add any pictures to your portfolio, be certain that you follow the policy of both your school and the teacher education program on photographing students. Make certain you have permission to use the photos for educational purposes.

4. *Organize your stuff.* You'll need a way to organize all of your documents. Our suggestion is to use a large accordion file and categorize your items. However, you may prefer piles on a table, a separate file cabinet, or some other method. What's important is that you organize your items so that you have a clear picture of what elements you have and how you will arrange them. Use whatever method works best for you; just be sure to be very organized before you begin. This is a key step that saves you a great deal of time in the end.

5. *Find your time.* If you think you can compile your portfolio in one night or over the weekend, know that you absolutely can. However, we wouldn't be very good Career Coaches if we didn't make it clear that anyone reviewing your portfolio will absolutely be able to tell that you compiled it within 48 hours. In other words, the amount of time you choose to spend on your portfolio is very apparent when evaluating your portfolio.

Remember, everyone looking at your portfolio has probably seen quite a few (as Career Coaches, we've seen over a thousand). It is very easy to spot a portfolio put together at the last minute.

Also, the portfolio is a representation of who you are as a teacher. The portfolio is a picture of you in your absence. It exemplifies all that you are as a teacher—your instructional style, your management style, and your overall approach to teaching. Don't you want this portrayal of you to look good even when you're not there in person? We know you do. That's why it's critical for you to schedule time to create your portfolio. As your Career Coaches, we want to warn you in advance that it's going to take much more time than you originally think, and often something goes wrong. Your computer crashes, your files become corrupted, the printer dies, coffee spills on your observation reports, your child gets the flu—you name it, and we've seen it happen to student teachers. So, allow not only enough time to skillfully create the portfolio, but also allow time to deal with any problems that inevitably arise.

6. *Find your reviewers.* You know to include only your best work in your portfolio; however, you are not always an objective judge of your own best work. So, before you submit your portfolio to any official audience (e.g., principal, university supervisor, or human resource representative), have objective reviewers look at your portfolio. The unit you taught on the duckbill platypus that culminated with your students making marshmallow sculptures might indeed be an engaging collection of lessons, activities, and assessments. Nonetheless, is it the best choice for your portfolio? Does it showcase your technology skills? Does it show how you incorporate reading across the curriculum?

Does it show how you help your students develop critical thinking skills? Does it show how you differentiate lessons? If you don't get some honest feedback on the documents you plan to include in your portfolio, you will do yourself a disservice. Therefore, ask your CT to review your lesson plans, the principal to review your résumé, and a friend to read your educational philosophy. Don't overwhelm any one person by asking him or her to review all of your items. Enlist several respected colleagues to review your portfolio, not just your friend, spouse, or classmate.

Who Looks at the Portfolio?

You may be considering directing your portfolio to different types of audiences, and if that is the case, it is extremely important that you tailor it for each specific audience. For example, as part of your student teaching requirements, your university supervisor and your cooperating teacher might formally or informally assess your portfolio to verify that you mastered program

Figure 9.1 Particularly Pertinent Portfolio Pointers

✓ *Make it simple.* Don't go overboard. Your portfolio is not a memory book or a photo album. It is a professional representation of your teaching.

✓ *Make it relevant.* Don't include class assignments or irrelevant documents in your portfolio just because you have them. Your goal is not to include EVERYTHING. You don't have to add it just because you have it.

✓ *Make it manageable.* Organize your portfolio so that it is reader friendly. Use a three-ring binder with tabs and plastic sleeves. Include a table of contents with page numbers so readers can access sections easily. Remember, quality is better than quantity.

✓ *Make it clear.* Every item you include in the portfolio should be well written and free of grammatical and mechanical errors. Include captions with pictures and documents; don't expect the reader to guess why you included an item.

✓ *Make it engaging.* The portfolio represents you, so it should leave a positive lasting impression. Make a cover that invites the reader to review it and add pictures to help show your teaching.

competencies. Although your CT and supervisor have seen you teach and have firsthand knowledge of your style and abilities, they still want concrete examples of your abilities to assess whether you can clearly articulate your ideas about teaching and education. Accordingly, you want to be sure to include the specific kinds of documents they specifically want.

Also, be certain not to include any documents that display you or your CT in a bad light. For example, never include documents that don't show you at your absolute best. Do not include any substandard lesson plans, below standard observations, or items with spelling, grammar, and/or mechanical errors. Also, don't include personal reflections that express your frustration with your CT, the students, the profession in general, or how you'll do EVERYTHING differently once you have your own classroom. Although this might be true (and it's probably not entirely true), do you really want your CT to read negative assessments of his or her teaching before writing your reference letter and/or recommending you to those principals you hope will be calling soon?

Often, administrators and teachers also review your portfolio during the interview process. This review can occur at any point in the interview process. Some systems review portfolios before the interview as a way to limit the pool of potential interview candidates. Others review portfolios during interviews and ask you questions based on your artifacts. Still other interviews might involve a review of the portfolio after the interview as a basis to confirm the decision to hold an additional interview or even to hire you. There is no way to determine how your portfolio is used during the process, so it's better to simply prepare the best portfolio possible so you are ready for any and all potential scenarios.

The portfolio you submit should be edited and revised to demonstrate that you meet the demands of a specific program or position. For example, you might have completed your student teaching internship in a kindergarten classroom; however, you've received a call to interview for a fifth-grade teaching position. It is important that you tailor your portfolio for that particular grade level and school. Revise a few of your kindergarten lesson plans to fit the curriculum standards for a fifth-grade class. Moreover, if you know the school is focused on technology, include plans that demonstrate your expertise with integrating technology into the curriculum. Do you get the idea? You want to make certain your portfolio demonstrates that you can teach to the needs and mission of the school where you are interviewing. If the focus is technology, show the people there you're a computer whiz. If the focus is basic skills, show them how you make the basics engaging. Whatever the focus is for the school, make sure your portfolio shows you can master it (e.g., teach second-language learners, use cooperative learning, incorporate character education, focus on global learning). Your portfolio should validate that you are exactly the candidate for them. You don't want any potential employer to wonder if you're a perfect match to their prerequisites; you want it to be obvious from review of your portfolio.

Electronic Portfolios

When we joined the teaching profession (back in the Stone Age), all of the documents for a student teacher's portfolio were expected to be neatly typed, placed in page protectors, and compiled in a three-ring binder. Usually, this was the only copy, and the student teacher carried it along to every interview and job fair. Times have changed drastically. Luckily, you don't have to carry around a huge notebook as your portfolio. In fact, many schools are switching to electronic portfolios (Strudler & Wetzel, 2008). An electronic portfolio allows your audience to view the sections they deem most appropriate, but it also allows you a great deal of options when it comes to compiling representations of your teaching. Figure 9.2 provides a description of the benefits of an electronic portfolio and suggested items for inclusion.

Figure 9.2   Benefits of Electronic Portfolios

Video Clips	Adding video clips of your actual teaching to your portfolio gives you an edge over other candidates. You are able to talk about your teaching, and also actually show your reviewers how you teach.
Pictures	Including pictures transforms your portfolio. Take pictures of student work, bulletin boards you've created, attendance at professional development workshops, service projects, and pictures of you teaching.
Testimonials	It may be appropriate to include interviews from your CT, university supervisor, and other teachers, as well as students and their parents, regarding your performance and successes as a teacher.
Hyperlinks	Hyperlinks within your electronic compact disc (CD) allow you to create links to detailed documents (e.g., lesson plans, unit plans) that a reviewer might want to access, but that adds bulk to a traditional paper portfolio. Hyperlinks also allow you to create links to websites and other resources on the Internet that you use as a teacher.
Portability	The best aspect of electronic portfolios is that they are lighter and easier to duplicate than traditional paper portfolios. You can make multiple copies within minutes and then leave them with potential employers. Also, consider buying an inexpensive software program that allows you to create CD covers, and use the CD to market yourself. Hand your CD portfolio out at job fairs, send them with cover letters to schools, and include them with a thank-you note after an interview.

Whether you choose to create an electronic or hard-copy portfolio, do not believe the rumors buzzing around in educational circles: Principals and hiring personnel don't take the time to look at your portfolio. As is true of most rumors, there is an element of truth in this statement. In all honesty, there are *some* school personnel who choose not to look at your portfolio—hard copy or electronic. However, there are still so many who review your portfolio during the interview because it serves as concrete evidence of your knowledge and skills. Isn't it better to have one, regardless? Remember, you want to do all you can to differentiate yourself from all the other teachers who've just finished their programs as well. Don't show up empty-handed. This is just like a lesson plan; don't be caught without one.

Résumés Rule

Although the decision to create a traditional three-ring binder portfolio or electronic portfolio is up to you (or perhaps your teacher education program), you absolutely must have a hard copy of your résumé. Résumés still rule. Having a portfolio simply is not a substitute for having a stellar résumé. However, don't make the mistake most student teachers make when creating their résumés—the résumé reads like a student teacher's (or worse, a student's) résumé rather than the résumé of an actual teacher. Keep in mind that you completed your student teaching internship successfully, which means that you have what it takes to enter the teaching profession. Your résumé should reflect this huge accomplishment and present a teacher ready to take on the challenges and responsibilities of being an independent educational leader in the classroom. Therefore, you need to make certain your résumé distinguishes you as a teacher (not student teacher) by clearly listing all of your accomplishments and experience in the teaching profession.

If you are a second-career student (also known as licensure-only or certification-only students) and had a very full career in a profession not related to teaching, be certain to incorporate in your résumé all of your professional skills and/or accomplishments that are applicable to teaching. For example, if you worked as a sales director, list relevant expertise, such as training new employees, operating your company's very complicated and sophisticated software programs, working well with colleagues, and transferable multitasking skills. It is essential that your résumé convince readers that you can transfer your previous job skills to the classroom.

Regardless of your work experience in education, whether it's just student teaching or serving as an instructional assistant for seven years, your résumé must show that you have the requisite skills necessary to be successful in the classroom. So, make certain you look at a few sample résumés of teachers and have a teacher friend or administrator give you feedback on your draft. You can never have too many eyes review this very important document. Examine these additional tips on creating your résumé and note that a sample résumé is provided in Appendix D.

BASIC RÉSUMÉ TIPS

✓ *Choose a well-known format.* Use one of the two most widely known types: chronological (categorized by sequence of events) or functional (categorized by type).

✓ *Include the basics.* These include name and contact information, objective, summary of qualifications, education, experience and skills, awards, and professional affiliations.

✓ *Use education terminology.* Using terms like *professional learning communities* (PLCs) shows that you participate in the greater educational discourse.

✓ *Describe all of your accomplishments related to teaching.* Don't list homecoming queen, but do list president of the service learning committee.

✓ *Make sure your résumé is concise.* Avoid using long narratives. Instead use bulleted lists or short summaries to convey information.

✓ *Check for errors.* Correct all grammar, pelling (oops, we meant *spelling*), and typing errors.

WHAT IS PRAXIS II, AND WHY DO I HAVE TO TAKE IT?

In addition to compiling a portfolio of your accomplishments and creating a résumé, taking and passing Praxis II is often required to obtain your teacher certification. The Praxis Series assessments provide educational tests and other services that the states use as part of their teacher licensure and certification process. The **Praxis II** tests measure general and subject-specific knowledge and teaching skills (see the Praxis website at www.ets.org/praxis). In short, the test is another hurdle for you to jump over to prove you know how to teach and know the content you'll be teaching. We're sure you're thinking, "Isn't completing student teaching enough to show that I'm qualified to be a teacher?" Remember, student teachers, once you complete this process, you'll be working in your own classroom without a cooperating teacher. Think of it this way. The bank doesn't just check to see if you have a job before it gives you a loan; it also runs your credit report and makes you show past and current pay stubs (at a minimum). It doesn't want to take any chance you might not be qualified for the loan. The education profession is exactly the same. You must take and pass the courses, successfully complete the student teaching internship, and take the Praxis II assessment tests. It's just another way to check that you are really qualified to become a teacher.

Depending on your content area and grade levels of certification, your state may not require the Praxis II examination for certification. So, be sure to investigate your state's requirements for certification. Your teacher education program can provide you with information regarding all of your requirements for certification, including whether you need to take and pass Praxis II.

Do I Have to Study for Praxis II?

There are competing viewpoints as to whether one should study for Praxis II exams. Many of our colleagues believe you can't successfully complete student teaching without having the knowledge necessary to pass Praxis II. However, as your career coaches, we understand that testing of any sort can cause anxiety and a great deal of stress for many students—even extraordinarily smart students. **Test anxiety**, excessive worry that negatively affects your performance on assessments, is a very real phenomenon that strikes many student teachers struggling to handle the challenges inherent in the internship (for more information about test anxiety and how to deal with it, see www.testtakingtips.com 2013).

Whether you decide to study or not, it is important that you be clear about what the test entails. At this point in your program, you want to use everything at your disposal to finish successfully. So, whether you study for 2 months or 2 days, be certain to check out what the test covers. It's appropriate to be confident and prepared so take this quick and easy step—visit the Praxis website (www.ets.org/praxis) and examine the sample questions and tips posted there for all to review.

What if I Fail Praxis II?

Unfortunately, some student teachers require more than one attempt to obtain the necessary score to pass Praxis II. If you are one of them, you are definitely not alone. Nonetheless, we know it can be disappointing when you are so close to meeting all requirements for certification, but stumble two steps from the finish line. Simply put, when you don't pass, it can be heartbreaking. Still, it's important to remember you have met all other requirements and not passing Praxis II is only a minor setback. With a few simple steps, you can get back on track. Just refer to Figure 9.3 and implement our field-tested strategies for eventual success.

Figure 9.3   Back on Track

1. *Don't panic.* Remain calm. As a teacher, you know that tests are not the only indicator of mastery. Remember, the score is just a number, not the totality of you as a teacher.

2. *Study this time, or study harder.* Revisit the Praxis website (www.ets.org/praxis). Spend some extended time examining the resources offered on the site.

3. *Talk to other students who passed.* Quiz them on their strategies for success with the test. Implement those you think will work for you.

4. *Study some more.* You've taken the test at least once, so you know what to expect. Were there questions you were a bit fuzzy on? Go back and look at some of your textbooks. Review, review, and review again. Purchase a Praxis II study guide in your content area and study consistently every day.

5. *Implement some of the confidence strategies from Chapter 5.* Failing the test can put a strain on your confidence. Remind yourself of your awesome abilities in spite of this minor postponement.

6. *Visualize yourself acing the test and receiving passing scores.* You know it will happen sooner or later. Just see it happening now (rather than later).

7. *Figure out the best method for you (paper and pencil versus computer-based).* If you hate typing, arrange to take the traditional version (with your favorite No. 2 pencil, of course).

8. *Start looking for a teaching job.* Request a letter from your teacher education program explaining that you've met all requirements except Praxis II. The reality of getting your own classroom is a great motivator.

9. *Enroll in a test preparation course.* There are educational agencies that offer courses or workshops on test-taking skills. If the issue is weak test-taking skills rather than a lack of content knowledge, a test preparation course is beneficial.

10. *Repeat the "back on track" process as many times as necessary.* You will ultimately pass Praxis II. Your success during student teaching is evidence you have what it takes to join the profession, so persevere. You might want to add a few additional strategies (like buying a big box of chocolates) to make this process a bit more palatable. Do what you have to do to get through.

HOW DO I GET MY LICENSE?

After you've finished the internship, created an exceptional portfolio, revised your résumé, and passed Praxis II, what's left? The next step involves additional paperwork required by your state. Because you've been teaching, you are not afraid of paperwork. Whether the paperwork entails lesson plans, notes home, report cards, permission slips, or running records—you know there are mounds and mounds of paperwork that must be completed during the school day. Surprisingly, these experiences come in handy as this last step requires you to complete a great deal of paperwork to complete your teacher education program.

Complete Required Paperwork

First, you need to look into the remaining paperwork necessary for you to graduate or exit your program. For traditional students, this could mean completing your graduation application, submitting your community service logs, completing exit surveys, or submitting your senior portfolio for review. The requirements vary by teacher education program; however, trust us, paperwork is always involved.

Once you have completed all necessary university paperwork, you'll need to file for your teaching license. Although some universities complete this process for you, the steps are fairly universal. You need to complete your state's licensure application packet. This usually includes an application, all official transcripts from every college and/or university ever attended, a license fee or copy of provisional license, and a form documenting successful completion of student teaching; official documentation of Praxis II scores may also be required.

Once your application is complete, either you or a representative from your teacher education program submits the application to your state's department of education. There, it joins a huge stack of other applications for processing. Usually, in less than 6 weeks, your teacher's license is mailed to the address you indicated on your application. Once you get it, show everyone you know. It's a symbol of all of your hard work and expertise. Feel free to celebrate as well because once you receive that certification (and you've verified your name is spelled correctly and they've listed your correct grade levels and content areas), you are officially done. See Figure 9.4 for a review of the process.

Figure 9.4   The Teaching License

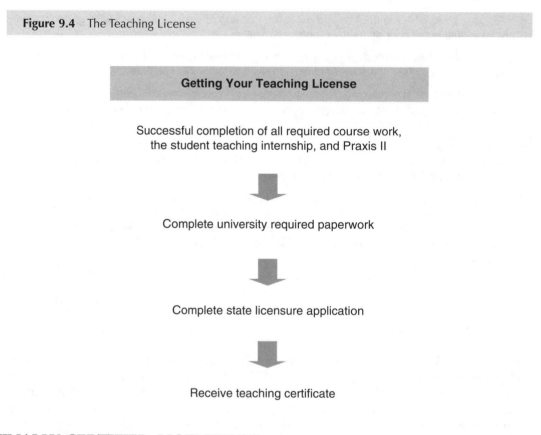

YOU'RE FINALLY CERTIFIED: NOW WHAT?

You can take a really deep breath now. All of your hard work has finally paid off. You've completed all requirements, and your teacher's certificate is on its way. So, other than taking a break, cleaning your apartment, catching up on all of those movies you missed, and reacquainting yourself with your friends, family, and pets, what should you do now?

Ask for reference letters now. Make your requests while your performance is still current and clear in the memories of your cooperating teacher, university supervisor, and others who may have observed your teaching. Although many school systems' applications contain a reference form (often an online form with a checklist and small area for comments), including a detailed reference letter (in addition to the required form) adds depth to your application. In order to not make constant requests for letters, ask for several signed copies at once. This strategy allows you to have letters for several applications without overburdening your reference.

Begin researching school systems and individual schools now. In Chapter 1, we discussed how all schools have a distinct culture. Your goal is to obtain a teaching position in a school that is a good fit for you. Access public records and school webpages; tour schools and communities; and talk to parents, students, and teachers. If possible, volunteer or work as a substitute teacher in schools you are strongly considering. Spending prolonged and consistent time in a school will give you a clear picture of whether the school is the right match for you.

Start applying for jobs now. As soon as you can, begin applying for teaching positions. Many states and school systems allow you to apply online; however, others require a hard copy obtained from a human resources representative. Attend employment fairs and visit career centers. The hiring process—from application, to interview, to employment offer—can take a very long time. Additionally, there are many other eager candidates searching for employment, so you'll want to begin the application process as soon as possible.

Join professional organizations and attend conferences now. Professional organizations offer new teachers a wealth of information and resources. For example, many publish journals or newsletters with current research and strategies in your field. They also offer information about conferences and professional development opportunities. Some professional organizations even offer job listings or assistance in obtaining employment. Potential employers can view membership in a professional organization as evidence of your commitment to teaching and continual development. So, join an organization, take advantage of the resources, and be sure to post your membership on your résumé.

Begin the balancing act now. You have firsthand experience with the demands of teaching. As you transition into a permanent position, consider how it will impact your personal life. Do you need to find care for your children? If you're commuting, do you need your car serviced? How will you budget your salary? Will you need to find a place to live? Now is the time to work on issues in your personal life important to your success as a teacher.

Getting to and Through the Interview

You've completed student teaching, created a professional résumé, passed Praxis II, and received your teaching license. You've also researched schools, acquired reference letters, applied for jobs, and have copies of your superior portfolio. You've been watching the news about how badly good teachers are needed in school classrooms, so why isn't your phone ringing or email buzzing nonstop with job offers? As your Career Coaches, we have to tell you that even with the intense demand for qualified teachers, most jobs won't just come to you. There are occasions where student teachers are offered positions at their internship sites, but for the majority of teachers, a principal won't call saying, "I know you've finished student teaching, and I have the perfect job waiting for you." You have to go after the job you want by snagging an interview and subsequent offer.

How to Get the Interview

Expand your search. We know you've already applied to your favorite school or district. Just remember that popular schools and districts receive a massive number of applications. So, why not broaden your chances for an interview by expanding your job search and applying to other school districts? Attend education job fairs that include several districts in one venue. The benefit of visiting education job fairs is that the personnel in attendance are there for one reason—to hire good teachers. Don't stop the search just at education job fairs. Investigate private, charter, and religious schools for teaching positions. Nonpublic schools advertise positions in the newspaper and on their websites. Finally, professional education organizations, university career centers, and state departments of education list information about teacher positions.

Network. You know you're a great teacher, so make sure everyone else knows as well! Networking means that all the people who can help you obtain an interview are aware of your interests, your qualifications, and your contact information. So, remain in contact with your university supervisor and other faculty members. They often receive targeted calls from school personnel, and you want your name to be the first name they state. Also, contact the administrators and teachers at your student teaching site. Make certain they all know you are looking for a position. Give them a copy of your résumé so they have your information accessible if a position becomes available at their school or another.

Make personal contact. You may need to do more to get the interview than just apply online. Remember, most schools and districts get many applications. As your Career Coaches, we suggest making a connection with those in position to hire you. Send cover letters to selected school principals indicating that you've applied. Call to see if you can meet with a principal or district human resource officer to get more information about the school or district. Use the meeting to acquire information about the school or district, but also use it to state your qualifications and express your enthusiasm in joining their team. Their job is to find qualified teachers who are assertive and passionate about teaching. Use the meeting to make certain they know you want an interview. Finally, use snail mail. That's right. Actually, type, print, place in an envelope with the requisite postage and mail your résumé and cover letter. Principals and HR personnel get so many email inquiries that they all begin to look the same. You want them to remember your name and qualifications. The rare hard copy from a qualified applicant gushing about joining their team just might make you more memorable.

Revise your materials. We know you've worked hard on your résumé and application because you followed the tips earlier in this chapter. Still, the one tip we've seen teachers not pay enough attention to is the very one that can determine whether you get an interview: check for errors. Unfortunately, it is often hard to see your own mistakes. It can be a bit like gaining weight, hard to see until someone gently (very gently) points it out to you. Hiring personnel weed out applicants based on poorly written cover letters and résumés. This means it doesn't matter how qualified you are as a teacher. Your accomplishments, skills, and passion for teaching will go unnoticed if your application, résumé, or cover letter has errors. So, we're reminding you to actually read and follow the directions for all applications. Have someone else review your materials. You need every item that represents you as a teacher to be clear, comprehensive, and, most important, correct.

Interview Basics

Say yes. We know you know some basics about professionalism because you've completed the student teaching internship. Still, as your Career Coaches, we must point out some important tips regarding interviewing. One critical piece of information is to give a professional and enthusiastic "yes" once you receive a call for an interview. Trust us; someone will call. Be excited. Say yes. Above all, accept EVERY invitation to interview. Yes, you read that correctly: Say yes to an interview even if it's for a school where you don't want to teach. You gain valuable experience every time you interview, and you just might change your mind

Figure 9.5   Get the Interview

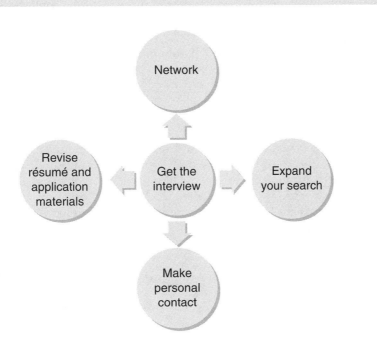

about that school that wasn't on your list. Plus, principals talk to each other. You may not be a good fit for one school, but a principal might send your information on to a colleague.

Dress to impress. Choose your attire carefully. You want to look professional and confident from head to toe. Even if the dress code at the school where you are interviewing is casual, you do NOT have the job yet. It's casual for employees, not interviewees! You are always safe with conservative attire: dark suit, white shirt, and black closed-toe shoes. However, you should also show your uniqueness. Add a great scarf or tie. It's okay to show some of your personality in a professional way. As your Career Coaches, we want to warn you about distractions: oversized earrings or bracelets, piercings, flashy ties, nail art, patterned tights, or extremely high heels. You are allowed to show your personal style, but you don't want your style to overshadow your answers. You attire and accessories should not be distractions. You want the panel to listen to you, not use the time admiring the zebra pattern on your nails or the fluorescent pattern on your tie. We suggest that you take a few pictures and show your outfits to current teachers. They'll tell you the truth about whether your choice is appropriate.

Time it right. It's important to arrive not on time, or in time, but EARLY. Find out the location of the school in advance. Drive the route prior to the time you'll complete the drive for your interview. Do not rely on Internet directions or your GPS to get you there without a test run (as there may be construction or traffic—or your navigation system may choose to take you on the scenic route through another state). Remember, you have to park, walk to the office, sign in at the front desk, and get a visitor's tag. Arriving early gives you a minute to freshen up in the restroom or to chat with the receptionist and build rapport immediately. Often the receptionist is part of the unofficial interview team, so be nice and friendly. Compliment the school or the directions that you were given.

Set the tone. As soon as you enter the building, set the tone. Start by smiling and reminding yourself that you are one step closer to getting your own classroom. Introduce yourself to everyone you contact. Tell them you are at the school for the interview and how excited you are at the possibility of joining the team. There are times that the people you meet before the interview will offer you a bit of inside information. You may learn that the principal loves teachers who implement service learning pedagogy, or who are strict disciplinarians. Whether you garner insider information or goodwill, offering a pleasant greeting to all you meet can only benefit you in the end. When you enter the interview space, do not sit down immediately. Walk to each panel member and shake his or her hand. Give each person a firm handshake, smile, make eye contact, get their names, and exude (or fake it if you must) confidence and positive energy.

Be prepared. Carry your portfolio and extra copies of your résumé. Interviewers may have copies already, but you want to be perceived as organized and prepared. Also, there are some basic questions asked in most interviews: "Tell me a little about yourself," "Why did you want to become a teacher," "How was student teaching," "Why do you want to work at our school?" Be prepared to answer these basic initial questions. Practice answering them with a teacher or good friend. The goal is to give the interview team a sense of who you are and why you might be a good fit for their school.

Audience is everything. Remember your audience. Those selected to participate on the interview team are often key stakeholders at the school. In other words, they have clout. Your job is to impress them so that you are selected for the job or the next round of interviews. They are looking for a teacher who is a good fit for the school, so do advance research about the school, its students and its community. Address ALL of them when you ask or answer a question. Whether you're in a room with one, two, or ten panelists, talk to all of them. Often there is one person who asks the majority of the questions. Don't make the mistake of directing your answer solely to the person who asked the question. Look around the room and engage everyone. Watch their body language to see if you are on track or if you need to redirect your answers. Also, remember that the panel might have been there all day and this is extra work for them. Although this may be your only interview of the day, it may be their tenth. Thank them for their time, dedication, and hard work. Assure them that you will work just as hard as they do, if you are offered a position.

Follow directions. As Career Coaches, we've interviewed countless hopeful student teachers. One common issue that arises during the interviews is whether a candidate can follow directions well. This seems like a minor detail, but often it can positively or negatively impact the interview. For example, if you are asked to give an example of a challenging experience during your student teaching, do just that. Most hiring teams are not trying to give you a trick question. They know that teaching is challenging. They are looking to see if you can genuinely manage the inherent challenges that are a part of the profession. Likewise, if you are given a scenario and asked to brainstorm a possible solution, do just that. Don't change or dismiss the scenario in an effort to avoid the question. Finally, and this is the most critical issue during the interview process, actually answer the question asked. One surefire way to lose the attention of your interview panel is to provide information that has nothing whatsoever to do with the question asked. Usually, panels have a list of questions that they ask all candidates. They need answers to those specific questions. If you don't understand the question, ask them if they can rephrase it. If you need more information to answer the question (e.g., about integrating technology into the classroom), ask clarifying questions. However, do your absolute best to answer the question asked.

Advertise yourself. Share your successes and skills. It is critical to answer the panelists' questions, but sometimes those questions do not allow you to share your biggest teaching successes. If that becomes the case, you need to work your accomplishments into the discussion. Discuss your achievements, particularly those that set you apart from other teachers interviewing for the position. Be sure to incorporate educational terminology, but know what terms mean and use them appropriately in the discussion. Discuss conferences you've attended, articles you've read, and workshops in which you participated. Do not leave an interview without making sure the hiring team knows exactly what you have to offer.

Finish strong. You arrived early, set the tone, answered all questions, and shared your accomplishments, now what? Well, the interview isn't over until you have the job! First, say thank you. Thank the panel for their time and the opportunity to interview. Send an email or handwritten note to ALL on the panel shortly after the interview. In this short note, extend your gratitude again and share any additional information relevant post interview.

Absolute no no's. Now that you know what to do, we do need to take a brief moment to address what NOT to do. Even if you've been on an interview every day for a year, we encourage you to read this section. Although we're sure you wouldn't commit any of these offenses, reading this section might give you the ammunition you need to help a teacher friend or two.

1. *Don't take your phone out.* Of course it's turned off (you do have it turned off or on vibrate, right?), but for many, it's a habit to check it to look at the time or an incoming text. Sure, you wouldn't mean to do it, but it does happen by accident. You want the panel to see you as focused and not distracted. Our suggestion is to leave it in the car where there is absolutely no chance that it will ring, buzz, or vibrate.

2. *Don't chew gum.* Yes, you'll be meeting quite a few people, and yes you want fresh breath. Still, you want the panel focused on you, not the color of your gum.

3. *Don't become too familiar with the panel.* It's great to be friendly, but don't forget you're in an interview.

4. *Don't request a specific grade level or ability group.* The panel knows your credentials, so they wouldn't have called unless there was an appropriate opening for you. Discuss these issues once you receive an offer.

5. *Don't discuss salary or benefits.* Trust that a fair offer will be made once they decide to hire you. Cross that bridge when you come to it.

SPECIAL FEATURE SECTION

Résumé Tips for Special Circumstances

What if...

"I've never worked in education?"

- Reflect on your work history and community experiences.
- Identify transferable skills and experiences desirable in the teaching profession.
- Write an objective that links your teaching goals to your past work history. For example, "Award winning staffing manager seeking to use training, technology, and multitasking skills in the teaching profession."

(Continued)

(Continued)

"I don't have a lot of teaching experience?"

- Fully highlight your accomplishments from your teacher education program—this includes all your volunteer and service learning activities, as well as the conferences and professional development sessions you attended.
- Describe in detail your student teaching internship. Indicate the school and duration of the internship. Also list all of your teaching assignments along with the number of students, grade levels, and content areas. Consider highlighting innovative lessons, extracurricular activities, and committee involvement.
- Express any interest you might have in supervising extracurricular activities. Your coaching skills or desire to start a recycling club helps add to your dimensions as a candidate.

"I've been out of the workforce for many years?"

- Demonstrate that you are proficient with current technology and that you have the skills to fully integrate technology into your teaching.
- Highlight your professional development activities. Describe in detail all relevant associated certificates, courses, conferences, and/or organizations.
- Carefully edit your résumé. Delete older, less relevant information. Emphasize your most recent accomplishments.

"I've been working as an instructional assistant?"

- Demonstrate mastery over your content area. Show that you are fully prepared to independently implement engaging lessons.
- Spotlight your leadership abilities. Show that you have the requisite skills to lead others to accomplishing a goal.
- Explain how your instructional assistant skills translate to success as a classroom leader.
- Use teachers and administrators as references. Their endorsement gives you additional credibility.

FINAL THOUGHTS

We know you're excited about completing the student teaching internship. However, don't forget that you still have some important tasks ahead of you. Complete your teacher portfolio and résumé to show your successes and skills. If you're required to take Praxis II, review what's on the test and prepare for it. Finally, complete the mountain of paperwork required for program completion. Once you've successfully accomplished all of these tasks, get to and through the job interview because you're ready for the joys and challenges of teaching.

BULLETIN BOARD

The Last STEP: Student Teacher Exit Plan

Create a portfolio of your best work.

Compile and organize documents and photographs showcasing your teaching talents. Remember, quality is better than quantity.

Create a teacher résumé, not a student teacher résumé.

Be sure to list and describe all of your teaching experience, including student teaching and past jobs where you used skills necessary for the profession. Edit and proofread your résumé carefully. Although school personnel may or may not examine your portfolio, your résumé will definitely be reviewed.

Complete all required paperwork.

The university, teacher education program, and/or state department of education have required forms for you to complete. Be sure to double-check the specific requirements for your certification and complete all paperwork accurately and in a timely fashion.

Use technology to create an electronic portfolio.

Video clips of your teaching, photographs, and audio clips can make your portfolio more engaging. An electronic portfolio also offers the ability to easily make multiple copies for networking and job hunting.

Praxis II may be a requirement for certification.

Check with your teacher education program to determine whether you need to pass Praxis II. Prepare for the exam by visiting the website (www.ets.org/praxis) and reviewing content area concepts with a study guide. If you don't pass, don't give up. Use strategies, such as a test preparation workshop, visualization, and additional content study to pass the exam the next time you take it.

Proceed quickly once you finish.

Ask for several copies of reference letters from your cooperating teacher and supervisor. Begin researching schools and applying for jobs. Join professional organizations and take advantage of professional development opportunities. Manage personal responsibilities that will impact your teaching position.

Get to and through the interview.

Network and extend your search for interviews. Accept every invitation to interview. Set a positive tone, be prepared, and follow directions during the interview. Remember to finish strong by sending thank you emails or notes. Avoid common interview blunders like distracting clothing/accessories, checking your cell phone, and making demands.

EXTRA CREDIT

Read About It

Transitioning

A+ Résumés for Teachers

http://resumes-for-teachers.com

Electronic Portfolios: Students, Teachers, and Life Long Learners

http://eduscapes.com/tap/topic82.htm

The Praxis Series

http://www.ets.org/praxis

Teacher Résumé

https://careercenter.depaul.edu/_documents/Resume%20Guide%20for%20Teachers%20final%20revised.pdf

More on Transitioning

Campbell, D. B., Cignetti, P. B., Melenyzer, B. J., & Nettles, D. H. (2010). *How to develop a professional portfolio: A manual for teachers.* Boston, MA: Pearson.

Educational Testing Service. (2010). *The Praxis Series official guide (2nd edition).* New York: McGraw-Hill.

Fredericks, A. D. (2012). Ace your teacher interview: 149 fantastic answers to tough interview questions. St. Paul, MN: Jist Works.

Grey, S., & Davis, A. P. (2011). *Praxis II elementary education: Curriculum, instruction & assessment.* Piscataway, NJ: Research & Education Association.

Think About It

What Do I Have to Offer?

Complete the following activity to help you to identify key information necessary to build an effective teacher résumé.

1. Describe all of your teaching experiences. Include those experiences from nontraditional settings, such as camps, tutoring, and mentoring.

2. Describe all of your professional development activities.

3. Describe your accomplishments during student teaching.

4. Describe the skills and qualifications you bring to teaching.

5. What sets you apart from all the other teachers certified in your content and grade level? What makes you unique? Ask your classmates about your strengths.

Try It

Next Steps: What to Do Now

Directions: Now that you've completed student teaching, you still have work to do. To begin the process, choose at least five activities from the next steps activities below. Then, discuss your progress and challenges with your classmates.

- Network now. Contact everyone you know in education. Let them know you've successfully completed student teaching, and you're ready for your own classroom.
- Examine your personal life. Do you have everything in order so that you can be successful once you get your teaching job? Now is the time to finish those unfinished projects. Make a list of three personal projects that, left undone, might interfere with your teaching success. Now, create a list of steps to complete one of the projects within one week. Your ultimate goal is to complete as much as you can before you get your own classroom.
- Xerox multiple copies of your awesome résumé and your best unit plan. You'll need them for all of your upcoming interviews.
- Tweak your résumé. Take a copy of your résumé and compare it to "real" teachers' résumés. Analyze how they are different and revise yours appropriately. Then, show your résumé to as many educators as possible. Listen to their feedback and implement it.
- Stay abreast of educational issues and trends. It's important you're aware of state and national trends that affect the profession. You'll be asked about them at interviews, and they will absolutely impact your teaching.
- Treat yourself to a few items that make you feel like a teacher, not a student teacher, whether it's buying a new teacher wardrobe or laptop, organizing a file cabinet with ideas about activities, or something else. Believe in yourself and your abilities, and do something that is a tangible manifestation of that belief.
- Examine potential schools. All schools have their own unique culture. Before accepting a teaching position, make certain that you examine the school to see if it's a good fit for you. You'll be spending a lot of time there, so make the best choice for you.
- Participate in professional development. Although you are no longer required to take classes at the university, don't stop learning. Talk to teachers to discover what professional organizations they joined and the benefits of membership. Research organizations in your field, and attend a local meeting or workshop. Take advantage of workshops, online trainings, and conferences. Go, participate, and learn.
- Spend time doing the things you love. You now know firsthand how demanding teaching can be. It's important for you to have some balance in your life. Make some time each day to have a little fun.

Glossary

Assessment: Formal and informal collection, review, and use of information regarding student learning; used to determine what students know, have learned, and should learn next

Blog: An online journal where individuals post regular entries about personal experiences and opinions; readers are often allowed to comment on the entries

Brain-friendly learning (also referred to as *brain-compatible teaching and learning*): Instructional methods grounded in research and understanding of how the brain functions, in an effort to increase student engagement and retention

Change: To cause a transformation

Classroom management: A complex yet organized matrix of variables teachers arrange to manage behavior and classroom processes, such as instruction and social interactions

Conflict: An actual or perceived opposition of needs, values, and interests

Consequence: Something that logically or naturally follows from an action or condition

Cooperating teacher (CT): An experienced teacher selected to be a mentor, model, and guide

Cooperative learning: Small-group work that requires input from each member to complete a task or solve a problem; key factors for success include interdependence, accountability, interpersonal skills, and skills for working effectively within a group

Council for the Accreditation of Education Preparation (CAEP): A national council created to ensure and raise the quality of teacher preparation and teacher certification programs at U.S. colleges and universities; a consolidation of the National Council for the Accreditation of Teacher Education (NCATE) and Teacher Education Accreditation Council (TEAC)

Differentiated instruction: Instruction that is adapted so that all students can reach their potential; it meets the needs of students with a variety of learning styles, those with learning disabilities or exceptionalities, academically gifted students, and English-language learners

Digital natives (also called *new millennials* or *Generation Z*): Individuals who have spent all or the majority of their lives surrounded by and using technology, including computers, cell phones, video games, and digital music players; *digital natives* can be compared to *digital immigrants* (i.e., individuals who began to use technology later in their lives and may or may not have adapted to its routine use)

Discipline: The act of training or punishment to obtain a certain behavior or outcome

Disposition: A tendency or inclination to act or behave a certain way under given circumstances

Ethical: Concerning what is moral or right

Experiential learning: The process of learning from direct experience

Flexible grouping: Grouping that is dynamic and allows for changes in student group composition based on such factors as task, interest, learning style, and readiness

Graphic organizers: Visual tools for providing structure for information; allow students to categorize, classify, and show relationships and processes

Growth: A progression in size or movement from simple to more complex forms

Internet scavenger hunt (also referred to as *web-based scavenger hunt*): An electronic version of the traditional scavenger hunt, where individuals or small groups learn about and review concepts by moving through a series of prompts or questions posed by the teacher, followed by links to specific teacher-approved websites where information can be found

Learning styles: Individual strengths and preferences for taking in information

Legal: Concerning the protections that laws or regulations provide

Lesson plan: A framework for presenting instruction in a clear and cohesive manner

Mission statement: A formal, short, written statement of the purpose of a company or organization

Motivation: The intrinsic or extrinsic activation of goal-oriented behavior

Multimedia project: A method for sharing knowledge that incorporates any combination of text, graphics, animation, video, and sound

Organizational structure: The form of an organization or entities that collaborate and contribute to serve one common goal

Pacing guide: A suggested sequence for effective implementation and delivery of the curriculum within a particular time frame (e.g., quarter, semester, school year)

Personality theory: A branch of psychology that studies personality and individual differences

Phase: The distinguishable part of a sequence or cycle occurring over time

Podcast: A digitally recorded session (e.g., of a lecture or presentation) that can be made available electronically via download for future viewing/listening; may include any combination of audio and/or video files

Portfolio: A collection of artifacts that summarize major teaching accomplishments and strengths

Praxis II: An examination that measures general and subject specific knowledge and teaching skills; it is sometimes required for teaching licensure

Procedures: A series of steps taken to accomplish an end

Professionalism: Adhering to a set of values composed of standards, obligations, formally agreed-on codes of conduct, and informal expectations

Race: The categorization of humans into populations or ancestral groups on the basis of various sets of heritable characteristics

Reward: The return for performance of a desired behavior; positive reinforcement

Rule: A principle or regulation governing conduct, action, procedure, or arrangement

School culture: The beliefs, attitudes, and behaviors that characterize a school

Socioeconomic status (SES): A basis or measure of a person's work experience and of an individual's or family's economic and social position relative to others, based on income, education, and occupation

Standard: A basis for comparison; a reference point against which other things can be evaluated

Standards: Uniform guidelines at the state and national level that outline the curriculum to be taught for different grades and courses; learners must master these standards in order to progress to the next grade or course

Strategic problem solving: A higher-order, cognitive process that facilitates progress toward a desired goal

Stress: The body's way of responding to different kinds of demands placed on it

Student achievement: An evaluation of performance based on a measurable standard; it may refer to academic disciplines or extracurricular activities

Student teacher (ST): A student who is teaching under the supervision of a certified teacher

Student teaching internship: A specific number of weeks spent teaching in an assigned classroom under the supervision of the classroom teacher and a university supervisor

Teacher education program (TEP): A program that provides the coursework and experiences necessary for completing requirements for teaching licensure and/or certification

Test anxiety: Excessive worry that negatively affects performance on assessments

Traits: A characteristic or property of an object or person

Transition: The act of moving from one thing to another

University supervisor (US): One who supervises or is in a leadership position and is employed by a university

Virtual field trip (VFT): A guided exploration of prescreened and thematically based web pages (including any combination of text, images, video, and audio content) that, when woven together appropriately, can create an effective online experience

WebQuest: A scaffolded learning experience using teacher-approved web resources to investigate a topic; includes an authentic, meaningful task and a structured group environment in which each member takes on a specific role and is responsible for searching for, discovering, and sharing specific information with the group

Wiki: A website that enables pages to be created and edited as a collaborative effort

Appendix A

Twenty Ways to Say No (or Not Right Now)

While you are participating in the internship, you may find yourself inundated with requests from friends, family, and colleagues to participate in various efforts. Some of these requests may be worthwhile (for example, your CT might ask you to assist with planning the service learning project for your grade level, or a classmate might ask you to proofread a unit plan that needs to be submitted), and some may be less meaningful or valuable at the time (such as a cousin asking you to spearhead this year's 20th annual four-day family reunion extravaganza). Sometimes it's great to be able to say yes, and other times you may have to find a tactful way to let everyone know that although you're still a team player, at the moment you are unable to commit to such time- and energy-consuming jobs. Remember: Student teaching is a juggling act, and it is only through careful selection of the items that you're juggling that you are able to keep everything in the air—and keep your sanity as well. To that end, we provide here a list of ways to let down or say no to your family, friends, and colleagues without destroying relationships that have to continue throughout and beyond the internship. (Please note that when it comes to your CT, we recommend you find more opportunities to say YES than NO!)

1. I am in the middle of several projects.

- Let people know when you have accepted other responsibilities.
- No need to make excuses if you don't have any free time.
- No one will fault you for having already filled your plate.

2. I am not comfortable with that.

- You might be uncomfortable with any of a number of issues.
- It could be the people involved, the type of work, the morale implications, etc.
- This is a very respectful way of avoiding a sticky situation.

3. I am not taking on any new responsibilities.

- You aren't saying that you will never help out again, just that you feel your schedule is as full as you would like now.
- Understanding your limits is a talent to be expected.

4. I am not the most qualified person for the job.

- If you don't feel that you have adequate skills, that's okay.
- It's better to admit your limitations up front.
- The best way to avoid feeling overwhelmed down the road.

5. I do not enjoy that kind of work.

- Life isn't about drudgery—If you don't enjoy it, why do it?
- Don't be afraid to let someone know you just don't want to.
- Someone else is bound to enjoy the work you don't.

6. I do not have any more room in my calendar.

- Be honest if your schedule is filled.
- "Filled" doesn't have to mean really filled.
- Know when you are scheduled as much as you are willing and then stop.

7. I hate to split my attention among projects.

- Let people know that you want to do a good job for them but that you can't when your focus is too divided or splintered.
- You will be more effective if you focus on one project at a time.

8. I have another commitment.

- It doesn't matter what the commitment is.
- It can even simply be time to yourself or with friends or family.
- You don't have to justify—you simply aren't available.

9. I have no experience with that.

- Volunteering shouldn't mean learning an entirely new set of skills.
- Suggest that they find someone who has experience in that area.
- Offer to help out with something that you already know how to do.

10. I know you will do a wonderful job yourself.

- People often ask for help because they doubt their own abilities.
- Let them know that you have confidence they will succeed.
- You are actually doing them a favor in the long run.

11. I need to focus more on my personal life.

- Don't be ashamed of wanting to spend time with your family.
- Having a strong family is an important priority in and of itself.
- Be willing to put your personal needs first.

12. I need to focus on my career right now.

- Often, you have to focus your energies on a work-related task.
- You may have to give up some civic or community duties.
- If you don't do it, someone else will take on the task.

13. I need to leave some free time for myself.

- It's okay to be selfish—in a good way.
- Treat your personal time like any other appointment.
- Block off time in your calendar and guard it with your life.

14. I would rather decline than do a mediocre job.

- Know when you aren't going to be able to deliver a quality product.
- The reason doesn't matter—not enough time, wrong skills, etc.
- Whatever the reason is enough for turning a request down.

15. I would rather help out with another task.

- Saying no doesn't mean that you can't help at all.
- If someone asks you to do something you really despise, refuse.
- Then offer to help with something you find more enjoyable.

16. Let me hook you up with someone who can do it.

- If you aren't available to help out, offer another qualified resource.
- Helping to connect people is a valuable service to offer.
- Make sure the person you refer will represent you well.

17. No.

- Sometimes it's okay to just say no.
- Just say it in a way that expresses respect and courtesy.
- Leave the door open for good relations.

18. Not right now, but I can do it later.

- If you really want to help but don't have time, say so.
- Offer to help at a later time or date.
- If they can't wait for you, they'll find someone else.

19. Some things have come up that need my attention.

- Unexpected things happen that throw your schedule off.
- Accept that you may need to make a few adjustments.
- It is temporary and you will have more time when life stabilizes.

20. This really is not my strong suit.

- It's okay to admit your limitations.
- Knowing what you can handle and what you can't is a skill.
- Your time will be more efficiently spent on something you do well.

Source: Content provided by www.RamonaCreel.com. Ramona Creel is a Professional Organizer and Simplicity Coach. Check out her website, particularly her "Beyond Organizing" page, for tips on how you can maintain control of your stuff and yourself during the internship and in other aspects of your life as well.

Appendix B

Sample Pacing Guides

Pacing guides help teachers pace themselves so that ample time is available for addressing the required content. The following samples give you an idea of how such guides might look. As you can see, they may be presented in a variety of formats, but the purpose is consistent: to give teachers (and often parents) an idea of exactly what is to be taught and learned at specific points in the school year. The guides included here come from Virginia (seventh-grade social studies curriculum) and North Carolina (high school algebra curriculum). Note that these are only selected portions of the curriculum guides.

SEVENTH-GRADE SOCIAL STUDIES PACING GUIDE

1st Nine Weeks	2nd Nine Weeks	3rd Nine Weeks	4th Nine Weeks
Geography (USII.2c) States grouped by region **Northeast: Maine, Vermont, New Hampshire, Connecticut, Massachusetts, Rhode Island, New York, New Jersey, Pennsylvania** **Southeast: Maryland, Delaware, West Virginia, Virginia, Kentucky, Tennessee, North Carolina, South Carolina, Georgia, Florida, Alabama, Mississippi, Louisiana, Arkansas** **Midwest: Ohio, Indiana, Illinois, Michigan, Wisconsin, Minnesota, Iowa, Missouri, Kansas, Nebraska, South Dakota, North Dakota** **Southwest: Texas, Oklahoma, New Mexico, Arizona**	**(USII.3e)** **Negative effects of industrialization** Child labor Low wages, long hours Unsafe working conditions **Rise of organized labor** Formation of unions—Growth of American Federation of Labor Strikes—Aftermath of Homestead Strike **Progressive Movement** workplace reforms Improved safety conditions Reduced work hours Placed restrictions on child labor **Women's suffrage** Increased educational opportunities Attained voting rights • Women gained the right to vote with passage of the 19th Amendment to the Constitution of the United States of America. • Susan B. Anthony worked for women's suffrage.	**(USII.5d)** **Causes of the Great Depression** People overspeculated on stocks, using borrowed money that they could not repay when stock prices crashed. The Federal Reserve failed to prevent the collapse of the banking system. High tariffs strangled international trade. **Impact on Americans** A large numbers of banks and businesses failed. One-fourth of workers were without jobs. Large numbers of people were hungry and homeless. Farmers' incomes fell to low levels. **Major features of the New Deal** Social Security Federal work programs Environmental improvement programs Farm assistance programs Increased rights for labor	**(USII.7c)** **Terms to know** Cold War: State of tension between the United States and the Soviet Union without actual fighting that divided the world into two camps **Origins of the Cold War** Differences in goals and ideologies between the United States and the Soviet Union (the two superpowers)—The United States was democratic and capitalist; the Soviet Union was dictatorial and communist. The Soviet Union's domination over Eastern European countries American policy of containment (to stop the spread of communism) North Atlantic Treaty Organization (NATO) versus Warsaw Pact **Major conflicts in the post–World War II era** South Korea and the United States resisted Chinese and North Korean aggression. The conflict ended in a stalemate.

Source: Accessed from http://www.pcva.us/cia/pacing_guides/Social_Studies/Middle_School/Seventh_Gradep.pdf

HIGH SCHOOL ALGEBRA I PACING GUIDE

Gaston County Schools

CCSS-M Implementation 2012-2013

Algebra I Pacing Guide

TIMELINE	UNIT	MAJOR CONCEPTS	CCSS-M	"I can…" STATEMENTS	ESSENTIAL VOCAB	TEXTBOOK CORRELATIONS
2 Weeks	**Unit 1** Data Analysis	• dot plots, histograms, box plots • key features of graphs • avg rate of change from graph • shape, center, and spread • outliers • two-way frequency tables • joint, marginal, and conditional relative frequency • compute joint, conditional, and marginal probabilities • correlation vs. causation	S.ID.1 S.ID.2 S.ID.3 S.ID.5 S.ID.7 S.ID.8 S.ID.9	• I can take a set of data and plot it on the number line. • I can compare data sets using statistics that are appropriate to the shapes of the distributions. • I can draw conclusions from the shape and individual points of a data set. • I can summarize two categorical variables using two-way frequency tables. • I can interpret the slope and intercept for a linear model. • I can find and explain the correlation coefficient for a linear model. • I can describe the difference between correlation and causation.	• association • categorical • causation • conditional distribution • conditional probability • distribution • correlation • explanatory variable • five number summary • interquartile range • joint probability • marginal distribution • marginal probability • maximum/minimum • measures of center • outliers • quantitative • relative frequency • residual • response variable • shape, center, spread • skew • standard deviation • trend • two-way table	• **Glencoe Algebra I** 1.9, 2.5-2.6, 3.7-3.8, 4.7-4.8, 5.7, 10.7, 13.3-13.5, 14.2-14.4
3 Weeks	**Unit 2** Solving & Graphing Linear Equations	• simplifying linear expressions • write and solve linear equations in one variable • algebraic proof • graphing in the coordinate plane • geometric terms, definitions, and symbols • define and name and lines using appropriate symbols • prove and lines using slope • writing equations of lines • midpoint	A.SSE.1.a A.SSE.1.b A.REI.1 A.REI.3 A.CED.1 A.CED.2 A.CED.3 A.CED.4 A.REI.10 G.CO.1 G.GPE.5 G.GPE.6	• I can identify the parts of linear expression. • I can identify and utilize the important parts of a linear expression or formula. • I can solve a simple linear equation in one variable. • I can solve linear equations in one variable. • I can write and solve a linear equation using one variable. • I can write a linear equation using two or more variables. • I can graph a linear equation with appropriate labels and scales. • I can determine whether a solution is viable to the given problem. • I can solve a literal equation (i.e. formula) for a specified variable. • I can determine the solution set for a linear equation from a graph. • I can identify, locate, and name points in the coordinate plane. • I can define and name parallel and perpendicular lines in the coordinate plane. • I can define and name line segments in the coordinate plane. • I can determine if two lines are parallel or perpendicular. • I can create linear equations using slope and any point on the line. • I can define the midpoint of a line segment. • I can determine the midpoint of a line segment.	• argument • assumption • bisect • coefficient • congruent • constant • dependent variable • equidistant • independent variable • line • line segment • literal equation • midpoint • parallel line • perpendicular line • properties of equality • proof • replacement set • slope • solution set • substitution • symbolic notation • T-chart • term • variable	• **Glencoe Algebra I** 1.1-1.2, 1.4-1.6, 2.1-2.4, 2.7, 8.1-8.8, 9.1-9.6, 11.1, 11.2-12.8 1.3, 1.8, 3.1-3.5, 3.6, 3.8, 4.1-4.3, 4.5-4.8, 5.1-5.6, 6.1-6.6, 12.9

Created by the GCS High School Teacher Leader Team

DRAFT - Revised 5/2012

To be Implemented 2012-2013

(Continued)

(Continued)

Gaston County Schools

CCSS-M Implementation 2012-2013

Algebra I Pacing Guide

SECOND SIX WEEKS

TIMELINE	UNIT	MAJOR CONCEPTS	CCSS-M	"I can…" STATEMENTS	ESSENTIAL VOCAB	TEXTBOOK CORRELATIONS
3 Weeks	**Unit 3** Linear Functions & Best Fit Lines	• domain/range • linear function • arithmetic sequences • recursive/explicit formulas • rate of change • comparing properties of functions • linear regression • scatter plots	F.IF.1 F.IF.2 F.IF.3 F.BF.1.a F.BF.1.b F.BF.2 F.IF.4 F.IF.5 F.IF.6 F.IF.7.a F.IF.9 F.BF.3 F.LE.5 F.LE.2 S.ID.6 S.ID.7 S.ID.8 S.ID.9	• I can distinguish between domain and range. • I can use and interpret equations written in function notation. • I can relate sequences and functions. • I can create functions that describe a relationship between two quantities. • I can model recursive and explicit formulas to create arithmetic sequences. • I can use recursive and explicit formulas to model and solve real-world and mathematical problems. • I can identify and interpret features of linear functions. • I can draw a sketch of linear function in the coordinate plane. • I can identify domains of a function in the context of a real-world or mathematical problem. • I can determine the average rate of change. • I can graph linear functions expressed symbolically. • I can identify and interpret key features of a linear function. • I can compare properties of two linear function, each represented in a different way. • I can create functions that describe a relationship between two quantities. • I can model recursive and explicit formulas to create arithmetic sequences. • I can use recursive and explicit formulas to model and solve real-world and mathematical problems. • I can construct a linear regression model. • I can interpret and explain the parameters of a linear model in context. • I can create and use scatter plots to describe how two quantitative variables are related. • I can interpret the slope and intercept for a linear model. • I can find and explain the correlation coefficient for a linear model. • I can describe the difference between correlation and causation. • I can use scatter plots and linear models to draw conclusions and make predictions to solve real-world and mathematical problems.	• arithmetic sequences • association • causation • correlation • domain • explanatory variable • explicit • fitted function • function • function notation • horizontal shift • impractical • intercepts • joint probability • marginal distribution • marginal probability • parent graph • practical • range • rate of change • recursive • regression model • relative frequency • response variable • residual • scatter plot • transformation • trend • two-way table • horizontal shift • parent graph • transformation • translation • vertical shift	• Glencoe Algebra I 1.9, 2.5-2.6, 3.7-3.8, 4.7-4.8, 5.7, 10.7, 13.3-13.5, 14.2-14.4
1 Week	**Unit 4** Linear Inequalities	• simplifying linear expressions • write and solve linear equations in one variable • algebraic proof • graphing in the coordinate plane • geometric terms, definitions, and symbols • define and name and lines using appropriate symbols • prove and lines using slope • writing equations of lines • midpoint	A.REI.3 A.REI.12 A.CED.1 A.CED.3	• I can solve linear inequalities in one variable. • I can determine the solution set for a linear inequality from a graph. • I can graph linear inequalities in the coordinate plane with appropriate labels and scales. • I can write and solve a linear inequalities using one variable. • I can write a linear inequalities using two or more variables. • I can determine whether a solution is viable to the given problem.	• bounded • dependent variable • independent variable • literal equation • solution • unbounded	• Glencoe Algebra I 6.1-6.6

Created by the GCS High School Teacher Leader Team   DRAFT- Revised 5/2012   To be Implemented 2012-2013

Source: Dr. Lory Morrow, Deputy Superintendent of Instruction, and the Gaston Co. Schools Instruction Department.

Appendix C

Sample Lesson Plan Templates

DETAILED LESSON PLAN TEMPLATE: GENERAL

Your Name:

Subject Area:

Lesson Topic:

Lesson Date(s):

Grade Level:

Duration of Lesson:

State and/or National Standards Addressed	
Standard:	
Obj. #:	Objective:
Obj. #:	Objective:

Key Vocabulary	Key Questions (at least 3)

Materials, Resources, Technology Needed

Procedure (Madeline Hunter's 6 or 7 steps)

Anticipatory Set

What will students learn or do—based on your objective? How does this relate to what they already know? Why do they need to know it? Focus on the objective. Write exactly what you will say.

Teacher Input/Modeling

You must model the concept or skill from your objective with at least three (3) examples for a new skill, and one clear example for a skill in review. Model exactly what you will have students doing in guided practice and independent practice. This section must be described in detail. Enough detail should be given such that another teacher can walk in and teach this lesson based on your description.

Example 1:

Example 2:

Example 3:

Guided Practice

Provide several opportunities for students to attempt the task with your guidance. This can be oral, board work, hands-on, small-group or paired work, or other active learning—but refrain from individual worksheets.

Check for Understanding

Write what you will do as students are attempting the task, in order to determine if they understand what they are supposed to do.

Independent Practice

Students are practicing the same skill or concept you taught during teacher input and that they practiced under guided practice. Students must exhibit the new skill or concept by themselves so you can see if they have mastered the criteria that you set in your lesson objective. Limited worksheets may be used at this time.

Check for Understanding

Write what you will do as students are attempting the task, in order to determine if they understand what they are supposed to do.

Closure

Summarization of the key points of the lesson facilitated by the teacher. Three (3) to five (5) explicitly designed questions must be written and asked of the students to check for understanding of key concepts and content taught in the lesson. Must link back to your objective and modeling.

Assessment

How will you measure your lesson objective? This can be formal or informal.

Additional Required Components

Meeting the Needs of All Learners

Include modifications and/or differentiation strategies of the designed lesson plan for other students in the classroom.

Fast-Finisher Activity

Provide another opportunity for those students who complete independent practice quickly to try the skill in a new or different way. This should be directly related to the original objective, but should not be another worksheet.

Infuse Cultural Diversity

State how you can infuse cultural diversity into the lesson plan (i.e., culturally responsive instruction, materials, and/or curricula). Go beyond the 3 F's: Food, Fun, & Family. Consider what is socially and culturally important to your students and how it can be connected to the lesson.

Infuse Technology

Cite websites used to design the lesson and infuse technology into the lesson presentation. Provide URLs for appropriate sites that learners can visit to practice the skill or to learn more about the concept.

Post-Teaching Reflection

After teaching this lesson, reflect on the following: What part of this lesson went really well? What might you change about this lesson if you use it again? What have you learned about teaching, learning, and children? How does this experience match with what you have been reading in the textbook and learning in class?

LESSON PLAN TEMPLATE: SMALL- OR WHOLE-GROUP READING

Book Title: Page or Chapter:

Group: Level:

ELA–(English Language Arts) Standards Addressed

Before Reading

Review/Preview

Help students call up important information using a picture walk, book preview, or summary/review of previous reading.

Challenging Content

Introduce concepts, vocabulary, language, and text features that may be unfamiliar. Preteach vocabulary that cannot be determined using context clues.

Focus Question

Help students focus their reading by providing a question that they will be able to answer on completion.

During Reading

Type of Reading

❑ Shared   ❑ Echo   ❑ Choral   ❑ Paired   ❑ Independent   ❑ Flexible

Check-In (Individual)

Tune into each student's reading skills and strategies, such as fluency, decoding, and comprehension. Ask questions that reflect reading comprehension. Take notes.

After Reading

Post-Reading Task (Individual)

Students will finish reading at different times, so have related and meaningful early finisher tasks ready. These should not be worksheets, but should relate to the use of strategies during real reading.

Post-Reading Discussion (Group)

Facilitate discussion about the main points from the selection. Be sure to use (and encourage the use of) vocabulary that was used in the text. Help students make connections to the text, themselves, and their world. Let the students do most of the talking.

Strategies (Group)

Focus on strategies that good readers use. This may be a review of a strategy, or explicit teaching of a new strategy. You may also want to point out strategies that you saw students using correctly during the reading.

Reflection

What worked well? What will you need to remember for the next time you meet with this group or use this text?

LESSON PLAN TEMPLATE: GUIDED DISCOVERY

Your Name:

Subject Area:

Lesson Topic:

Lesson Date(s):

Grade Level:

Duration of Lesson:

State and/or National Standards Addressed	
Standard:	
Obj. #:	Objective:
Obj. #:	Objective:

Key Vocabulary	**Key Questions (at least 3)**

Materials, Resources, Technology Needed

Procedure (Guided Discovery Steps)
Set the Stage—But Don't State Objectives Yet!
Begin by providing just enough background information (tap into students' own prior knowledge) to provide a context for the upcoming task.
Provide Instructions
Tell students exactly what they are to do—without revealing what they will learn, discover, or observe. Be very clear. It may be helpful to have instructions displayed. Be prepared to repeat them as needed.
Guided Practice (e.g., a lab experiment)
Students attempt the task. Write what you will do during this time, in order to determine if they understand what they are to do and to see if they are reaching the expected outcomes.

Regrouping for Instruction

Stop the activity briefly. As a class, talk about what was learned or observed. Take time to clear up any misunderstandings.

State the Objectives

Tell students (or clarify) the purpose for the task. What were they supposed to learn? Why is it important? Allow opportunities for students to share their own insights, but always steer them back to the intended objective.

Independent Practice

Allow opportunities for students to reflect on their learning in their journals or small-group discussions. As you listen to or read about their learning, be sure to clear up any remaining misunderstandings.

Closure

Students should assist with summarization of the key points of the lesson. Three (3) to five (5) explicitly designed questions should be written and asked of the students to check for understanding of key concepts and content presented in the lesson. This must link back to your objective, guided practice, and regrouping for instruction.

Assessment

How will you measure your lesson objective(s)? This can be formal or informal.

UNIT PLAN ESSENTIALS

An effective unit of instruction can last from a few days to several weeks. Regardless of the time frame or the content covered, there are several components that should be included in any unit:

- a *rationale* that justifies teaching the unit. It should argue the merits of your unit's theme and include a list of anticipated student learning outcomes, key course activities, and culminating project(s). Include the grade level standards as part of your rationale.
- a set of *5 to 7 measurable objectives* that provide a framework for the unit; these objectives will be woven throughout your series of planned lessons and activities, as well as guide your formative and summative assessments.
- a *professional resource list* compiling all sources used to create the unit (e.g., methods textbooks, teacher manuals, web-based sources, journal articles)
- a list of *materials* to be read (fiction and nonfiction books, poems, plays, student-produced texts), to be viewed (art, sculpture, films, PowerPoint presentations), and to be heard (music, audio tapes, podcasts) by students during the unit as they explore the unit's key ideas and problems.
- an *introductory activity* that engages students in the unit, taps prior knowledge, and serves as a scaffold for students before they begin exploring the instructional materials.
- a series of *lesson plans* arranged in an appropriate sequence to prepare students to take increasing responsibility for their own learning. The unit's lessons should feature brain-friendly teaching strategies or other research-based methods of differentiated instruction, diversity components/extension activities, and reteaching elements. Lessons should be constructivist and include student choice, opportunities for collaboration, and technology components. They should be written thoroughly enough that someone else could teach the lesson from the plan. Each lesson should include clear student learning outcomes and link to the state standards.
- a set of formative and summative *assessments* (and accompanying *assessment rubrics*) that allow students to demonstrate the new knowledge they have constructed regarding the unit's key concepts. Prompts and formative/summative assessments must be authentic, varied, and culturally responsive. When possible, they should incorporate collaboration and problem solving.

Appendix D

Sample Résumé

DIANA M. WESLEY

Telephone: (H) 555-234-6789 or (C) 555-333-1360   **Email:** dmw@gmail.com

Address: 123 Elm Street, Small Town, NC 27789

Qualifications

NC Elementary Education Teaching License, May 2010, North Carolina Central University (GPA 4.0)

Bachelor of Arts (Education), June 1998, University of the Free State, South Africa (GPA 3.86)

Related Experience

1st-Grade Student Teacher, Ridge Road Elementary School, Durham, NC (January 2010–May 2010)

- Plan and implement developmentally appropriate lessons and learning experiences for 1st-grade students, aligned with the NC Standard Course of Study.
- Guide students in classroom discussions in order to scaffold their learning.
- Design and facilitate cooperative learning groups focused on specific learning outcomes.
- Provide small-group instruction in literacy and math to meet diverse educational needs.
- Provide classroom management to enhance the learning experience of a cohesive classroom community.

3rd-Grade Instructional Assistant, Penny Road Elementary School, Cary, NC (August 2007–December 2009)

- Give small-group instruction and tutoring in literacy and math for ethnically and economically diverse 3rd-grade students.
- Implement lesson plans in the absence of lead teachers in Grades 3 through 5.
- Provide administrative assistance for three 3rd-grade teachers.

Substitute Teacher, Wake County, NC Grades 2–7 (April 2007–August 2007)

- Implement lesson plans in the absence of classroom teachers in Grades 2 to 7.

Kindergarten Literacy Center Volunteer, Baucom Elementary School, Apex, NC (August 2006–June 2007)

- Lead literacy and reading centers two days per week for kindergarten students.
- Lead math or thematic centers one to two days per week, as requested by the lead teacher.

Self-Employed Home Daycare Provider, Apex, NC (January 2001–April 2005)

- Provide care for two children ages 4 months through 3 years.
- Provide developmentally appropriate educational experiences for infants through pre-schoolers, including read-aloud activities, prereading and premath skills, arts and crafts, and weekly field trips.

4th-Grade Sunday School Teacher, Bloemfontein, South Africa (1996–1998)

Volunteer Music Teacher, St. Boniface Primary School, Kimberley, Republic of South Africa (1994)

- Plan and implement lessons in basic music theory and soprano recorder technique for disadvantaged children ages 7 to 12.

Volunteer Drum Majorette Trainer, St. Boniface High School, Kimberley, Republic of South Africa (1994)

- Design and teach choreographed team drills to a squad of 50 girls in Grades 8 through 12.
- Teach baton and flag handling skills, in addition to proper posture, self-confidence, and music interpretation.

Other Work Experience

- *Armed Nuclear Security Officer,* Harris Nuclear Plant, New Hill, NC (April 2004–April 2005)
- *Armed Nuclear Security Officer,* Harris Nuclear Plant, New Hill, NC (September 1999–July 2000)
- *Office Assistant III,* Division of Prisons, Program Services, Raleigh, NC (1999)
- *Waitress* in Family Restaurants, Kimberley and Bloemfontein, South Africa (1993–1996)

I appreciate your time in considering my application for a teaching position.

References and Further Readings

CHAPTER 1

Campbell, E. (2013). Cultivating moral and ethical professional practice: Interdisciplinary lessons and teacher education. In M. N. Sanger & R. D. Osguthorpe (Eds.), *The moral work of teaching and teacher education: Preparing and supporting practitioners* (p. 29). New York: Teachers College Press.

Cherubini, L. (2008). Teacher-candidates perceptions of school culture: A mixed methods investigation. *The Journal of Teaching and Learning, 5*(2), 39–54.

Cherubini, L. (2009). Reconciling the tensions of new teachers' socialisation into school culture: A review of the research. *Issues in Educational Research, 19*(2), 83–99.

Deal, T. E., & Peterson, K. D. (2010). *Shaping school culture: Pitfalls, paradoxes, and promises.* San Francisco, CA: Jossey-Bass.

Geertz, C. (1973). *The interpretation of cultures.* New York: Basic Books.

Hazard, W. R. (1976). *Student teaching and the law.* (ERIC Document Reproduction Service No. SP009739). Washington, DC: American Association of Colleges for Teacher Education.

Peters, A. (2011). Small urban high school success: A case study. *Journal of Education for Students Placed at Risk, 16*(2), 89–99.

Schuck, S., Aubusson, P., Buchanan, J., & Russell, T. (2012). The way we do things around here: School culture and socialisation. In S. Schuck, P. Aubusson, J. Buchanan, & T. Russell (Eds.), *Beginning Teaching* (pp. 39–53). Dordrecht, Netherlands: Springer.

Strike, K. A., & Ternasky, P. L. (Eds.). (1993). *Ethics for professionals in education: Perspectives for preparation and practices.* (Eric Digests #377 589). New York: Teachers College.

Sundell, K., Castellano, M., Overman, L. T., & Aliaga, O. A. (2012). The role of school culture in improving student achievement in POS. *Techniques: Connecting Education and Careers, 87*(1), 28–31.

Thomas, H. (2011). The effect of school culture on student achievement in restructured high schools. (Doctoral dissertation). Valdosta State University Graduate School, Valdosta, GA.

Wolk, R. (2010, April). Education: The case for making it personal. *Educational Leadership, 67*(7), 16–17.

Zhu, C., Devos, G., & Li, Y. (2011). Teacher perceptions of school culture and their organizational commitment and well-being in a Chinese school. *Asia Pacific Education Review, 12*(2), 319–328.

CHAPTER 2

Council for the Accreditation of Teacher Preparation. (2010). *CAEP Draft Standards.* Retrieved from http://caepnet.org/commission/standards/

Johnson, S. (1998). *Who moved my cheese? An amazing way to deal with change in your work and in your life.* New York: Putnam.

Kitchel, T., & White, C. C. (2007). Barriers and benefits to the student teacher–cooperating teacher relationship. *Proceedings of the 2007 AAAE Research Conference, 34,* 710–712.

Rando, R. A. (2000). *Adaptive supervision in counselor training.* Retrieved from http://ccvillage .buffalo.edu/Village/ElecProj/Rando.htm

Russell, M. I., & Russell, J. A. (2011). Mentoring relationships: Cooperating teachers' perspectives on mentoring student interns. *The Professional Educator, 35,* 16–35.

Weasmer, J., & Woods, A. M. (2003). The role of the host teacher in the student teaching experience. *The Clearing House, 76*(4), 174–177.

CHAPTER 3

Allport, G. W., & Odbert, H. S. (1936). Trait names: A psycholexical study. *Psychological Monographs, 47,* 211.

Carver, C. S., & Scheier, M. F. (2013). Goals and emotion. In M. D. Robinson, E. Watkins, & E. Harmon-Jones (Eds.), *Handbook of cognition and emotion.* New York: Guilford Press.

Cattell, R. B. (1965). *The scientific analysis of personality.* Baltimore, MD: Penguin.

Cattell, R. B. (1970). Advances in Cattellian personality theory. In L. A. Pervin (Ed.), *Handbook of personality: Theory and research* (pp. 101–110). New York: Guilford Press.

Conn, S. R., & Rieke, M. L. (1994). *The 16PF fifth edition technical manual.* Champaign, IL: Institute for Personality and Ability Testing.

Diehl, M., & Hooker, K. (2013). Adult personality development: Dynamics and processes. *Research in Human Development, 10*(1), 1–8.

Draguns, J. G. (2012). Personality theory and research: International issues and trends. In F. T. L. Leong, W. E. Pickren, M. M. Leach, & A. J. Marsella (Eds.), *Internationalizing the psychology curriculum in the United States* (pp. 95–130). New York: Springer.

Fairweather, A. (2005, January 29). *Dealing with difficult people.* Retrieved from http:// ezinearticles.com/?Dealing-with-Difficult-People&id=12110

Lawley, J. A. (2012). *Pairing of pre-service and cooperating teachers during student internship: Opinions of collaborative relationships* (Doctoral dissertation). The University of Alabama, Tuscaloosa, AL.

CHAPTER 4

Johnson, S. (2013). Administrative supports that reduce teacher stress. *Research VIU's: Educational Leadership in Action, 3*(1).

Joseph, R. (2000). *Stress-free teaching: A practical guide to tackling stress in teaching, lecturing, and tutoring.* London, UK: Routledge.

Kyriacou, C. (2011). Teacher stress: From prevalence to resilience. In J. Langan-Fox & C. L. Cooper (Eds.), *Handbook of stress in the occupations* (pp. 161–173). Cheltenham, UK: Edward Elgar.

CHAPTER 5

Albert, L. (1996). *Cooperative discipline.* Circle Pines, MN: American Guidance Service.

Albert, L. (2003). *Cooperative discipline* (3rd ed.). Circle Pines, MN: American Guidance Service.

Apple, M. (1995). *Education and power.* New York: Routledge.

Berliner, D. C. (1988). Effective classroom management and instruction: A knowledge base for consultation. In J. L. Graden, J. E. Zins, & M. J. Curtis (Eds.), *Alternative educational delivery systems: Enhancing instructional options for all students* (pp. 309–325). Washington, DC: National Association of School Psychologists.

Brophy, J. E., & Good, T. L. (1986). Teacher behavior and student achievement. In M. C. Wittrock (Ed.), *Handbook of research on teaching* (3rd ed., pp. 328–375). New York: Macmillan.

Byrne, R. (2006). *The secret.* Hillsboro, OR: Artria Books/Beyond Words.

Canter, L., & Canter, M. (2009). *Assertive discipline: Positive behavior management for today's classroom.* Santa Monica, CA: Canter & Associates.

Doyle, W. (1986). Classroom organization and management. In M. C. Wittrock (Ed.), *Handbook of research on teaching* (3rd ed, pp. 392–431). New York: Macmillan.

Glasser, W. (1999). *Choice theory.* New York: HarperCollins.

Jones, F. (1987). *Positive classroom discipline.* Santa Cruz, CA: Jones & Associates.

Jones, F. (2007). *Tools for teaching: Discipline, instruction, motivation.* Santa Cruz, CA: Jones & Associates.

Kohn, A. (1999). *Punished by rewards: The trouble with gold stars, incentive plans, A's, praise, and other bribes.* New York: Houghton Mifflin.

Kounin, J. (1970). *Discipline and group management in classrooms.* New York: Holt, Rinehart & Winston.

Marzano, R. J., Marzano, J. S., & Pickering, D. J. (2003). *Classroom management that works: Research-based strategies for every teacher.* Alexandria, VA: Association for Supervision and Curriculum Development.

Moskowitz, G., & Hayman, J. L., Jr. (1976). Success strategies of inner-city teachers: A year-long study. *Journal of Educational Research, 69,* 283–289.

Tate, M. (2006). *Shouting won't grow dendrites: 20 techniques for managing a brain-compatible classroom.* Thousand Oaks, CA: Corwin.

Wong, H., & Wong, R. (2009). *The first days of school: How to be an effective teacher.* Mountain View, CA: Harry K. Wong.

CHAPTER 6

Anderson, R. C. (1977). The notion of schemata and the educational enterprise: General discussion of the conference. In R. C. Anderson, R. J. Spiro, & W. E. Montague (Eds.), *Schooling and the acquisition of knowledge* (pp. 415–431). Hillsdale, NJ: Erlbaum.

Bodkin, R. (2006, November 5). How to make your students WANT to pay attention in class. *Associated Content.* Retrieved from http://www.associatedcontent.com/article/80395/how_to_make_your_students_want_to_pay.html? cat=4

Bowman, S. (2008). *Preventing death by lecture.* Glenbrook, NV: Bowperson.

Dunn, R., & Dunn, K. (1978). *Teaching students through their individual learning styles: A practical approach.* Reston, VA: Reston.

Dunn, R. S., & DeBello, T. C. (1999). *Improved test scores, attitudes, and behaviors in America's schools: Supervisor's success stories.* Santa Barbara, CA: Greenwood.

Elias, M. (2005, March 30). So much media, so little attention span. *USA Today.* Retrieved from http://usatoday30.usatoday.com/news/education/2005–03–30-kids-attention_x .htm

Guthrie, J. T. (2001, March). Contexts for engagement and motivation in reading. *Reading Online, 4*(8). Retrieved from http://www.readingonline.org/articles/handbook/guthrie/

Hootstein, E. W. (1995). Motivational strategies of middle school social studies teachers. *Social Education, 59*(1), 23–26.

Jensen, E. (1995). *Super teaching.* San Diego, CA: The Brain Store.

Jensen, E. (2000). *Brain-based learning.* San Diego, CA: The Brain Store.

Johnson, L. (2005). *Teaching outside the box: How to grab your students by their brains.* San Francisco, CA: Jossey-Bass.

Marzano, R. J., Pickering, D. J., & Pollock, J. E. (2001). *Classroom instruction that works: Research-based strategies for increasing student achievement.* Alexandria, VA: Association for Supervision and Curriculum Development.

Nolen, S. B., & Nicholls, J. G. (1994). A place to begin (again) in research on student motivation: Teachers' beliefs. *Teaching & Teacher Education, 10*(1), 57–69.

Nunley, K. F. (2003). *A student's brain: The parent/teacher manual*. Kearney, NE: Morris.

OECD, Organisation for Economic Co-operation and Development. (2008). *New millennium learners: Initial findings on the effects of digital technologies on school-age learners*. Paper presented at the OECD/CERI International Conference, "Learning in the 21st Century: Research, Innovation and Policy," Paris, France.

Office of the Press Secretary. (1990, July 18). *Decade of the Brain*. (George H. W. Bush Proclamation #6158). Washington, DC: Author. Retrieved from http://www.loc.gov/loc/brain/proclaim.html

Prensky, M. (2001). *Digital natives, digital immigrants*. Retrieved from http://www.marcprensky.com/writing/prensky%20-%20digital%20natives,%20digital%20immigrants%20-%20part1.pdf

Richards, W. (2009). *Blogs, wikis, podcasts, and other powerful web tools for classrooms* (2nd ed.). Thousand Oaks, CA: Corwin.

Sousa, D. A. (2001). *How the brain learns* (2nd ed.). Thousand Oaks, CA: Corwin.

Sylvester, R. (1995). *A celebration of neurons: An educator's guide to the human brain*. Alexandria, VA: Association for Supervision and Curriculum Development.

Warlick, D. (2007). *Classroom blogging: A teacher's guide to blogs, wikis, & other tools that are shaping a new information landscape*. Raleigh, NC: The Landmark Project.

Zahorik, J. A. (1996). Elementary and secondary teachers' reports of how they make learning interesting. *Elementary School Journal, 96*, 551–565.

CHAPTER 7

Elksmin, L. K. (2001). Implementing case method of instruction in special education teacher preparation programs. *Teacher Education and Special Education, 24*, 95–107.

Sands, D. I., & Barker, H. B. (2004, Fall). Differentiating instruction in teacher education. *Teaching and Learning, 19*(1), 26–49.

Whitaker, S. D. (2001). Supporting beginning special education teachers. *Focus on Exceptional Children, 34*, 1–18.

CHAPTER 8

Bray, J. (1995). *A comparison of teacher concerns for the nontraditional student teacher and the traditional student teacher*. Retrieved from http://eric.ed.gov/?id=ED390844

Bridges to success. (2002). *Developmental phases of beginning educators*. Retrieved from http://www.tr.wou.edu/bridges/contact.htm

Bullough, R. V., Jr. (2011). Critical practice in teacher education: A study of professional learning. *Journal of Education for Teaching, 37*(4), 503–506.

Bullough, R., & Gitlin, A. (1995). *Becoming a student of teaching: methodologies for exploring self and school context.* New York: Garland.

Chism, N. V. N. (2011). Learning and teaching in higher education: The reflective professional. *The Review of Higher Education, 34*(3), 506–508.

Cook, J. (2012). Examining the mentoring experience of teachers. *International Journal of Educational Leadership Preparation, 7*(1), 1–10.

Dewey, J. (1933). *The question of certainty.* New York: Capricorn.

Kolb D. A. (1984). *Experiential learning: Experience as the source of learning and development.* Englewood Cliffs, NJ: Prentice Hall.

Lee, D. (2011). Changing course: Reflections of second-career teachers. *Current Issues in Education, 14*(2), 1–17.

Lee, E. D., & Mark, A. (2011). Non-traditional entrants to the profession of teaching: Motivations and experiences of second-career educators. *Christian Perspectives in Education, 4*(2), 3.

Lewin, K. (1951). *Field theory in social science: Selected theoretical papers* (D. Cartwright, Ed.). New York: Harper & Row.

Lowman, J. (1984). *Mastering the techniques of teaching.* San Francisco, CA: Jossey-Bass.

Meijer, P. C., de Graaf, G., & Meirink, J. (2011). Key experiences in student teachers' development. *Teachers and Teaching: theory and practice, 17*(1), 115–129.

Moir, E. (1990). Teaching phases. Unpublished article originally written for publication in the newsletter for the California New Teacher Project, California Department of Education (CDE). Santa Cruz, CA: New Teacher Center. Retrieved from http://www.newteachercenter.org/blog/phases-first-year-teaching

National Center for Education Information (NCEI). (2005). *Alternative routes to teacher certification.* Retrieved from http://www.ncei.com/Alt-Teacher-Cert.htm

National Center for Education Statistics. (2008). *Special analysis: Non-traditional undergraduates.* Washington, DC: Institute of Educational Sciences, U.S. Department of Education.

CHAPTER 9

Campbell, D. B., Cignetti, P. B., Melenyzer, B. J., & Nettles, D. H. (2010). *How to develop a professional portfolio: A manual for teachers.* Boston, MA: Pearson.

Darling-Hammond, L. (2006). *Powerful teacher education: Lessons from exemplary programs.* San Francisco, CA: Jossey-Bass.

Delandshere, G., & Arens, S. A. (2003). Examining the quality of evidence in preservice teacher portfolios. *Journal of Teacher Education, 54*(1), 57–72.

Educational Testing Service. (2010). *The Praxis Series official guide* (2nd edition). New York: McGraw-Hill.

Fredericks, A. D. (2012). *Ace your teacher interview: 149 fantastic answers to tough interview questions.* St. Paul, MN: Jist Works.

Goodson, F. T. (2007). The electronic portfolio: Shaping an emerging genre. *Journal of Adolescent & Adult Literacy, 50*(6), 432–434.

Grey, S., & Davis, A. P. (2011). *Praxis II elementary education: Curriculum, instruction & assessment.* Piscataway, NJ: Research & Education Association.

Knapper, C. K. (1995). The origins of teaching portfolios. *Journal on Excellence in College Teaching, 6*(1), 45–56.

Lee, H., & Herner-Patnode, L. (2011). Reflecting on portfolio development: How does the portfolio facilitate a preservice teacher's growth? *International Journal of Online Pedagogy and Course Design, 1*(1).

Shore, B., Foster, S., Knapper, C., Nadeau, G., Neill, N., & Sim, V. (1986). *The teaching dossier: A guide to its preparation and use.* Ottawa: Canadian Association of University Teachers.

Strudler, N., & Wetzel, K. (2008). Costs and benefits of electronic portfolios in teacher education: Faculty perspectives. *Journal of Computing in Teacher Education, 24*(4), 135–142.

Wetzel, K., Strudler, N., Addis, A., & Luz, T. (2009). Trends in the use of electronic portfolios for accreditation purposes. In I. Gibson, R. Weber, K. McFerrin, R. Carlsen & D. A. Willis (Eds.), *Proceedings of Society for Information Technology & Teacher Education International Conference 2009* (pp. 233–237). Chesapeake, VA: AACE, Association for the Advancement of Computing in Education.

Zeichner, K., & Wray, S. (2001). The teaching portfolio in U.S. teacher education programs: What we know and what we need to know. *Teaching and Teacher Education, 17,* 613–621.

Index

About the Authors

Kisha N. Daniels has worked extensively for 26 years in the areas of teaching and learning with children, public school teachers, administrators, and university students. She holds a BA in Elementary Education, a MEd in School Counseling, a MSA in School Administration, a specialist certification in curriculum and instruction, and an EdD in Educational Leadership from the University of North Carolina at Chapel Hill. As a teacher and administrator in large, urban school districts, Kisha has devoted her work to utilizing engaging curriculum to support diverse learning styles. She is currently an Associate Professor at North Carolina Central University in the Department of Education Leadership's MSA program, where she teaches courses in instructional and organizational leadership and supervises administrative interns. Kisha is actively involved with building and sustaining community partnerships in an effort to extend the scholarship of teacher leadership through service learning. This focus has guided her research and writings, where she is credited with many journal articles on teacher quality and the impact of collaborative teaching and community engagement.

Gerrelyn C. Patterson earned a BA in English Literature from North Carolina Central University, a MEd in English Education from the University of Virginia, and a PhD from the University of North Carolina at Chapel Hill in Curriculum, Culture and Change with an emphasis on teacher education and race, class, and gender issues. She has more than 17 years of P–12 and university teaching experience as a teacher educator and literature and composition instructor. Gerrelyn has worked as a consultant and researcher with the Comer School Development Program at Yale University, taught in the Master's in Teaching Program (MAT) at the University of North Carolina at Chapel Hill, and added to the body of work documenting school desegregation in North Carolina as a researcher with the Southern Oral History Program at the University of North Carolina at Chapel Hill. Currently, she is an Associate Professor at North Carolina Central University, where she teaches undergraduate and graduate courses in lesson planning, classroom management, and middle school philosophy. As the Middle Grades Education Coordinator, she has the opportunity to supervise student teachers in urban and rural middle schools and build service-learning partnerships between university faculty and P–12 teachers. Her passion involves training P–12 and university faculty in the areas of effective and practical classroom management, engaging instructional strategies, and service learning.

Yolanda L. Dunston has 21 years of experience in P–12 and higher education in the state of North Carolina. She earned a BA in Elementary Education, a MEd in Special Education— Literacy Studies, and a PhD in Literacy, all from the University of North Carolina at Chapel Hill. Her focus is on effective teaching for both preservice and practicing teachers, particularly in the area of literacy. She has been a teacher at the preschool and elementary level, a private consultant for struggling middle and high school students, and an adjunct instructor at UNC–Chapel Hill teaching undergraduate emergent and early literacy courses. Yolanda has prepared instructional materials for Pearson Prentice Hall and is a contributing author for the text *Aftermath of Hurricane Katrina: Educating Traumatized Children Pre-K Through College* with a chapter dedicated to using literacy and language strategies to help children cope and progress academically after a tragedy. Currently, she is a tenured Associate Professor at North Carolina Central University in the Department of Curriculum and Instruction in the School of Education, where she coordinates the Elementary Education program, teaches undergraduate and graduate methods courses in literacy, facilitates the student teaching seminar, and supervises student teachers in the field.

SAGE researchmethods

The essential online tool for researchers from the world's leading methods publisher

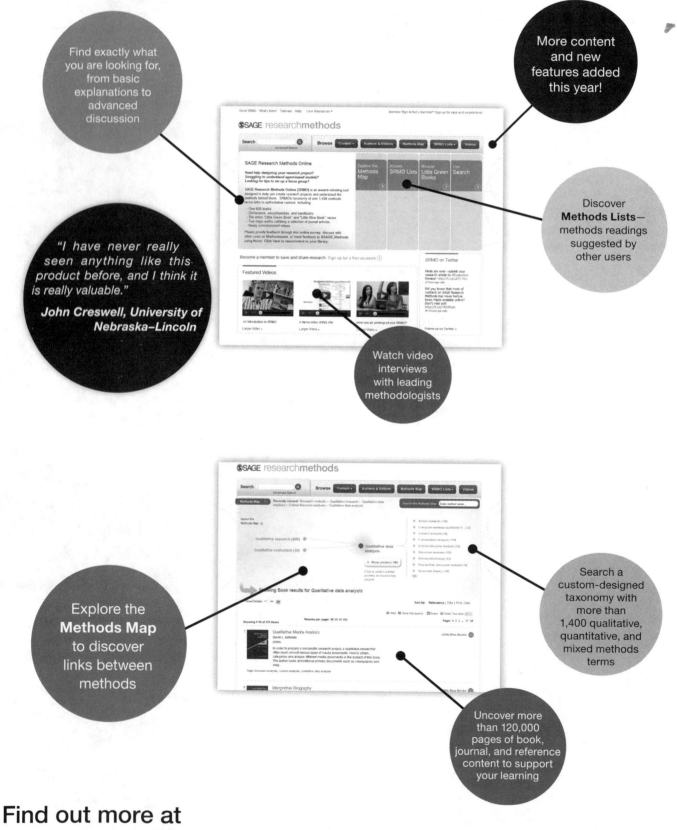

Find exactly what you are looking for, from basic explanations to advanced discussion

More content and new features added this year!

Discover **Methods Lists**— methods readings suggested by other users

"I have never really seen anything like this product before, and I think it is really valuable."

John Creswell, University of Nebraska–Lincoln

Watch video interviews with leading methodologists

Explore the **Methods Map** to discover links between methods

Search a custom-designed taxonomy with more than 1,400 qualitative, quantitative, and mixed methods terms

Uncover more than 120,000 pages of book, journal, and reference content to support your learning

Find out more at
www.sageresearchmethods.com